John Bloundelle-Burton

In the Day of Adversity

A Romance

John Bloundelle-Burton

In the Day of Adversity
A Romance

ISBN/EAN: 9783744675475

Printed in Europe, USA, Canada, Australia, Japan

Cover: Foto ©Thomas Meinert / pixelio.de

More available books at **www.hansebooks.com**

IN THE DAY OF ADVERSITY

A ROMANCE

BY

JOHN BLOUNDELLE-BURTON

AUTHOR OF

THE HISPANIOLA PLATE, THE ADVENTURES OF VISCOUNT ANERLY,
HIS OWN ENEMY, THE DESERT SHIP, A GENTLEMAN-ADVENTURER,
THE SILENT SHORE, ETC.

" If thou faint in the day of adversity, thy
strength is small "   PROVERBS

NEW YORK
D. APPLETON AND COMPANY
1896

.

PREFACE.

Those who are acquainted with the delightful
Mémoires Secrets de M. Le Comte de Bussy Rabutin
(particularly the supplements to them), and with Rous-
set's Histoire de Louvois, will, perhaps, recognise the
inspiration of this story. Those who are not so acquainted with these works will, I trust, still be able
to take some interest in the adventures of Georges
St. Georges.

J. B.-B.

CONTENTS.

viii CONTENTS.

IN THE DAY OF ADVERSITY.

THE FIRST PERIOD.

CHAPTER I.

"THE KING'S COMMAND."

ALL over Franche-Comté the snow had fallen for three days unceasingly, yet through it for those three days a man—a soldier—had ridden, heading his course north, for Paris.

Wrapped in his cloak, and prevented from falling by his bridle arm, he bore a little child—a girl some three years old—on whom, as the cloak would sometimes become disarranged, he would look down fondly, his firm, grave features relaxing into a sad smile as the blue eyes of the little creature gazed upward and smiled into his own face. Then he would whisper a word of love to it, press it closer to his great breast, and again ride on.

For three days the snow had fallen; was falling when he left the garrison of Pontarlier and threaded his way through the pine woods on the Jura slopes; fell still as, with the wintry night close at hand, he approached the city of Dijon. Yet, except to sleep at nights, to rest himself, the child, and the horse, he had gone on and on unstopping, or only stopping to shoot

1

once a wolf that, maddened with hunger, had sprung
out at him and endeavoured to leap to his saddle;
and once to cut down two footpads—perhaps poor
wretches, also maddened with hunger—who had striven
to stop his way.

On and on and on through the unceasing snow he
had gone with the child still held fast to his bosom,
resting the first night at Poligny, since the snow was
so heavy on the ground that his horse could go no
further, and another at Dôle for the same reason,
until now he drew near to Dijon.

"A short distance to travel in three days," he muttered to himself, as, afar off, his eye caught the gleam
of a great beacon flaring surlily through the snow-
laden air—the beacon on the southern watchtower of
the city walls—"a short distance. Yet I have done my
best. Have obeyed orders. Now let me see for further
instructions."

There was still sufficient light left in the wintry
gloom to read by, whereon, shifting the child a little as
he drew rein—it needed not much drawing, since the
good horse beneath him could hardly progress beyond
the slowest walk, owing to the accumulated snow—he
took from his holster a letter, and, passing over the beginning of it, turned to the last leaf and read :

"At Dijon you will stay at the château of my good
friend and subject the Marquis Phélypeaux, avoiding
all inns; at Troyes, at the manoir of Madame la Marquise de Roquemaure; at Melun, if you have to halt
there, at the château of Monsieur de Riverac. Between
these, if forced to rest, you are to select the auberges
which offer; but at these three towns you are to repose
yourself as stated. Above all, fail not to present your-

self at the manoir of Roquemaure. The marquise will deliver to your keeping a message for me. Therefore, be sure you travel by the route indicated, and not by that which passes by Sémur, Tonnerre, and Sens. On this, I pray God to have you, M. Georges St. Georges, in his holy keeping. Written at Paris, the 9th of December, 1687.

"*Signé*, LOUIS.   *Soussigné*, LOUVOIS."

"So," said M. Georges St. Georges to himself, as he replaced the letter in his holster, "it is to the Marquis Phélypeaux that I am to go. So be it. It may be better for the child than at an inn. And I cannot gossip, or, if I do, only to my host, who will doubtless retail it all to the king." Then addressing himself to the watchman on the southern gate, he cried:

"Open there, and let me in!"

"'Tis too late," the man replied, looking down at him through the fast-gathering night. "None enter Dijon now after four of the evening. Ten thousand devils! why could you not have come half an hour earlier? Yet there is a good auberge outside the walls, and——"

"Open, I say!" called up the horseman. "I ride by the king's orders, and have to present myself to the Marquis Phélypeaux. Open, I say!"

"*Tiens!*" exclaimed the watchman, peering down at him through the gray snow and rime with which was now mixed the blackness of the oncoming night. "You ride in the king's name and would see the marquis. *C'est autre chose!* Yet I must be careful. Wait, I will descend. Draw up to the *grille* of the gate."

The horseman did as the watchman bid him, looking down once at the child in his arms, whose face had become uncovered for a moment, and smiling again into its eyes, while he muttered, "Sweet, ere long you shall have a softer couch"; then, as the *grille* opened and the watchman's ruddy face—all blotched with the consumption of frequent *pigeolets* of Macon and other wines—appeared at the grating, he bent down toward him as though to submit his own face to observation.

"Your name and following?" grunted the man.

"Georges St. Georges. Lieutenant in the Chevaux-Légers of the Nivernois. In garrison at the Fort de Joux, between Verrières and Pontarlier. Recalled to Paris by order of the king. Ordered to visit the Marquis Phélypeaux. Are you answered, friend?"

"What do you carry in your arms? It seems precious by the way you clasp it to you."

"It is precious. It is a child—my child."

"*Tiens!* A strange burden for a soldier *en route* from the frontier to Paris. Where is the mother?"

"In her grave! Now open the gate."

For answer the bolts and bars were heard creaking, and presently one half of the great door swung back to admit the rider. And he, dismounting, led his horse through it by one hand, while with the other he clasped his child to his breast beneath the cloak.

Standing in the warder's lodge was a woman—doubtless his wife—who had heard the conversation; for as St. Georges entered she came forward and exclaimed gently:

"A cold, long ride, monsieur, for such as that," and she touched with her finger the rounded back of the child as it lay curled up on his arm beneath the cloak. Then, still femininely, she went on: "Ah! let me see the *pauvrette*," and without resistance from him she drew back the cloak and gazed at it. "Mon Dieu!"

she exclaimed, "a pretty little thing. Poor little *bebé*. And the mother dead, monsieur?" her eyes filling with tears as she spoke.

"Dead," he replied—"dead. In giving birth to her. I am father and mother both. God help her!"

The woman stooped down and kissed the little thing, whose soft blue eyes smiled up at her; then she said:

"The Marquis Phélypeaux is a solitary—dwelling alone. There is little provision for children there. What will monsieur do?"

"As I have done for three years—attend to all its wants myself. There is none other. It had a nurse in the fort; but I could not leave it nor bring her with me. In Paris I may find another. Now tell me where the house of this marquis is?" and he made a movement to go forward.

"And its name, monsieur?" the kindly woman asked, still touched with pity for the little motherless thing being carried on so long and cold a journey. Two or three of her own children were already in their beds of rags that were none too clean, but they, at least, were housed and warm, and not like this one.

"Her name," he replied, "is Dorine. It was her mother's." Then turning to the warder, who stood by, he exclaimed again, "Now direct me to the marquis's, I beg you."

The man's method of direction was to seize by the ear a boy who at that moment had come up—he was one of his own numerous brood—and to bid him lead the monsieur to the marquis's.

"'Tis but a pistol shot," he said, "at the foot of the Rampe. Be off!" to his son, "away! Escort the gentleman."

Certainly it was no great distance from the southern

gate, yet when Monsieur St. Georges had arrived there, still leading his horse by one hand and carrying his precious burden by the other, or by the other arm, the house had so deserted a look that it seemed as though he was hardly likely to be able to carry out the orders of the king and his minister to quarter himself upon the marquis instead of going to an inn. Therefore, he gazed up at the mansion before which he stood waiting, wondering what kind of man was this who dwelt in it.

The house itself was large and vast, having innumerable windows giving on to a large, open, bare *place* in front of it, while the great *porte cochère* had a lock which looked as though it would resist an attack either of battering rams or gunpowder if brought against it. But the blinds, or shutters, were all closed; the great door itself looked as though it had not been opened for a century; the knocker—a Christ upon the cross!—as though it had not been raised for as long a time.

"Phélypeaux," muttered St. Georges to himself. "Phélypeaux! I know the name; what do I know of him? Let me think. Ha! I have it. A soldier like myself. Also another, a brother, a priest, Bishop of Lodève—which is my host, I wonder? For choice the soldier, if all is true of the bishop that is told. *Mon enfant*," turning to the urchin, "is the marquis soldier or divine?"

The boy laughed, then said:

"Divine, monsieur. But *en retraite*. Oh! *avez ça* —they say droll things. Only I am young—I do not know." Whereon he grinned. Then he exclaimed: "*Voilà!* the door is opening."

It was, in truth, or rather a wicket in the door large enough to admit a man who should stoop, or the urchin by the side of St. Georges; but certainly by no means large enough to admit of the passage of his horse if that was also to be entertained for the night.

At that wicket appeared a face, wine-stained and blotchy, but not so good-humoured-looking as that of the watchman at the southern gate. Instead, a scowling face, as of a man on whom good liquor had no improving effect, but, rather, had soured and embittered him.

"What want you?" he asked, staring out moodily at the soldier before him and at his horse, and observing the great sword, hat, and cloak of the former with— beneath the latter—its burden; and also the military trappings of the steed. "What want you?"

"An audience of the marquis. By order of the king. Also food and lodging by the same authority. *Ma foi!* if I had my way I should not demand it. There is a good auberge over there to all appearances," nodding his head toward the white-walled inn on the other side of the *place*, before which hung a bush and on which was painted the whole length of the house: "*L'Ours de Bourgogne. Logement à pied et à cheval.*" "Doubtless I could be well accommodated."

"Take your horse there, at any rate," said the sour-faced man; "there is no accommodation for *it*. Then come back. We will see later about you." And turning to the boy he cried, gesticulating with his hands: "*Va t'en.* Be off!"

The lad did not wait to be bidden a second time to depart, but scampered across the open *place*, while St. Georges, regarding the morose-looking man in front of him, said: "My friend, neither your courtesy nor your hospitality is of the best. Does your master bid you treat all who come to visit him in this manner?"

"I am obeying my master," the other replied; "the

only one I acknowledge—when I parley with you. Show me your warrant, however, for coming to this house."

"There it is," replied St. Georges; "take it to your master, bid him read it, and then bring me whatever message he may send me. Perhaps"—regarding the servitor through the wicket, as he gave him the paper—"if the master is like the man I had best wait until he has read the king's letter ere I seek shelter for my horse. It may be that I shall have to demand it for myself also at the inn."

Then, to his amazement, he saw that the other had opened the leaves of the king's letter and was calmly reading them. "Fellow!" he exclaimed, "how dare you make so bold? You read a letter from the king to me—to be shown to your master——"

"Pish!" replied the other. "Be silent. I am Phélypeaux."

"You!" exclaimed the soldier, stepping back—"you!" and his eye fell on the rusty-brown clothing of the man half in, half out, the wicket. "You!"

"Yes, I. Now go and put your horse up at the inn. Then come back. But stay—what have you beneath your arm?"

"A child."

"A child! Does Louis think I keep a nursery? What are we to do with the child while you stay here?"

"I will attend to that. If you give me a bed the child will share it, and if you have some white bread and milk it is enough for its food."

"Best get that at the 'Ours,'" replied he who said he was Phélypeaux. "Bread I have, but no milk. *Ma foi!* there is no babes' food here. Now, I counsel you, go seek the inn. Your horse may take a chill. Then come back. And "— as the soldier turned to lead his animal across the snow-covered, deserted *place*—"leave the child there. The *patronne* is a motherly creature with half a dozen of her own brood. 'Twill be better there than here. Ring loudly when you return—I am somewhat deaf," and he banged the wicket in St. Georges's face.

"Humph!" muttered the latter, as he crossed to the inn; "the counsel is good. That seems no place for a child. Yet, how to leave it? Still, it is best. It has slept often with its nurse; maybe will sleep well at the inn. Well, let me see what the *patronne* is like."

He entered the yard of the "Ours" as he meditated thus, engaged a stall for the animal, saw it fed and rubbed down, and, then taking his pistols and the king's letter from the holsters and putting them in his belt, entered the hostelry and called for a cup of wine. And, seeing that the woman who served him—evidently the mistress from the manner in which she joked with one or two customers and gave directions to a servant—was a motherly looking woman, he asked her if the child he carried would be safe there for the night?

"A child," she exclaimed, "a child, and in the arms of a soldier! Why, sir, whence come you with a child? *Mon Dieu!* Of all burdens, soldiers rarely carry such as that."

"Nevertheless, I carry such a one. I am on the road from Pontarlier to Paris with my child, and I sleep to-night across the way at the Marquis Phélypeaux's. It seems there is no accommodation there for infants."

"*Hein!*" screamed the woman, turning to the customers in the place; "you hear that?" Then addressing herself to St. Georges, she continued: "You speak

2

well, monsieur; that is no place for children. *Ma foi!*
the old *scélérat* would be as like to eat it."

CHAPTER II.

HOSPITALITY!

" Wно, then, is Phélypeaux?" asked St. Georges as
he sat himself down in front of the great kitchen fire—
the kitchen serving always in a Burgundian inn as the
general place of assembly and serving room. " Who is
Phélypeaux ? "

" Monsieur does not, in truth, know?" she replied,
with a glance at the customers—one a mousquetaire,
himself *en route* to Bar to join his regiment, and the
other evidently a shopkeeper of the place. The former
had risen and saluted St. Georges as he entered, seeing
by his accoutrements and lace * that he was an officer,
and now he joined in the conversation deferentially.

" In truth, monsieur, he is a rarity, an oddity. He
is priest and bishop both——"

" So," interrupted St. Georges, " he is the Bishop of
Lodève. I have heard of him. He has a brother, I
think, comrade, who follows our profession."

" That is true, monsieur. One who will go far.
'Twas but last year the king sent him ambassador to
Cologne; now they say he goes to Turin."

" So, so. But this one here—this bishop? And if
Bishop of Lodève, what does he do in Burgundy? "

---

* The various *chevaux-légers* had not as yet been put by Louis
into uniform, as was the case a few years before with most of the
French regiments.

"Villainies, *scélératesses*," interrupted the hostess, turning away from the fowl she was basting on the spit and emphasizing her remarks with her great wooden spoon. "Oh! figure to yourself—he is a villain. *Ma foi, oui!* A bishop! Ha! A true one. Boasts he believes not in a God, yet rules Languedoc with a rod of iron since Cardinal Bonzi fell off his perch; entertains the wickedest *mondaines* of Louis's court as they pass through Lodève; has boys to sing to him while he dines and—and— But there," she concluded as she turned to the fowl again; "he is a Phélypeaux. That tells all. They are sacred with the king."

"But why?" asked St. Georges, as he rose from his seat—"but why? What does he here if he rules Languedoc, and why should Phélypeaux be a charmed name? Tell me before I go."

He had made arrangements with the good woman to leave his child there for the night, she swearing by many saints that it should sleep with her own and be as carefully guarded and as precious as they were. So he had confided it to her care, saying: "Remember, 'tis motherless, and, besides, is all I have in the world, all I have left to me of my dead wife. Remember that, I beseech you, as you are a mother yourself"; and she, being a mother and a true one, promised. Therefore it was now sleeping peacefully upstairs, its little arms around the neck of one of her own children.

"Why, monsieur, why is he here and why does he bear a charmed name?" repeated the other customer, the *bon bourgeois*, joining in the conversation for the first time. "I will tell you. First, he comes regularly to take his rights of seigniorage, his rents, his taxes, his fourths of all the produce of his vineyards and arable lands on our Côte d'Or. They are rich, these Phély-

peaux; have been ever since the days of Charles the
Bold, and they are greedy and grasping. Also they are
great and powerful—they are of the Pontchartrain blood,
and are of the court. One was minister to the late
king under the cardinal. And for being bishop, *tiens!*
he was priest under Mazarin, who had been a cavalryman, as monsieur is himself. It was Barberini who told
him the gown was better than the sword. And it was
Mazarin who made Phélypeaux bishop. To silence him,
you understand, monsieur—to silence him. He knew
too much."

"What did he know?" asked the soldier, lifting his
cup to his lips for the last time, though with his eyes
fixed on the *bourgeois* as he spoke.

"Ha! he knew much. The king's first love for La
Beauvais—his first love—then for Marie de Mancini and
for La Mothe Houdancourt. Also he knew Turenne
and Condé—and also much more than the world knew
or will ever know."

"Turenne and Condé!" St. Georges echoed. "Two
great captains. Two great rivals and friends! So!
Perhaps he will tell me something of them to-night.
They are names for a soldier to respect. *Bon soir, la
compagnie,*" and he made toward the door.

They wished him good-night, the hostess telling him
to have no fear, the child should be well attended to,
and the mousquetaire saluting him; then the latter said:
"Monsieur rides north again to-morrow, as I heard him
say. I too go forward to Bar. 'If monsieur permits,
and since the roads are bad and often infested with vile
characters, I will ride part way with him."

St. Georges looked at the young man; observed his
stalwart frame—as big as his own—his honest face and
clear gray eyes, the former ruddy with many a march

and much exposure; then he said: "*Soit!* We will ride together; Bar is more than twenty leagues on the journey I have to make. We must part before it is reached. Still, let us set out together. At what hour do you leave?"

"As soon after daybreak as possible, monsieur, if that is convenient."

"It shall be. I will quit Phélypeaux at the dawn." Then St. Georges added aside: "Comrade, I leave here in the inn the two things dearest to me in the world— my child and horse. I confide them to you. Will you accept the trust until the morning?"

"With the greatest will, monsieur. Trust me. Ere I sleep to-night I will see that all is well with both. You may depend on me."

"So be it," replied St. Georges. "I do depend on you. Farewell till dawn," and he strode across the great, gaunt *place*, on which the snow still fell and lay.

"'Ring loud!' the old man said," he muttered to himself; "well, here's for it," and he pulled a peal on the bell chain hanging by the side of the door that might have waked the dead. Then, as he stood there musing on why the king should have given him orders to put up at such a place as Phélypeaux's instead of enjoying the solid, if rough, comfort of a Burgundian inn, the wicket opened again and the old man's sour face appeared once more at it.

"So!" he said, "you have come back. And I per- ceive you have left the child behind you. 'Tis well. We have no room for children here. Come in, come in," he added snappishly.

Obeying an invitation given in none too warm a tone, St. Georges stepped through the wicket into the court- yard of the house—a place filled with snow that had

lain there and increased since the first flake had fallen
until now, and through which a thin path or track had
been trodden from the great doorway to a smaller one
that admitted to the house.

"You perceive," remarked Phélypeau, "this is not a
luxurious halting for you, monsieur. Still, the *chevaux-
légers* are doubtless used to an absence of luxury."

"The *chevaux-légers* can make shift with anything,"
replied the soldier. And shrugging his shoulders as he
spoke, he said : "*Monseigneur l'Évêque*, why do you imagine his Majesty has instructed me to become your
guest for a night?"

He spoke without any of that respect usually shown
to exalted members of the Church in the days of Louis
XIV—a monarch who considered himself a religious
man, and demanded that the most scrupulous reverence
should be paid to all things ecclesiastical. But, in
truth, the Bishop of Lodève was known to be a scandal
to the sacred calling he belonged to; and now that
Georges St. Georges was aware that he was face to face
with the man himself, he refused to testify a respect for
him that he could not feel.

"Humph! 'Monseigneur l'Évêque!' Ha! So you
know me?" St. Georges nodded, whereon the other
went on :

"Why the king has sent you to me? Eh? Perhaps because he thinks I am a good host, and because
he loves his troops to be well treated. So I am a good
host—only it is when I am in Languedoc. Here, *mal-
heureusement*, I must be perforce a bad one. I have no
servants but those I have brought with me, and one or
two women who look after the château during my absence."

He had by this time opened the door into the house

and escorted his visitor into a large, desolate-looking
saloon, on the walls of which the damp hung in huge
beads and drops, and in which there was a fireplace of
vast dimensions that gave the appearance of never having had a fire lighted in it for years. Yet before this
fireplace there stood two great armchairs, as though to
suggest that here was a comfortable, cosey spot in which
to sit.

" We'll soon have a fire," said this strange creature,
whereon he went to a corner of the room in which hung
some arras, and, thrusting it aside, brought forth a
handful of kindling wood, two or three green, newly
cut logs of different sizes, and some shavings, to which
he applied the tinder after he had thrown them all pell-
mell into the grate together. Then, when the smoke
which arose from the damp green wood had thoroughly
permeated the whole of the room, he looked round at
St. Georges and said :

" You were gone some while to the ' Ours.' Did
you sup there ? "

" Nay," replied the other, glancing at him through
the smoke and by aid of the single candle by which the
room was illuminated, for it was now night. " Nay,
monseigneur, I thought to sup with you."

"And so you shall," exclaimed Phélypeaux, with an
assumed air of hilarity—" and so you shall. Only—I
cannot entertain you as in Languedoc. Now, if we
were there——"

" Well," said the soldier, " we are not. We are in
Burgundy. The land of good cheer. We must take
what Burgundy offers."

" *Hélas !* it offers little. At least in this house.
However, I will see." Saying which he opened a door
at the other end of the room, and calling, " Pierre,

Pierre!" loudly, he cried out, after a harsh voice had
answered him from some distant room: "Bring some
supper for Monsieur St. Georges and myself. For Monsieur St. Georges and myself. You understand! For
Monsieur St. Georges and myself."

"Why emphasize 'Monsieur St. Georges' so strongly,
monseigneur?" the other demanded. "The respected
servitor can hardly care much whether he bring supper
for you and Monsieur St. Georges or for you and Monsieur the dev— I beg your pardon, monseigneur."

The Bishop of Lodève laughed a kind of grim,
uncanny laugh as St. Georges said this, then he remarked :

"Surely you don't believe in—in—the gentleman
you were about to mention. Let me see, there is a
musty proverb that he who sups with that personage
needs a long spoon. Well, I would not sup with him—
if he exists. Our supper will be none too profuse as it
is," and again he laughed.

So, indeed, it seemed, judging by what Pierre
brought in later. The soup, served in a handsome
silver tureen, whose antique form and chasings must
have dated back to the days of Henri de Navarre at
latest, was so thin that it was nothing but boiling water
with a greasy flavour, and St. Georges twisted his long
mustaches with dismay as he gazed into the stuff before him. Moreover, the bread with which he endeavoured to fortify this meagre commencement was half
baked, so that it was of the consistency of dough. Next,
the meat which was brought to table must have been
unkilled at the time he rode into Dijon, so tough and
tasteless was it; and the wine was a disgrace to France,
let alone to Burgundy, where every peasant can obtain
a drink that is palatable if weak. And, to add to the

other miseries of this *régale*, the tablecloth and napkins were so damp that, affected by the tureen and
plates, which were hot if they possessed no other virtues
—such as eatable food upon them—they smoked so
much that the guest could scarcely see his host across
the table.

"Not the fare of Languedoc," this worthy divine
muttered, once or twice, "not the fare of Languedoc.
Ah, Monsieur St. Georges, you must come and see me
in my bishopric if you want to live well. I can give
you a good supper there."

"So I have heard, monseigneur. With many other
things as well. Music, I hear, accompanies your feasts;
the voices of silver-tongued lads——"

"Ha!" chuckled the other, "you have heard that.
Well, why not? The choir is lazy, and—since it costs
me nothing—may as well sing at my table. Now, since
I cannot persuade you to eat more," St. Georges having
pushed his plate away from him with an action of disgust, "let us have a little talk.—Pierre, go away; we
wish to be alone. Though—stay—first of all bring a
bottle of the old clos from the buffet—the old clos,
you understand, the '79 bottling."

The cavalryman wondered if the "old clos" was
likely to be any better than the vinaigrous stuff he had
just been treated to, and sat waiting its arrival with
curiosity, if not impatience. Meanwhile, he regarded
his host from under his eyelids as well as he could
through the mist made by the still steaming napkins,
and also by the wet, hissing logs which spluttered and
reeked in the grate close by which the table had been
drawn up. The old man, he saw, was perfectly cognizant that he was being observed; occasionally from
under *his* eyelids he would shoot a glance in his turn at

the great form of the *chevau-léger* near him, and
would then smile in what he evidently intended to be
an engaging manner; while at other times he would
swiftly remove his eyes and gaze meditatively into the
green wood that smouldered on the andirons.

Then Pierre came back with a bottle that appeared,
outwardly at least, to give promise of containing good
liquor within it, since it was covered with dust and cob-
webs, and, uncorking it and placing two long, thin,
tapering glasses by its side, withdrew—yet not before
Phélypeaux, with that remarkable persistency in mentioning his guest's name which the latter had previously
remarked, had called out:

"Fill Monsieur St. Georges's glass, Pierre. Fill it,
I say. Fill the glass of Monsieur St. Georges.—Monsieur St. Georges," raising his own, "I drink to you.
To your good health and prosperous ride to Paris. And
afterward, Monsieur St. Georges—afterward."

CHAPTER III.

IT IS THE MAN.

THE wine *was* good! Worthy of whatever *clos* it
had ripened on! A glass of it went far to repay St.
Georges for any discomfort he had suffered during the
wretched meal just concluded, and made amends for all
that had passed hitherto. As for the Bishop of Lodève,
he drank two glasses rapidly in succession, smacked his
lips, and peered at the ruby liquid held between the

---

* Cheval-léger is a modern rendering of the old term.

guttering candle and his eye in the most approved fashion, and seemed to be making or receiving amends for the miserable meal he had also partaken of, though so sparingly that the soldier thought he must either have made a better one recently or be about to make one later on.

Then, after he had put three of the logs together—which seemed at last as though about to burn with some effect—by the summary method of kicking them close to each other with his foot, he said quietly, though quite unexpectedly on the part of the other:

"His Most Christian Majesty—or rather Louvois for him—wrote me that I might expect a visit from you on your way from Franche-Comté to Paris."

"Indeed!" said St. Georges, looking, as he felt, astonished. After which he added: "Truly, for a poor lieutenant of horse, such as I am, the king seems much interested in my doings. I marvel much that he should be so."

"Family interest, perhaps?" said the bishop, glinting an eye at him from behind the glass which he was again holding up to the light of the guttering candle. "Family interest is useful at court."

"Family interest!" exclaimed the other, pushing his glass away from him. "Monseigneur, it is evident you know nothing of Georges St. Georges, or you would not mention that. Still, how should you know my affairs?"

"How, indeed!" replied Phélypeaux, though again there was a flash from the eye—"how, indeed! I—I never heard of you until his Majesty said you would honour me with a visit. Yet, Captain—I mean Monsieur—St. Georges, there must be something which guides Louis in sending for you—in removing you from the miserable garrison in the Jura to Paris. Ah,

Paris!" he interjected with an upward glance. " Paris!
Paris!" But having recovered from this fervent ec-
stasy, he continued: " And if not family interest—I am
a believer in family interest myself—what can it be?
Unless, of course, you have been selected because of
your military promise."

" Nor can it be that either," replied the guest. " I
have been in garrison at Pontarlier for a year, and as
for my service, why I have done nothing to distinguish
myself. No more than thousands of his Majesty's
troops have done—nay, not half so much."

" How old are you, may I ask?"

" Thirty-three."

" Ah," replied monseigneur, "and this is the third
day of '88. So you were born in 1655. Ah!" and he
leaned back in his chair and muttered to himself, though
once he said quite audibly: " Yes, yes. That would do
very well."

" What would do very well, monseigneur?" asked
the other, looking at him.

" Pardon me," replied the bishop, and St. Georges
could not help remarking how much more courtly his
manner had become by degrees, so that, while heretofore
it was quite in keeping with what he had originally imagined him to be—a servitor—it was now thoroughly
suitable to his position—the position of a member of an
old French family and of a father of the Church; "pardon me, my mind rambles sometimes when—when I
throw it back. I was reflecting that—that—it was in
that year I was made bishop. So you were born in
1655? And how—since you say you have none of that
valuable family interest—did you become a *chevau-
léger?*"

" It is somewhat of a story, and a long one. Hark!

surely that is the cathedral clock striking. It is too late to pester you with my affairs."

"Not a jot," exclaimed Phélypeaux—"not a jot. Nay, tell the story, and—shall we crack another bottle of the clos? It is good wine."

"It is, indeed," replied St. Georges, "excellent. Yet I will drink no more. Three glasses are all I allow myself after supper at the best of times. And, after all, my history will not take long in telling. At least such portions of it as I need tell you."

"Tell me all. I love to hear the history of the young and adventurous, as you are—as you must be. The *chevaux-légers* encounter adventure even in garrison," and he leered at him.

"I have encountered none, or very few. A few indecisive campaigns against Holland in the year the king gave me my commission—namely, fourteen years ago— then the Peace of Nimeguen, and since then stagnation in various garrisons. Yet they say the time is coming for war. Holland seeks allies everywhere against France; soon a great campaign should occur."

"Without doubt, when his Most Christian Majesty will triumph as he has done before. But why—how— did you obtain your commission? You do not tell me that."

"No, I had forgotten. Yet 'tis not much to tell. My mother—an English woman—excuse me, Monseigneur l'Évêque, but you have spilt your wine."

"So, indeed, I have," said the bishop, sopping up the wine which his elbow had overturned by a sudden jerk while the other was speaking, "so, indeed, I have. But 'tis not much. And there is still that other bottle uncorked." Then with a sidelong glance he said : "So your mother was an English woman. *Ah! mon Dieu, elles sont belles, ces Anglaises!* An English woman. Well, well!"

"Yes, an English woman. Daughter of a Protestant cavalier who left England when the Commonwealth was declared. He had done his best for the king, but with his death he could do no more. So he quitted his country forever."

"Most interesting," exclaimed the bishop, "but your father, Monsieur St. Georges. Who was he? Of the St. Georges's family, perhaps, of Auvergne! Or another branch, of Dauphiné! A noble family is that of St. Georges!"

"He was of the branch in Auvergne. A humble member, but still of it. I know no more."

"No more?"

"No."

"Humph! Strange! Pardon me, monsieur, I would not ask a delicate question—but—but—did not the family recognise the marriage of Monsieur St. Georges?"

"They did not recognise it for the simple reason that they were never told of it. It did not please my father to divulge the marriage to his family, so they were left in ignorance that it had ever taken place."

"And was Monsieur St. Georges—your father—a soldier like yourself?"

"He was a soldier like myself. And served against Condé."

"Against Condé. Under Turenne, doubtless?" and once more he cast a sidelong glance at his visitor.

"Yes. Under Turenne. They were, I have heard, more than commander and subordinate. They were friends."

"A great friendship!" exclaimed the bishop. "A

great friendship! To his influence you doubtless owe your commission, obtained, I think you said, in '74, the year before Turenne's death."

"Doubtless. So my father said. He died in the same year as the marshal."

"In battle, too, no doubt?" Then, seeing a look upon the other's face which seemed to express a desire for no more questioning—though, indeed, he bowed gravely at the question if his father had died in battle—monseigneur with a polite bow said he would ask him no more impertinent questions, and turned the conversation by exclaiming:

"But you must be weary, monsieur. You would rest, I am sure. I will call Pierre to show you to your room. Your child will sleep better at the 'Ours' than you will do here, since my accommodation is not of the first order, owing to my being able to inhabit the house so little. But we have done our best. We have done our best."

"I thank you," the soldier said, rising from his chair. "Now, monseigneur, let me pay my farewells to you at the same time I say 'Good-night.' I propose to ride to-morrow at daybreak, and if possible to reach Bar by night. Though much I doubt doing so; my horse is jaded already, and can scarce compass a league an hour. And 'tis more than twenty leagues from here, I take it."

"Ay, 'tis. More like twenty-five. And you have, you know, a burden. You carry weight. There is the little child."

"Yes, there is the child."

"You guard it carefully, Monsieur St. Georges. By the way, you have not told me. Where is its mother, your wife?"

Again the soldier answered as he had before answered to the watchman's wife—yet, he knew not why, he felt more repugnance in speaking of his dead wife to this strange bishop than he had when addressing either that simple woman or the landlady of the "Ours." But it had to be done—he could not make a secret of what was, in fact, no secret. So he answered, speaking rapidly, as though desirous of getting his answer over :

"She is dead. Our existence together was short. We loved each other dearly, but it pleased God to take her from me. She died a year after our marriage, in giving birth to the babe."

Phélypeaux bowed his head gravely, as though, perhaps, intending thereby to express sympathy with the other, and said, " It was sad, very sad." Then he continued :

"And madame—*pauvre dame!*—was she, too, English, or of some French family?"

"She was, monseigneur, a simple French girl. Of no family—such as you, monseigneur, would know of. A girl of the people, of the *bourgeoisie.* Yet I loved her; she became my wife, and now—now"—and he looked meditatively down into the ashes of the (by this time) charred and burnt-out logs—"I have no wife. That is all. Monseigneur, permit me to wish you good-night."

The bishop rang the bell, and while they waited for Pierre to come, he said :

"You asked me, Monsieur St. Georges, this evening, why his Most Christian Majesty should have thought fit through Louvois to direct you to stay at my house in Dijon? I shall not see you to-morrow ere you depart; let me therefore be frank. The king—and Louvois also—are in correspondence with me on a political matter, which must not even be trusted to the post, nor to courier, nor messenger. Nay, we do not even write what we have to say, but, instead, correspond by words and signs. Now, you are a trusty man—you will go far —already I see your captaincy of a troop looming up before you. Therefore I will send by you one word and one alone. You cannot forget it, for it is perhaps the simplest in our or any language. You will convey it?"

"I am the king's servant. What is the word, monseigneur?"

"The word '*Yes.*'"

"The word '*Yes,*'" the *chevau-léger* repeated. "The word '*Yes.*' That is it? No more?"

"Nothing more. Simply the word '*Yes.*' Yet stay, remember my instructions. The word is sent as much to Louvois as to the king. It is a common message to both. And there is one other thing. The Marquise de Roquemaure is also concerned in this matter; she will without doubt ask you what the word is I have sent. And, monsieur, there is no need of secrecy with her. You may frankly tell her."

Again with military precision the other made sure of his instructions.

"I may say that the word you send is '*Yes*'?"

"Precisely."

"I shall remember."

And now, Pierre coming in, the bishop bade him farewell and good-night.

"The bed, I trust," he said, addressing the servant, "is as comfortable as may be under the circumstances. Also properly aired. For Monsieur St. Georges must sleep well to-night. He rides to Troyes to-morrow or as far upon his road as he can get. He must sleep well."

"So! he rides to Troyes to-morrow," repeated the

3

domestic, surlily—" to Troyes, eh? And at what hour does Monsieur St. Georges set forth? I must know, so that he shall be called."

"At daybreak," St. Georges replied.

The man led him after this up some great stairs, evidently the principal ones of the mansion, and past what were the chief salons, holding the lantern he carried above his head all the way and casting thereby weird shadows on to walls and corners. Then up another flight they went—their feet echoing now on the bare, uncarpeted stairs, and so along a corridor until at the end the man opened a door and ushered the guest into a moderately sized room very sparsely furnished in all except the bed, which was large enough for three men to have slept in side by side. Next, lighting a taper which looked as though it might burn ten minutes but not longer, he gruffly bade St. Georges "Goodnight," and, saying that he should be called before daybreak, he strode away, while the other heard his heavy footfall gradually grow fainter and fainter until, at last, there was no further sound in the house except the banging of a door now and again.

"*Nom d'un chien!*" exclaimed the soldier, as he unbuckled his spurs, drew off his long riding boots, and, unsheathing his sword, laid it along the side of the bed nearest the wall, "this is a pleasant hole for a man to find himself in." And throwing himself on the bed, and discovering that, as he drew the counterpane up about his shoulders, it was so short that it did not reach below his knees, he wrapped up the lower part of his body in the great cloak in which he had carried the . child all day, and so, shivering with cold, went at last to sleep.

Down below, while this had been going on, Pierre

had rejoined his master, and, standing before him, was answering several questions put with great rapidity.

"Your horse is sound?" the bishop asked, as now he partook of a glass out of the second bottle.

"Ay, it is sound," replied the other. "It has not left the stable for three days."

"You can, therefore, ride forth to-morrow."

"Further than he can, weather permitting."

"Good. Therefore ride ahead of him until you meet the Marquis de Roquemaure. Then you can deliver to him a message somewhat similar to the one he will deliver to the mother of the noble marquis."

"What is the message?"

"The message he will deliver to madame la marquise —if he is fortunate enough to see her—is the word '*Yes.*' The message you will deliver to her son, whom you *must* see, is also '*Yes.*' And, if you can remember, you may also say to the marquis, 'It is the man.' *Can* you remember?"

"Without doubt I can. The words are: 'Yes. It is the man.'"

"Those are the words."

CHAPTER IV.

"HER LIFE STANDS IN THE PATH OF OTHERS' GREED."

AWAKENED in the dark of the morning by a loud knocking on the door, St. Georges sprang off the bed and called lustily to know who was there?

"It is near dawn," a female voice answered. "Monsieur was to be awakened."

"Where is the man called Pierre?" asked St. Georges, perceiving that the tones were not his gruff ones.

"He has gone forth to one of the bishop's farms at Pouilly. He bade me call monsieur."

"And the bishop?"

"Monseigneur is not yet risen. There is a meal prepared for monsieur below, if he will partake of it."

Monsieur so far partook of it on descending—after he had made a rapid toilet, cleaned his sword by passing the folds of his cloak over it, and (good soldier as he was!) having said a prayer at his bedside ere leaving the room—as to drink a cup of thick, lukewarm chocolate. But beyond this he would wait no longer, being very anxious to regain the custody of his child. Also he thought that the "Ours" would offer a more satisfying meal than that now set before him, which, in truth, was nothing but the selfsame chocolate, some bread, and a half-finished *saucisson* which did not look particularly appetizing.

Therefore he tossed on the table a silver crown to the miserable-looking old woman who had called him, and who afterward escorted him downstairs, and, following her across the more than ever snow-covered courtyard, emerged on to the great *place*.

And still, as he observed, the snow fell, must have been falling all night, since it lay upon this open space in great tussocks, or mounds, while across the *place* itself no footmark was to be seen. It was, indeed, as though a vast white sea stretched from the house of Phélypeaux over to where the "Ours" stood.

Beneath a dull leaden canopy of cloud the wintry day was, however, coming; from the chimneys of the inn he could see the smoke, scarcely more dull and

leaden than that canopy itself, rising; at the door of
the inn he saw the mousquetaire standing, looking up
at what should have been the heavens.

" Is all well?" he asked as he drew close to him now.
" Have you seen the child?"

" All well, monsieur," the other replied, saluting as
he spoke—" all well, both with child and horse. Yet,
ma foi! what a day for a journey! Must monsieur,
indeed, continue his?"

" Ay!" replied St. Georges, "I must. My orders
are to pause no longer than necessary on the route to
Paris, to report myself to the Minister of War, the
Marquis de Louvois." Then turning to the mousquetaire, he asked: "What are your orders? Do you ride
toward Bar to-day?"

" Since monsieur proceeds, so do I. Yet I doubt if
we get even so far as Bar. *Ciel!* will the snow ever
cease to fall?"

But in spite of the snow, in half an hour both were
ready to set out. The little child, Dorine, had slept
well, the *patronne* said, had lain snug and close with
two of her own all through the night, while she had
seen to its nourishment and had herself washed and
fed it.

" Heaven bless you, for a true woman," St. Georges
said, "Heaven bless you!"

But the woman would hear of no thanks; she reiterated again and again that she was a mother herself and
had a mother's heart within her; she only wished monsieur would leave the little thing with her until he came
back; she would warrant it should be well cared for
until he did.

" I doubt my ever coming back this way," he said,
as he ate his breakfast—a substantial one, far different

from that which the bishop's servant had been able to
set before him—and she ministered to his wants, "unless the future war rolls toward Burgundy. I am *en
route* for Paris, and Heaven only knows where to afterward."

"Find a good home for her, monsieur," she said, "a
home where she may at least be safe while you are away
campaigning. Nay," she continued, "if I might make
so bold, meaning no offence, find a new mother for her.
It would be a sad life for her even though monsieur
followed a stay-at-home existence; 'twill be doubly
hard when you are separated from her."

But St. Georges only shook his head and said mourn-
fully there was no other wife for him; a statement from
which she dissented vehemently. Then she asked:

"Does monsieur know of any one in Paris to whom
the little Dorine might be confided? If not," she continued—"she intended no liberty!—she could recommend one with whom it would always be safe. A woman
of Dijon like herself, married and settled in Paris; married, indeed, to a cousin of her late husband, who, rest
his soul! had been dead eighteen months. This woman's
husband was a mercer in a large way of business in the
Rue de Timoleon, lived well, and had children of his
own; it would be an *abri* for the child if monsieur cared
to consider it."

"Care to consider it!" exclaimed St. Georges, "why,
it is the very thing I should wish." Then he paused a
moment, reflecting deeply and looking round the kitch-
en, as though to see that they were alone, which they
were with the exception of the mousquetaire, who sat
by the great fire warming himself.

"Hark you, dame," he said, lowering his voice a
little, though not from any fear of the mousquetaire

hearing, but more from instinct than anything else. "You have done me one great kindness in being so tender to my poor little motherless babe. Will you answer me, therefore, a question? Will—will—suppose, I would say, that I wished the whereabouts of this, my child, unknown to any one—would she be safe in the house of this mercer you speak of? Also—if you—should be asked by any one—high or low, here in Dijon —if, *par hasard*, you know, or could guess, had indeed the faintest suspicion, where that little child might be— would you hold your peace? Would you let this be a secret locked only in your own honest heart?"

"Would I? Ay, monsieur, I would! Your child has slept with my little *fillettes ;* when I went to arouse them ere dawn they all lay cheek to cheek, and with their arms entwined. She is as one of mine, therefore; she shall be as sacred. *Je le jure.*"

"Give me your friend's name and address," St. Georges made answer. "What you have said is enough. I trust you as I should have trusted her dead mother." And he took his tablets from his pouch as he spoke.

"Write," said the woman, "the name of Le Sieur Blecy, 5 Rue de Timoleon. That is sufficient. His wife Susanne will arrange with you for the safety of the little one when she knows that I have sent you."

"But," exclaimed St. Georges, "can you give me no line, no word, to her or him? Surely she will not accept me on my own assurances. Besides, 'tis much to ask. She will scarcely receive my child into her house, into her family, without some proofs from you."

"How," exclaimed the woman, "can I send such proof? I can not write—alas! I can not even read." She blushed as she spoke—though truly she need not have done so, since in all Burgundy, in the days of

Louis *le Dieudonné*, not one in a hundred could do more than she—and he himself reddened at having so put her to shame, and muttered some sort of excuse under his thick mustache.

" Send some trifle that she will recognise—some little thing she will know to have been yours," exclaimed the mousquetaire from his seat in the chimney-piece.   " She will know that."

" Ha ! " she said, recovering instantly from her confusion, " and so I will."   Then, casting her eyes round the great stone-floor kitchen and seeing nothing therein that she could send to her friend, she ran up the stairs and came back bearing in her hand a little missal, with her name written in it.

" It was given to me by Susanne's mother on my wedding day, she saying that, though I could not follow the service with it, my children might learn to do so— as they shall !—as they shall ! "

St. Georges took the book—a tiny one—and put it in his pouch also, along with his tablets ; then he said to the mousquetaire : " Friend, if you have still a mind to depart, let us set out.   Yet I would not take you from your comfortable nook if duty does not make it absolutely necessary for you to go."

" I will go," the other said, springing to his feet. "All is ready ; my horse has rested for two days ; at least we can get some distance on our route.   Come, monsieur, let us away."

Therefore St. Georges paid the reckoning due, not forgetting among other things to give the woman's children—who were now all up and ready for their breakfast—some little sums to buy things with ; and so he bade the woman farewell, thanking her again and again for her goodness, and promising that he should certainly seek the Sieur de Blecy on his arrival in Paris.

"Also," he said, as he shook her by the hand, "I shall find some means of letting you know of her welfare. Burgundy is far from Paris, yet there is always continuous passing to and fro from one to the other—you shall hear from me."

"I hope so," she said, "and, *tenez!* De Blecy is himself of Burgundy; his old mother lives near here—not a league away—send through him. He corresponds often with her and others. A word to me will reach. Farewell, monsieur;—farewell, mousquetaire. Adieu!"

Yet the last word was not said; for while the soldier went into the inn yard to fetch the horses and St. Georges brought down from the room she slept in his little child—who prattled in her baby way to him while her soft blue eyes smiled up in his—and wrapped it in his great cloak preparatory to mounting the block before the inn door, she asked:

"Why, why, monsieur, do you desire that no one should know where she is? Why keep her existence a secret? Surely there are none who would harm so innocent a little thing as that?"

He paused a moment, looking down at her from his great height as though meditating deeply; then he said:

"I will trust you fully. I wish her whereabouts—not her existence, that is already known—kept secret until the time comes that either she shall be in safety out of France or I can be ever near to guard and watch over her; for her life—after mine—stands in the path of others' greed—perhaps of others' ambition. My life first, then hers. I know it, have known it long; until a day or so ago I thought none other knew it——"

"And?" she asked, glancing up at him, while she stole her hand into the folds of his cloak and again softly patted the child's little dimpled cheek— "and——?"

"And," he continued, "I am sure now that against her life, or at least her liberty, some attempt will be made—as it will against mine. That," he said, sinking his voice to a whisper, "is why I am recalled to Paris. Farewell!"

CHAPTER V.

THE GRAVEYARD.

By the time that the wintry night was about once more to close in upon them they were nearing Aignay-le-Duc, having passed through the village of Baigneux some two or three hours previously.

A change in the weather had set in; the snow had ceased to fall at last; right in their faces from the north-northwest there blew a cold, frosty wind; from beneath their horses' hoofs there came a crisp sound, which told as plainly as words that the soft, feathery snow was hardening, while the ease with which the animals now lifted their feet showed that the travelling was becoming easier to them every moment.

"Courage! courage!" exclaimed St. Georges; "if we proceed thus we may reach Chatillon-sur-Seine to-night. What think you, Boussac?"

On their road the men, as was natural between two comrades of the sword, had become intimate, St. Georges telling the mousquetaire some of that history of his life which will be unfolded as these pages proceed, while the

other had in a few words given him his own. His name
was Boussac—Armand Boussac—the latter drawn from
a little village or town in Lower Berri, wherein his
father was a *petit seigneur.*

" A poor place, monsieur," he said, " a rock—fortified,
however, strongly—and with a castle almost inaccessible
except to the crows and hawks. A place in which a
man who would see the world can yet scarce find the
way to study his fellow-creatures. *Ma foi,* there are
not many there! A priest or two—those always!—some
farmers whose fields lie at the foot of the rock, some
old crones who, no longer able to earn anything in those
fields, are kept until they die by those who can. And
on the rock a few soldiers drawn from the regiment of
Berri—men who eat their hearts out in despair when
sent to garrison it."

" A cheerful spot, in truth!" said St. Georges, with
a smile; " no wonder you left the rock and sought the
mousquetaires. And I see by your horse that you are
of the black regiment.* How did you find your way
to it?"

" Easily. I descended once to Clermont, having bade
farewell to my father and intending to join the Regiment de Berri, when, lo! as I entered the town, I saw
our *grand seigneur* of Creuse in talk with an officer of
the Mousquetaires Noirs. Then as I saluted him he
called out to me: ' Boussac! Boussac! what have you
crossed the mountains for and come to Clermont?'
' *Pardie!* ' I replied, ' monsieur, to seek my fortune as
a soldier. I hear there are some of the Regiment of
Berri here. And the *arrière-ban* is out, the summons

---

* " Les mousquetaires tiraient leur noms de la couleur de leur
chevaux."—*St. Simon.*

made.' 'And so it is,' replied the seigneur, 'only the
Regiment of Berri is complete, has all its complement.
Now, here is the colonel of the mousquetaires; if he
would take you, why, your fortune's made. Ask him,
Boussac. Ask him.' So, monsieur, I asked him, telling him I could ride any horse; would do so if he
brought one; knew the *escrime*—*ma foi!* many a time
had I fenced in the old castle with those of the regiment; was strong and healthy, and, *voilà!* it was done.
Even the Mousquetaires—the king's own guard, the
men of the *Maison du Roi* were recruiting—it needed
only that one should be of gentle blood, as the Boussacs
are. So, monsieur, I am mousquetaire; have fought
when they fight; we, of Ours, were at Mulhausen,
Turckheim, and Salzbach——"

"Did you see Turenne killed?" asked St. Georges,
turning on his horse to look at his comrade.

"Nay, not killed, but just before the battle. Ah!
he was a soldier!" Then he went on with his recollections, finishing up by saying: "But, alas! since then the
peace has come, and we have naught to do but to dance
about the galleries of Versailles and be in attendance
on the king and his court. That," he said, patting his
horse's coal-black neck, "is no work for a soldier."

"It will change ere long," said St. Georges, "if all
accounts be true. Louis is threatened from all sides by
the Dutchman, William, above all. It will come."

"Let us hope so, monsieur. Peace is no good to us."

"No! peace is no good to us. My only hope is,
England may not be drawn into the game."

"And wherefore, monsieur?"

"I am half English—my mother was of that country. To draw a sword against the land that gave her
birth would be no pleasure to me."

"Yet, on the other—and the greater—side, monsieur is French. How should you decide, therefore, if war comes?"

St. Georges rode on silently for a little while ere he answered this question, and the mousquetaire could see that he was pondering deeply. Then he seemed to shake himself clear of his doubts, and said:

"My allegiance is to France. I have sworn fidelity to the king. To him consequently I belong. If, therefore," he continued, "my fidelity to him brings no harm to one whom I love best of all in the world"—and Boussac saw his arm enfold more closely the little child he carried—"I draw my sword for him."

"Can your fidelity do that—bring harm to her?" he asked.

"It might," replied the other, "it might. In serving Louis, in serving France, it may be that I put her in deadly peril. But as yet, Boussac, I can tell you no more."

That Boussac was bewildered by this enigmatical remark he could plainly see. The soldier had wrinkled his brow and stared at him as he made it. Now he rode quietly by his side, saying no further word, yet evidently turning it over in his own mind. And so, as they progressed, the night came nearly upon them, and had the weather not now changed altogether and become fine and clear, there would have been no daylight left.

Suddenly, however, as they rode thus silently but at a good pace—for the frosted snow on the path or road shone out clear and distinct now to their and their horses' eyes in spite of the oncoming night—St. Georges became sure of what at first he had only imagined—namely, that Boussac suspected something, was watching for something—perhaps an ambush or an attack.

"What is it?" he asked in a low voice, as the mousquetaire tightened his hand upon the rein of his horse and, bending forward over its jet-black mane, peered into the bushes of the side on which he rode; and also he noticed that his comrade put his hand to his long sword and, drawing it an inch or two from its scabbard once or twice, loosened it. "What is it, Boussac?" But as he spoke he, too, made his weapon ready in the same way.

"Take no notice," muttered the mousquetaire, "ride straight ahead, look neither to left nor right. Yet— listen. All day from the time we were a league outside of Dijon—*ma foi!*" in a loud tone that might have been heard fifty yards off, "a fine night, a pleasant night for the season!"—then lowering it again, "a man has tracked us, a man armed and masked, or masked whenever we drew near him—*si, si*, monsieur"; again in the loud voice assumed for the purpose, "the *vin du pays*, especially of Chantillon, is excellent; a cup will cheer us to-night."

"Doubtless," replied St. Georges, in a similar voice; then sinking it, he asked beneath his teeth, "Why not warn me before?"

"Oh! red wine, monsieur, above all," replied Boussac, loudly. "There is little white grows here." Again lowering his tone: "I feared to distress, to alarm you. You had the child. Now I am forced to do so. He has been joined by five others at different points since we passed Flavigny. All armed and all masked. Yes," in the loud voice, "and with a *soupe à l'oignon*, as monsieur says. They are around us," sinking it again. "I judge they mean attack. Well, we know *we are* soldiers:

they should be brigands, *larrons!* Shall we encounter them, give them a chance to show who and what they are?"

"Ay," said St. Georges. "Observe, here is a small church and graveyard; wheel in and let us await them. I see them now, even in the dusk."

Swiftly, as on parade, the order was given, and as swiftly executed. The black horse wheeled by the side of the chestnut of the *chevau-léger* into the open graveyard—the gate of the place hung on one hinge down toward the road from which the church rose somewhat—and then St. Georges in a loud voice said :

"Halt here, comrade. Our horses are a little blown. We will breathe them somewhat."

It was a wretched, uncared-for spot into which they had ridden, the church being a little, low-built edifice of evidently great antiquity, and doubtless utilized for service by the out-dwellers of Aignay-le-Duc, which lay half a league further off, and some sparse lights of which might be now seen twinkling in the clear, frosty air beneath a young moon that rose to the right of the village. In the graveyard itself there was the usual heterogeneous accumulation of tombstones and memorials of the dead; here and there some dark-slate headstones; in other places wooden crosses with imitation flowers hanging on their crossbars, covered with frozen snow; in others, huge mounds alone, to mark the spots where the dead lay.

"Not bad," said the mousquetaire, as he glanced his eye round the melancholy spot, "for an encounter, if they mean one.—Steady, *mon brave,*" to his horse, "steady!—Ah! here comes one. Well, we have the point o' vantage. We are in the churchyard; they have to come up the rise to attack us. *Peste!* what can they want with two soldiers?"

St. Georges arranged his child under his arm more carefully, gathered his reins into the hand of that arm, and then, with the other, drew his long sword—it glittered in the rays of the young moon like a streak of phosphorus!—and was followed in this action by Boussac. After which he whispered: "See! All six are coming. Which is the one who, you say, followed us from Flavigny?"

"He who hangs behind all the others. The biggest of all."

As the mousquetaire answered, the men of whom he had spoken, and who had gradually come from behind the hedges and trees that grew all along the way, formed up together, five of them being in a body behind one who was evidently their leader and who rode a little ahead. And all were, as Boussac had said, masked, while one or two had breastpieces over their jerkins and some large gorgets. As for the leader himself, he wore what, even for the end of the seventeenth century, was almost now obsolete, a burganet with the visor down.

As he advanced until his horse's head was where the graveyard gate would have been, had it hung properly on its hinges and been closed, he spoke, saying—while his voice sounded hollow by reason of the band of steel which muffled it: "Who are you who ride on the king's highroad to-night? Soldiers, I see, by your accoutrements, and one a mousquetaire. Answer and explain why neither are with your regiments."

"First," replied St. Georges, "answer you, yourself. By what right do you demand so much of a *chevau-léger*, whose cockade is his passport, and of a mousquetaire who is of the king's own house?"

"I represent the governor of the territory of Burgundy, and have the right to make the demand."

"That we will concede when you give us proof of it. Meanwhile, take my assurance as an officer that we ride by the king's orders. That order I carry in my pocket for myself; my comrade goes to join the Mousquetaires Noirs at Bar."

"Still we must see your papers."

"As you shall," said St. Georges, "when you produce your own. Otherwise we intend to proceed to night to that village ahead."

"You do? How if we prevent you?"

"Prevent!" echoed St. Georges, with a contemptuous laugh. "Prevent! Come, sir, come. You are no representative of the governor, as you know very well. He scarcely, I imagine, sets spies, such as that skulking fellow behind you, to track the king's soldiers from village to village, from daybreak to night." Then raising his voice authoritatively, he said: "Stand out of our way!—Boussac, *avancéz!*" and he urged his horse forward to the leader so that the animals' heads touched.

"So be it," exclaimed the other, and, turning his head to those behind, the two comrades heard him say: "The bait takes. Fall on."

In an instant the *mêlée* had begun—in another St. Georges knew what he had from the first suspected. It was his life and the life of his child that was aimed at!

All hurled their horses against him—except the sixth man, he who had tracked them all day, and who now, masked and with his sword drawn, sat his horse outside of the fray, looking on at what was being done by the others.

The leader dealt blow after blow at St. Georges without effect, owing to the latter's skilful swordsmanship;

4

the remaining four directed theirs at the arm which
bore and shielded the child, and which, had Armand
Boussac not been by, would have been pierced through
and through.   But the adroit swordsman perceived the
intention of these murderers—the would-be murderers
of a little child!—and foiled them again and again,
beating off their weapons with his own, and at the same
time losing no opportunity of attacking them.   And so
far was he successful that already he had put two *hors
de combat.*   One was by now off his horse, lying across
a snow-covered grave which was rapidly becoming red
from the blood that poured from his lungs, through
which the mousquetaire's sword had passed two minutes
before; the other, lying forward on his horse's neck,
was urging the animal out of the press of the fight.

And now the odds were but three to two—for still
the man who took no part in the attack sat on his animal's back, and, indeed, from the glances he cast round
him appeared to be meditating flight.

Yet withal they were unequal odds, especially since
their three antagonists were skilful swordsmen, the
leader in particular wielding his weapon with remarkable craft.   Moreover, by his possession of the burganet
he wore, the odds were still greater in his favour—it had
saved his life more than once already from the blows
dealt at his head by St. Georges.

Yet now those odds were soon further diminished—
the chances became at last equal.   As one of the two
followers thrust at the arm of the *chevau-léger*, meaning to strike the burden he carried beneath, Boussac
with a quick parry turned his weapon off, and thus glid-
ing it along his own blade, brought its hilt with a clash
against his own.   Then in a moment the mousquetaire
had seized the sword arm of his antagonist, and, holding

it a moment, struck through the man's body with his own weapon, which he shortened in his grasp. A second later the fellow was writhing on the ground beneath the feet of the various steeds, and helping to crimson the snow, as the others had done who had fallen previously.

"*Pasquedieu!*" the comrades heard the leader mutter through the bars of his helmet, "we fail." Then, as he and St. Georges wheeled around on their horses, while still their weapons clashed and writhed together, he shouted to the man who had taken no part in the affray, "Hound! cur! come and render assistance!"

"Ay," exclaimed Boussac, "come and render him assistance. The chances are even without you. We shall defeat him ere long if you assist not!" and with a mocking laugh he again attacked his own particular adversary, taking heed at the same time to insure that no thrust nor blow of his should strike the precious burden under St. Georges's arm.

In truth, the fellow skulking on the horse seemed to think that matters tended in the direction indicated, for, instead of responding to the leader's orders, he shook up the reins of his own horse, and in a moment had vanished into the night, leaving the four combatants equally matched—except that on the side of St. Georges and Boussac there was the child to be protected.

And now those four set grimly to work—though had there been an onlooker of the fray in that deserted churchyard he would have said that the defenders, and not the attackers, had most stomach for the fight! St. Georges, his blood at boiling point at the assaults made on his little child—now screaming lustily at the noise and clash of steel, and perhaps at the unwonted tossing about to which it had been subjected—fought determinately, his teeth clinched, his eyes gleaming fire. He had sworn to kill this assassin, who had led his band against him. He meant to kill him!

Yet it was hard to do—the other was himself a swordsman of skill. But, skilful as he was, one good thing had now happened: neither he nor his follower could any more threaten harm to the little Dorine! They had sufficient to do to protect themselves from the two soldiers—to protect themselves from the blows and thrusts that came at them; so that, at last, they were forced to retreat down the slope to the road—driven back by the irresistible fury of St. Georges and his follower. And, eventually, seeing that he had got the worst of it, the leader, after one ineffectual thrust at his antagonist, wheeled his horse round and, with a cry to the other to follow him, dashed off down the road in the same direction that the man who had skulked all through the fight had taken.

Yet such an order was more easily given than obeyed, since, at the moment he uttered it, Boussac had by a clever parry sent the other's sword flying out of his hand, while, an instant afterward, he dealt him such a buffet with his own gantleted hand as knocked him off his horse on to the top of those lying on the ground beneath.

CHAPTER VI.

A LITTLE LIGHT.

THE first thought of both the victors was to see to the child, who, while still screaming piteously, was un-harmed—though a deep cut in St. Georges's sleeve and, as he afterward found, a slight sword thrust in the forearm, showed how great had been her peril and how near her little body to being pierced by one of the ruffians' swords. Still she was safe, untouched, and her father muttered a hasty thanksgiving to God as he found such was the case.

Then they addressed themselves to Boussac's vanquished antagonist—the last living and remaining remnant of their foes. For of those who had been overcome earlier in the fray, all three were dead, lying stark and stiff on the frozen ground across the graves where they had fallen. As for him, the living one, he presented as ghastly a spectacle as they who were gone to their doom —sitting up as he now did, and endeavouring to stanch the blood that flowed from his lips and nose in consequence of the blow dealt him by Boussac.

"Stand up," said St. Georges, as he towered over him, his drawn sword in his hand, while by the light of the moon, such as it was, he was able to see the fellow's face. "Stand up and answer my questions."

"What are you going to do to me?" asked the man, staggering to his feet at the other's command.

"Hang you to the nearest tree," replied St. Georges, "in all likelihood. Especially if you trifle with me. I will have the truth from you somehow. Now, *spadassin*, the meaning of this attack. Quick!"

"Monsieur, I know no more than you—monsieur, I——"

"No lies. Answer!" and he lifted his arm and drew his sword back as though about to plunge it into the other's throat. "Answer, I say! Who are you all, you and this carrion here?" and he spurned the dead with his foot. "Above all, who is the fellow in the antique morion, the man who takes double precautions to guard his head and, *ma foi!* to hide his features!"

"Again, I say monsieur, I know not. Nay, nay," he cried, seeing once more the threatening aspect of the other, and again the sword drawn back. "Nay, I swear it is the truth. Let me tell my tale."

"Tell it and be brief."

"Monsieur," the man, therefore, began, as St. Georges stood in front of him and Boussac never took his eyes off his face, while at the same time he held the horses' reins, "there came into our village—not this which you see down there, but Reccy, two leagues off—yesterday the man you call the leader, he who wears the burganet. And accompanied by one other—this," and he looked down at the dead men lying across the graves and touched one with his toe, thereby to indicate him. "Then," the fellow went on, "when he had drunk a cup and made a meal he spake to us sitting round the fire; to him, Gaspard," pointing to a dead man, "and to him, Arnaud," pointing to another, "and said that he and his follower were in search of a brigand riding to Paris from the Côte d'Or who had stolen a child from its lawful parents—a child, he said, whom the brigand desired to make away with, since it stood between him and great wealth."

"He said that?"

"Ay, monsieur, and more. That he must save the child at all costs, wrench it away from the man who had it."

"Now," exclaimed St. Georges passionately, "I know you lie! Neither he nor you endeavoured to save it, to wrench it away from me. On the contrary, all aimed at that harmless child's life, endeavoured to stab it through my cloak, under my arm. Villain! you shall die," and this time he made as though he would indeed slay the fellow.

"No! no! monsieur!" the man howled, overcome with fear of instant death—death that seemed so near now—"hear my story out; you will see I do not lie. It was not until later—when he had bought us—that we knew what he truly wanted. Let me proceed, monsieur."

"Go on!" said St. Georges, again dropping the point of his weapon.

"Also, he said," the man continued, "that he needed more men to make certain of catching him and hauling him to justice and releasing the child. Those were his very words. And he asked us, Gaspard, Arnaud, and myself, if we would take service with him. We looked strong and lusty, he thought—soldiers, perhaps. If we would take part in the undertaking there were fifty gold pistoles for us to divide. Was it worth our while? We said, Yes, it was worth our while; we were disbanded soldiers of the Verdelin Regiment—our time expired, and we looking for a fresh recruiting. If what he said was true—that we were wanted to arrest a kidnapper—we would join. But for no other purpose. Then he swore at us, told us we were *canaille*, that he explained not his movements nor made any oath to the truth of his statements; there was a bag of pistoles, and if we had horses and weapons—but not without—he would employ us. So we took service. Arnaud had two horses at his mother's farm; he lent one to Gaspard, I borrowed mine for two *écus*. *Voilà tout.*"

"Is that all?" asked St. Georges quietly.

"All of importance. The pact was made, and then he said we must, this morning, move on toward Aignay-le-Duc. Le Brigand—as he called monsieur—would pass that way to-night, he thought. But, later on, he would know. A messenger from Dijon would arrive to tell him."

"A messenger from Dijon!" Both St. Georges and Boussac started at this and looked at each other in the uncertain light. A messenger from Dijon! Who could it be? Who was there who knew of St. Georges's where-abouts? Yet, as the man spoke, they guessed that the fellow whom Boussac had noticed, who had tracked them all day, mostly masked, must have been that messenger.

"He came at last," the narrator continued, "an hour or so before monsieur and his companion. And he told us that there were two, so that we had to do more than we had undertaken. Yet, we thought not much of that. We were five to two, for he, the messenger, averred he would take no part in the fight unless absolutely neces-sary. He was not well, he said; he had ridden all day— fighting was not his business; he was a messenger, not a soldier. So our employer cursed him for a poltroon, but told him he might stand out of the attack. We were five without him—that was enough."

"Go on," said St. Georges once more, seeing that again the man paused as though his narrative had con-cluded. "Go on. There is more to be told."

"But little, monsieur. Only this. As you wheeled into this graveyard he gave us one final order. 'They will resist,' he said, 'therefore spare not. Dead or alive they must be taken. Child and man. Dead or alive. You understand!'"

"And it was for that reason that all endeavoured to plunge their swords into this innocent child! My God!" And St. Georges paused a moment ere he went on; then he said to Boussac: "What shall we do to him? He merits death."

"*Ma foi!* he does," replied the mousquetaire, while he grimly added, "For my part, I am willing to execute it on him now."

At this sinister remark, uttered with the callousness which a brave soldier would naturally feel for the existence of such a creature, the other flung himself on his feet before them and began to howl so for mercy that St. Georges, more for fear that he would call the attention of some who might be about the village than aught else, bade him cease the noise he was making or he would indeed take effectual steps to stop it. Then, when this remark had produced the desired effect, namely, a cessation of the man's shouts, though he whimpered and whined like a beaten hound, the other continued :

"In spite of your villainy, of your assaults on one so harmless as the child I carry, you are too vile for us to stain our weapons with your blood. Yet, what to do with you?"

"Throw him in there," said Boussac with *sang froid*. "That will keep him quiet for some time at least," and he pointed to an open grave which yawned very near where they stood, and into whose black mouth he had been peering for some time. He added also: "It will be his only chance of ever occupying one. Such as he end by hanging on roadside gibbets or rotting on the wheel they have been broken upon—the peaceful grave is not for them."

St. Georges turned his eyes to the spot indicated, exclaiming that it would do very well. It was no newly made grave, he saw, prepared for one who had recently departed, but, instead, an old one that had been opened, perhaps to receive some fresh body; for by the side of it there lay a slab that had, it was plain to see, been pushed aside from where it had previously rested, as though to permit of it being so opened.

"Ay," echoed Boussac, sardonically, " it will do very

well. Add when he is in—as we will soon have him—
the stone shall be pushed back to keep him safe. Then
he may holla loud enough and long: no one will hear
him."

His hollas began again at once, however, for at the
terrifying prospect of being thus incarcerated in so
awful a manner he flung himself once more on his
knees, and bellowed out:

"Nay! Nay! In pity, I beseech you. You know
not what you do—what terrors you condemn me to.
A plague, a horrible one, a sweating sickness, passed
over this province a year back—it took many, among
others him who laid here. He was of Chantillon—a
seigneur—and is now removed by his friends. Mercy!
Mercy! Mercy! Condemn me not to this. Think, I
beseech you. The grave is infected, impregnated with
contagion. Mercy! Mercy! Mercy!"

The fellow had thrust at his child's life—St. Georges
remembered it even as he spoke!—yet, being a brave
soldier himself, he could not condemn the ruffian to such
horrors as these. Revenge he would have taken earlier,
in the heat of the fight; would have killed the man
with his own hand, even as he would have killed that
other, the leader, had the chance arisen; but—this was
beneath him. Therefore, he said:

"Bind him, Boussac, to this old yew. Bind him
with his horse's reins and gag him. Then he must take
his chance—the night grows late. We must away."

It was done almost as soon as ordered, the mousquetaire detaching the coarse reins of the man's horse—
which was itself wounded and seemed incapable of
action—and lashing him to the tree, while he took one of
his stirrup leathers and bade him open his mouth to be
gagged.

"To-morrow," he remarked to the unhappy wretch, "at matins you may be released. Meanwhile, heart up! you are not alone. You have your comrades for company." And he glanced down at the others lying still in death.

"Stay," said St. Georges, "ere you put the gag in his mouth let me ask him one question.—Who," turning to the shivering creature before him, "who was your leader? Answer me that, and even now you shall go free. Answer!"

For a moment the man hesitated—doubtless he was wondering if he could not invent some name which might pass for a real one, and so give him his freedom—then, perhaps because his inventive powers were not great, or—which was more probable—his captor might have some means of knowing that he was lying, he answered:

"I do not know. I never saw him before."

"You do not know, or will not tell—which?"

"I do not know."

"Whence came he to your village? From what quarter?"

"The north road. The great road from Paris. He had not come many leagues; his horse was fresh."

"So! What was he like? He did not wear his burganet all the time—when he ate, for instance."

"He was young," the man replied, hoping, it may be, that by his ready answers he would earn his pardon even yet, "passably young. Of about monsieur's age. With a brown beard cropped close and gray eyes."

"Is that all you can tell?"

"It is all, monsieur. *Ayez pitié*, monsieur."

"Gag him," said St. Georges to Boussac, "and let us go."

So they left the fellow gagged and bound, and rode on once more upon their road, passing swiftly through Aignay-le-Duc without stopping.

"For," said St. Georges, "badly as we want rest, we must not halt here. To-morrow those dead men will be found, with, perhaps, another added to their number if the frost is great to-night, as it seems like to be. We must push on for Chatillon now, even though we ride all night. Pray Heaven our horses do not drop on the road!"

So through Aignay-le-Duc they went, clattering up the one wretched street, their animals' hoofs waking peasants from their early slumbers, and the jangling of their scabbards and steel trappings arousing the whole village. Even the *guet de nuit*—who because it was his duty to be awake was always asleep—was roused by the sound of the oncoming hoofs, and, rushing to his cabin door, cried out, "Who goes there?"

"*Chevau-léger en service du roi*," cried St. Georges; and "*Mousquetaire de la maison du roi*," answered Boussac; and so, five minutes later, they had passed the hamlet and were once more on their road north.

"Yet," said St. Georges as, stopping to breathe their horses, he opened the cloak and gazed on his sleeping child, "I would give much to know who our enemy is— who the cruel wretch who aimed at your innocent little life. 'A young man with a fair beard and gray eyes!' the ruffian said. Who, who is he?"

And, bending over, he brushed her lips with his great mustache.

"My darling," he whispered, "I pray God that all attacks on you may be thwarted as was this one to-night; that he may raise up for you always so stout and true a protector as he who rides by my side."

"Amen!" muttered Boussac, who among his good qualities did not find himself overwhelmed with modesty. "Amen! Though," he exclaimed a second after, "he who would not fight for such an innocent as that deserves never to have one of his own."

CHAPTER VII.

A REASON.

MIDNIGHT was sounding from the steeples of Chatillon as the soldiers rode their tired beasts across the bridge over the Seine and through the deserted street that led up to the small guard-house, where, Boussac said, would be found the Governor of the Bailliage with some soldiers of the Montagne Regiment.

As they had come along they had naturally talked much on the attack that had been made upon them outside Aignay-le-Duc, and St. Georges had decided that, as Chatillon was the most important town on this side of Troyes, it would be his duty here to give notice to any one in authority of that attack having taken place.

"For," said he, "that it was premeditated who can doubt? The leader spoke of me as a brigand who had stolen a child, while he himself was the brigand who desired to steal my child. Then, see, Boussac, we were followed—or preceded—from Dijon by that man who warned him we were coming—merciful heavens! who could he have been?—so that it shows plainly that I am a marked man. Marked! tracked! known all along the route."

"But why? Why?" interposed Boussac. "Why is your life, the life of the *pauvrette*, aimed at? Across whose path do you and she stand?"

"That I can but guess at," replied the other; "though I have long suspected that I have powerful enemies to whom my existence was hateful." Then, since their tired horses were now walking side by side across a wide plain, at the end of which rose Chatillon, he leaned over, and, putting his hand on the mousquetaire's saddle, said gravely:

"Boussac, you have shown to-night the true metal you are made of. Listen to me; hark to a secret; though first you must assure me you will never divulge to any one that which I tell you until I give you leave. Will you promise?"

"Ay," replied Boussac. "I will." Whereon he stretched out his own hand, drawing off first the great riding gantlet he wore, and said, "There's my hand. And with it the word of a brother soldier, of a mousquetaire."

"So be it," taking the offered hand in his own. "Listen. I believe that I am the Duke de Vannes."

"What!" exclaimed Boussac, "you the Duke de Vannes! *Mon Dieu*, monsieur, this is extraordinary. But stay. You bewilder me. Your name is St. Georges —if it is as you say, it should be De la Bresse. I knew him—your father. He died at Salzbach the same day as Turenne did. And *you believe*—do you not know? Or —or did—or was——"

"Stop there, Boussac. I can suppose what you are going to say. To ask if my mother was—well, no matter. But be sure of this: if I am what I think, I am his lawful son. His heir, and myself a De Vannes, the De Vannes."

"But 'what you think!' 'what you believe yourself
to be!' Do you not know?"

"No. I may be his son, I may in truth be only Monsieur St. Georges. Yet—yet—this attack on me and
mine points to the presumption that I am what I believe myself to be. The cavalry soldier, St. Georges,
and his helpless babe would not be worth waylaying,
putting out of existence forever. De Vannes's heir
would be."

"Only—again—you do not know. Does not a man
know whose son he is?"

Chatillon still lay far off on the plain through which
they were riding; the flickering flambeaux on its gate
and walls were but little specks of light at present, and
St. Georges decided that he would confide in the mousquetaire who had shown himself so good a friend that
night. Moreover, Boussac had said he was of gentle
blood; his being in the Mousquetaires proved it, since
none were admitted who had not some claim to good
birth—above all, he wanted a friend, a confidant. And
as, in those days, there was scarcely any gulf between
the officers of the inferior grades and the soldiers themselves, Boussac was well fitted to be that friend and confidant. Also he knew, he felt now, since the attack of
the evening, how insecure his own life was; he recognised that at any moment the little motherless child he
bore on his breast might be left alone unfriended in the
world. Suppose, for instance, he fell to-night in a second attack, or ere he reached Paris, in a week, or a
month hence. Well! a mousquetaire whose principal
duties were in Paris near the king's person would be a
friend worth having!

So he told him his tale.

"My mother, a Protestant cavalier's daughter, was

in Holland with her father after the execution of the
king. As you know, that country was full of refugees
from England. There she met my father, 'Captain St.
Georges.' But at that time De Vannes was out of favour
with the court; he was allied with the party of the
Fronde, also he was a Protestant. And I believe he was
'Captain St. Georges,' I believe he was my mother's
husband."

"Always you 'believe,' monsieur. Surely there must
be proofs! Your mother, what does she say?"

"She died," went on St. Georges, "when I was two
years old—suddenly of the plague that spread from Sar-
dinia to many parts of Europe. It was because of her
memory that I spared that fellow we have left behind
from the infected grave. I would not condemn him to
the death that robbed me of her."

"Therefore," exclaimed Boussac, "you gathered nothing from her!"

"Nothing. I cannot even remember her. Nay,
some more years had to pass ere I, growing up, knew that
my name was St. Georges. Then, as gradually intelligence dawned, I learned from the man with whom I lived,
a Huguenot pastor at Montéreau, that I had no mother,
and that my father was a soldier who could rarely find
time to come and see me. Nay, was not often in Paris,
and then not always able to make even so short a journey as that to Montéreau. Yet," went on St. Georges,
meditatively, "he came sometimes, loaded with presents
for me which he brought in the coach, and passed the
day with us, being always addressed as Captain St.
Georges by the pastor. Those were happy days, for he
was always kind and good to me, would walk out with
me hand in hand, would spend the day with me in the
Forest of Fontainebleau, hard by, and would talk about

my future. Yet he was sad, too; his eyes would fill with tears sometimes as he looked at me or stroked my hair, and always he asked me if I would be a soldier as he was. And always in reply I answered, 'Yes,' which seemed to please him. So I grew up, treated with more and more respect mingled with affection from the pastor as time went on; and, also, I was now taught military exercises and drilled in preparation for my future career. But as the time went on my father came less and less, though he never failed to send ample sums to provide for my education and also for my pleasures. When I asked the pastor why he never came near us, he said he was occupied with his profession, that he was away in the Palatinate with Turenne. Now, at that period, I being then about eighteen, there came frequently to Paris the story of all that was doing in the Palatinate—stories that made the blood run cold to hear. Stories of villages and towns burnt, so that never more should that region send forth enemies against Louis."

"They penetrated further than Paris and Montéreau," interrupted Boussac, " ay, even to our out-of-the-way part of France. And not only of villages and towns burnt and destroyed, but of fathers and bread-winners burnt in their beds, women ill treated, ruin everywhere. There were those who said it was not war, but rapine."

"And so I said," replied St. Georges; " once even I went so far as to say that I regretted that my father followed so cruel and bloodthirsty a man as Turenne. But the pastor stopped me, rose up in his chair in anger, bade me never say another word against him—told me that I, of all alive, had least right to judge him."

"But," exclaimed Boussac, " this does not show that

5

the duke was your father, monsieur. The worthy pastor
may have thought it wrong to encourage you in speaking ill of one——"

"Nay; listen," said St. Georges. "The year 1674
arrived, my twentieth year, when there came one night
my commission in the regiment—the Nivernois. You
have perhaps never seen one of these documents, Boussac, but you will ere long, I make no doubt, when your
own is made out for the Mousquetaires. Therefore, I
will tell you of its strange character and wording. It
was that the king, at the request of the Duc de Vannes,
had been graciously pleased to appoint me to the position of *porte-drapeau* in the Nivernois under De Mailly-
Sebret—a brave man, now dead—and that I was to join
it in Holland. I did so, and, from that day to this, have
prosecuted many inquiries as to why De Vannes should
have procured me that commission. But up to now I
have never received positive proof that he was my father
—though still I do believe it."

"But why, why, why?" asked Boussac impatiently.
"A man must have some friend who obtains him his
presentation to a regiment—even I had our grand
seigneur. And I never suspected *him* of being my
father!"

"Doubtless you had no reason to do so. Yet, again,
listen. De Vannes was killed in 1675; in the same year
—a month before him—died my old friend and protector—the one man who had ever stood in the light of
a parent to me. His successor found among his papers
and chattels a packet addressed to me, and forwarded it
by a sure hand to Holland. When I opened it I found
therein a miniature of my mother—though I should not
have known it was she had he not informed me of it—
and also instructions that I should myself seek out the

Due de Vannes at the first opportunity and boldly ask him who my father was. 'For,' he wrote, 'he can tell you if he will, and he ought in justice to tell you. I would do so only the most solemn promise binds me to keep silence—a promise which, had I never given it, would have stood in the way of my ever being to you all that I have been—of having my life cheered by you, my dear, dear one.' I was preparing to seek the duke out, had obtained leave to do so and to join Turenne in the campaign, when, lo! the news came that both he and De Vannes were killed on the same day."

"And you know no more?" asked Boussac, as now the plain was passed, and from the watch towers of Chatillon they could hear the guard being changed. And also, as they rode up to the gate, the challenge of " Who comes there?" rang out on the frosty air.

Again the usual answer was given, "Chevau-Léger" and " Mousquetaire," and then, while the bolts were heard creaking harshly in their sockets as the gate was being opened for them, St. Georges turning to his comrade said, in answer to his last question:

" I know no more, though still my belief is fixed. But, Boussac, she at whose manoir I am bidden to stay at Troyes—the Marquise de Roquemaure—may be able to enlighten me. She was, if all reports are true, beloved by De Vannes once, and I have heard loved him. Yet they never married—perhaps because they were of different faith—and she instead married De Roquemaure, De Vannes's cousin and heir. He left a son by his first wife, who is now that heir in his place. Boussac, does any light break in on you now—can you conceive why I and my little darling asleep under my cloak should run hourly, daily risks of assassination—ay! even as to-night we have run them?"

"*Mon Dieu!*" exclaimed Boussac, "yes. You stand in the path of——"

"Precisely. Hush! See, the gate is open. We may enter."

The soldiers of the guard saluted St. Georges as he rode in, followed by the mousquetaire, while the officer of the night, after bowing politely to him, held out his hand, as greeting to a comrade.

"Monsieur has had a cold journey, though fine— Heavens!" he exclaimed, as he saw that the other had a strange burden under his cloak, "what does monsieur carry there?"

"A harmless child," St. Georges said, while the men of the garrison gathered round to peer at the little creature whose blue eyes were now staring at them in the rays of the great lantern that swung over the gateway. "My child, whose life would have been taken to-night by five desperadoes had it not been for this honest mousquetaire who, by Heaven's providence, happened to be riding my road."

From the soldiers around the newcomers—some risen half asleep from their wooden planks in the guard room, some already on duty and with every sense awake to its utmost—there rose a murmur of indignation that was not at all extinguished by Boussac's description of the attack in the graveyard, and at the passes made more than once at Dorine under his own guard and the *che-vau-léger's* arm.

"*Grand Dieu!*" exclaimed the officer, "five men attack two, and one burdened with a little child under his arm. Of what appearance were these assassins?"

St. Georges described them as well as he could— mentioning in particular the leader, who wore the bur-

ganet, and the fellow who skulked outside the fight—the
man who, the comrades knew, had brought the news
from Dijon that they were on the road. And then from
all who surrounded those fresh comers there arose a
hubbub, a babel of sound that drowned everything like
intelligible question or answer.

"A man who wore a burganet," one cried; "a rusty
thing that would have disgraced the days of the Bear-
nais." "*Fichte!*" hissed another, "you have come an
hour too late." "'Twas but at midnight," exclaimed a
third, "that he rode through—ten minutes of midnight. And, by good chance for him, it was to-night,
since 'tis the last of our New-Year carousals; to-morrow
the town will be closed at dusk as usual."

"But where—where is he gone?" asked St. Georges.

"*Corbleu!*" exclaimed the officer, "we had no right
to ask him, since both this and the other gates were
open. Yet, stay; has he left the town yet? It may be
not."

"Ay! but he has, though," exclaimed a boyish
young officer who at this moment joined the group.
"In truth, he has. I was at the north gate as he clattered up to it, calling out that he must go through.
'And why the devil must you?' I asked, not liking the
fellow's tone, which sounded hollow enough through the
rusty iron pot on his head. 'I have been attacked,' he
said; 'nigh murdered by some ruffians, and am wounded.
I must get me home.' 'And where is your home?' I
asked. 'Beyond Bar,' he replied; 'for Heaven's sake,
do not stop me!' Whereon," continued the young officer, "since I had no right whatever to prevent his exit,
I let him go, and a second afterward the clock struck
midnight, and we clapped the gate behind him. Yet,
ere that was done, I saw him spurring along the north

road as though the devil, or a king's exempt, were after him."

"The north road!" St. Georges said in a low voice to Boussac. "The north road! You hear? And the north road leads to De Roquemaure's manoir."

CHAPTER VIII.

DRAWING NEAR.

Two days later, when again the wintry evening was fast approaching, St. Georges, by now alone, drew near to the ancient city of Troyes. So near, indeed, had he arrived that its walls and fortifications were plainly visible to him, and from its steeples the bells could be heard, either chiming the hour or summoning the inhabitants to evening worship. Beneath his cloak, as ever, he bore his precious burden, who showed no signs of being fatigued by the long journey she had made in so rough a fashion, but often woke up and, thrusting her little head from out the folds of the cloak, smiled up into the face of her father.

He had parted with Boussac at Bar, leaving him there surrounded by his comrades of two troops of the Mousquetaires Noirs, from whom he had received the joyful intelligence that they were soon to move on to Paris, to be quartered at Versailles, while two other troops of the "Gris" were to replace them—a piece of news that had given St. Georges almost as much pleasure as it had done to the other. For it seemed to him that, should aught take him away from Paris when he had left the child in the house of the Sieur Blecy in the Rue de

Timoleon, there was one faithful friend on whom he could rely to keep watch over it and see to its welfare.

"And be sure," said the mousquetaire, "that I will do so. Monsieur St. Georges, we are friends now in spite of our difference in military rank; we have fought side by side; if you are not there to guard your child, I shall be. Meanwhile, prosecute your inquiries as to the rank and position—ay, and the fortune!—you believe, is yours, and may the good God put you in the right way! Farewell, monsieur, and Heaven bless you! You know where I may be communicated with; let me know also where I may send to you," and he stooped down and kissed the child ere he grasped the other's hand as he prepared to mount his horse.

"Adieu," St. Georges said, "adieu, friend. You helped me to save her life once. For that I thank you, am bound to you forever. I pray Heaven that, if she should need it, you may be by to do so again." Whereon, with a farewell to his new friend and to several officers and men who had all testified as much interest in him and his charge as those others had done at Chatillon, he set forth once more upon another stage of his journey.

Both at Chatillon and in Bar, which he was now leaving behind, he and Boussac had spoken to those whose duty it was to keep an eye to the safety of the highroads, and had informed the captain of the maréchausse—or mounted patrol of the highroads—of the attack that had been made on them. But this official had only shrugged his shoulders and remarked that "it was possible, very possible."

"Louvois," he said, "is responsible for all. Either he denudes the country of men to send on his campaigns, so that none are left to guard it, or, the cam-

paigns being over, he pours back into it thousands of
disbanded soldiers who, for want of aught else to do,
become *filous* and *spadassins*. What would you? And
according to your own account, monsieur, you and your
friend, the mousquetaire, could take good care of yourselves."

"These were neither *filous* nor *spadassins*," replied
St. Georges, "or at least the leader was not. Oh! that
I may meet him again, and when I am not encumbered
with a harmless child to protect!"

"You know him, then, monsieur?"

"No. And since he carefully disguised his face as
well as protected his head, I may not even assert that I
have ever seen him. But I suspect."

"Tell me the name of him you suspect, and I may
do something—may call upon him to answer your
charge."

"Nay," replied St. Georges, "that cannot be. For
I must not tarry here; I have the king's orders to ride
straight for my destination, halting no more than is
necessary; and so, perforce, I must go on. But should
you hear of a man wearing an ancient burganet whose
appearance in your neighbourhood seems suspicious, and
who"—remembering the description given by the man
they had gagged and left tied to the tree at Aignay-le-
Duc—"is young, with a brown beard cropped close and
gray eyes, I pray you question him as to his doings two
nights ago. It may save your roads from further brigandage, and—should you confine him for any length
of time—his life from my sword. For, I promise you,
if ever I encounter him again, and am sure of my man,
he shall not escape a second time."

"*Mon Dieu!*" replied the captain of the *maréchausse*, "if he falls into our hands I will warrant him

against your sword. If we can but bring his attack on you at Aignay-le-Duc home to him, it will be the wheel and not the sword with which he will find his account."

"So best. Yet I doubt your catching him, and must believe and hope the punishment he deserves shall reach him through my hand. If it is he whom I think, he is of high position."

"Many of high position have come to the wheel when in our grip," said the fierce old captain, a man who had followed his trade under Condé. "*Ma foi!* we have great powers, we of the *maréchausse*, and for brigandage on the king's highway we use those powers swiftly. Poof! If we catch him and bring his vagabondage home to him, he will be broken all to pieces before his position is of any avail."

So in this frame of mind St. Georges left the old man, and now, as night drew on, he neared Troyes.

All day he had pondered on the meeting that was before him—on the fact that he was about to encounter the woman who had once loved so dearly the man he believed to be his father. For, that he would meet her, stand face to face with her, he supposed was certain. She would scarce let an officer of the *chevaux-légers* stay in her house—sent there by the king's orders—and not summon him to her presence. Moreover, did he not go there, as that evil-seeming bishop had said, so that he might also hear a word possessing great significance to both the king and his minister? A word of similar import to the one the bishop had himself sent!

"Yet," he pondered, as now the hum from the busy old city reached his ears and he saw its smoke rising in the evening air, "yet, does she know who I am, whom I believe myself to be? Ha!" as a thought struck him, "how else should it be? If De Roquemaure, her son, or

stepson, knows, then she must know too. And—and
does she, too, wish me dead—and you—you, also, my
darling," with a pressure of his arm against his burden,
" as well? *Mon Dieu!* If that is so, then it is to the
lion's jaws I am going in entering this manoir of hers.
No matter! I will do it. It is in the king's name I
present myself; let us see who dares assault his messenger. And," he muttered fiercely to himself, "if her
whelp, De Roquemaure, is the man with the brown
beard—the man whose voice I shall know in a thousand,
although it reached me before through iron bars—he
shall have one more chance at my life in spite of his
lady mother." And he clinched his white teeth as he
reflected thus.

Knowing what he did, namely, that "the whelp, De
Roquemaure," as he had termed him, was heir in a year
or two to De Vannes's great fortune, and coupling with
that fact that he and his child had been attacked in a
neighbourhood at no great distance from Troyes, he had
begun on his solitary ride this day to speculate as to
whether the whole of his journey, his sudden summons
from Pontarlier to Paris, was not some deeply devised
plot to remove him out of existence. For, although he
had long suspected who and what he was, might it not
be the case that those in whose light he stood had only
recently learned that such was the case? And, if such
were the fact, what a revelation, what a blow, such
knowledge would be to them! They had doubtless
long looked forward to the enjoyment of the Duc de
Vannes's wealth; if they had now discovered that the
possession of that wealth might be disputed, what more
likely than that they should endeavour to remove for
ever from their path the two—himself and his child—
who could so dispute it with them?

"Yet," he had mused all through that day, "how know it since I, of all people, have no certain knowledge; how, above all, learn that their opportunity had come? How know that I who stand between them and their greed should pass upon their way, come across their path? Bah!" he finally exclaimed, "it is a coincidence that I should so travel their road, seek shelter in the house that my father's heir dwells in. It may be that when I see this young De Roquemaure he shall in no way resemble that night assassin who attacked me; it may be that his mother no more dreams that she is about to see the son of the man she loved than that she will ever see him again in life."

Yet, even as he so decided, he knew that there was more than coincidence in it. He knew that those who had attacked him and Boussac at Aignay-le-Duc were more than common bravos. Otherwise the child's life would not have been sought as fiercely as his own; the spy, whomsoever he might be, would not have ridden so many leagues from Dijon to carry the news of his approach.

Therefore, in spite of his attempted dismissal of all his doubts and suspicions, he resolved that, above all, he would be cautious as regarded one thing—his child. She, at least, was under no orders to seek shelter in the manoir; the roof that covered this marquise and her stepson should never be slept under by Dorine.

"All women's hearts," he murmured, " go out to my motherless babe, strangers though they be. There must be many such in this old city, and one such I will find. If as—God help me!—I must suppose, this she-wolf and her husband's son seek our lives, at least they shall get no chance at hers. The mistress of a common inn, a warder's wife, will keep her in greater

safety than she may be under the roof-tree of madame
la marquise."

The gates of Troyes were not yet shut—the city having too much traffic with the outlying hamlets to permit
of their being closed early—so that St. Georges rode in
without any formalities beyond replying to the usual
questions as to who he was and what was his business,
and, passing slowly into the quaint streets, soon came to
a great *auberge* which looked as though suitable for
the purpose he required, a shelter for the child. In the
vast kitchen, or hall, through whose diamond-paned
windows he could see perfectly, he perceived a young
bare-armed woman cooking at a large fireplace, while
around her at wooden tables sat the usual company of
such places—men drinking in groups or eating from
platters which another woman brought from the first
and set before them. So he rode in under the great
gateway and called loudly for an hostler to come.

At his summons a man came forth who, seeing his
soldierlike appearance, asked if he desired to rest there
for the night, and stated at the same time that the inn
was very full.

"That may be so," replied St. Georges, "yet, perhaps, not so full but that a child can be sheltered here
for one night. See, friend," he continued, opening his
cloak, "I bear one here who has been carried far by me.
Think you the hostess will give her protection? She
needs a good bed sorely."

As it always was—to the credit of humanity—the
sight of the little helpless thing sleeping on its father's
arm roused this man's sympathy as it had roused that
of all others.

"*Ma foi!*" he said, stooping to gaze at it as it
lay on that arm, "a rude cradle for *la petite*. Yet—

there is no hostess; the landlord's wife is dead. And why — why — do you leave it? Why not stay yourself?"

"I have to present myself to the Marquise de Roquemaure at her manoir. Where is that manoir? Heaven grant I have not passed it on the road!"

"Half a league outside the city—to the north, on the Paris road. If you have come from the south, you have not passed it."

"So! It is from the south I come. Now, quick, can I leave the child here—in safety?"

"I will see. Wait." And he went away toward the kitchen, leaving St. Georges standing by his horse easing its saddle, and then holding a bucket of water, which he had picked up, to its thirsty mouth with his disengaged hand.

Presently the man came back, followed by one of the young women whom St. Georges had seen waiting on the company—a dark girl with her arms bare—a girl whose face looked kind and honest. And again with her, as with the others, her heart went out to the little child in the great man's arms. The sense of helplessness, of dependence on so unusual a nurse, touched all those hearts, especially feminine ones.

Briefly as might be he explained to her what it was he required—a night's shelter for and watchfulness over the child, he having to visit the Manoir de Roquemaure. Also, he said, he would come back early in the morning to fetch it away.

"If," said the girl, a little hesitatingly, for she was but a waitress at the inn, "monsieur will intrust the child to me—it is a pretty thing, and see—see—how tired it is!—how it yawns!—then I will do my best. It may sleep with me, and I am used to children. I have several little sisters whom I saw to after my mother's death and before I took service."

"I will intrust it to you most thankfully," St. Georges replied. "Your face is honest, my girl, and true."

So—telling her, as he had told others on his road, that the child was motherless—he kissed it, and bade it good-night, saying inwardly, as he ever said when he parted from it, a little prayer that God would guard and have it in his keeping, and so let the waitress take it away. But, because something told him he was in a dangerous neighbourhood, he impressed upon her that she should in no way leave it more than was absolutely necessary; above all, he begged her and the hostler, who was a witness to the proceedings, to remember that they need say nothing about a child having been left in her care. And they, with many protestations that they would not chatter, assured him that he need be under no apprehension.

"I take my rest," the girl said, "at the close of day. The child shall not leave me till I rise at dawn, nor, indeed, until monsieur returns. I promise."

Then he let her go away with it, and busied himself next with his horse, seeing that it was rubbed down and freshened with a feed. "For," said he, patting its flank, "you have another league to do, my friend, ere your rest comes." And the animal being refreshed, he gave the hostler a piece of silver as earnest of more in the morning if he found he had not been chattering, and so made for the North Gate.

"And now," he said to himself as he passed out, "for the house of the woman De Vannes loved, the house of the man who, I believe, thirsts for my life and the life of my child."

CHAPTER IX.

A ROYAL SUMMONS.

"La plus cruelle de toutes les voies par laquelle le roi fut instruit bien des années fut celle de l'ouverture des lettres. Il est incroyable combien des gens de toutes les sortes en furent plus ou moins perdus."

St. Simon.

A FORTNIGHT before St. Georges had set out upon his long and, as it had already proved, hazardous ride from Pontarlier to Paris, four men were busily employed in a small, neatly furnished *cabinet* at Versailles —a little apartment that partook more of the appearance of a bureau, or office, than aught else.

Two were seated at a table facing each other; behind each of these was one of the others, who handed them papers rapidly drawn from portfolios which they carried. Of the men who were seated, the one with his hat on and wearing a costume of brown velvet—because already the days were very cold—was Louis the Fourteenth; the other, whose manner was extremely rough and coarse—indeed brutal, except when addressing the king himself—was Louvois, the Minister of War, ostensibly, but in reality the one minister who had his fingers in all the business of the state. Those standing behind each of the others were Pajot and Rouillier, who farmed the postal service from the crown.

" *Finissons*," said Louis, in the low clear voice that expressed, according to all reports, more authority than even the trumpet tones of many of his great commanders—*finissons*. The morning wears away. What remains to be done?" Then in a rich murmur he said: " It has not been too interesting to-day. My subjects are losing the art of letter-writing."

On the table there lay five large portfolios bound in purple leather and impressed with a crown and the letters L. R. Also upon each was stamped a description of its contents. On one was inscribed, in French of course, "Letters opened at the Post"; another "Conduct of Princes and Lords"; a third bore upon it "Private Life of Bishops and Prelates"; a fourth, "Private Life of Ecclesiastics"; and the fifth, "Report of the Lieutenant of the Police."

Furnished thus with these five reports, which reached his august hands and were inspected weekly by his august eyes, Louis considered that the whole of his subjects' existences were, if not known to him, at least very likely at some period or other to come under his supervision. What he did not know, however, was that Louvois, who was the originator of the odious system of opening letters sent through the post, did not always show to him those epistles which came first into his own hands. Therefore in this case, as in many others before and after the days of Louis *le Dieudonné*, the valet was a greater man than his master.

It was the case now—as it had often been!—the king had seen some threescore letters marked with the senders' names or initials; and there was one he had not seen.

He seemed a little weary this morning—nay, had he not been so great a king, as well as a man who had almost every impulse under control, it would almost have appeared that he was a little irritated at the contents of the first portfolio, that one inscribed "Letters opened at the Post." "For," he continued, after descanting on the art of letter-writing which his subjects appeared to have lost, "the responsibility given to the masters of our royal post seems to me, my good Louvois, to be greater than their minds—provincial in most cases—appear able to sustain. They mark letters from the local seigneurs as worthy of perusal by us in Paris ere being forwarded to their destination, which, in truth, are barren of interest. To wit," he went on, with that delicate irony for which he was noted, " we have opened fifty-five letters, and in not one of them is there the slightest hint of even murmuring against our royal authority, no suggestion of resisting our, or the seigniorial, imposts, not even the faintest suggestion of an attack against our royal person. They are harmless, and consequently wearisome."

" I regret," replied Louvois, softening his raucous voice to the tones absolutely necessary when addressing Louis, " that your Majesty finds the system so barren of interest. But, I may with all deference suggest, perhaps, that it has one gratifying result. All these letters are from the most important persons among your Majesty's subjects, yet there is, as your Majesty observes, no one word hostile to your rule or sacred person. The system—my system—testifies at least to that agreeable fact."

" Yes," replied the king, in the calm, unruffled voice, " it testifies to that. You are right. What else is there to do ?"

" But little, your Majesty. Yet, with your permission, something. May I also suggest that Monsieur Pajot and the Vicomte de Rouillier may retire ?"

Louis signified by a bend of his head that they might do so, whereon the two " farmers," after profound obeisances, left the room, and the king and his minister again applied themselves to the work before them.

It was of a multifarious nature, since it dealt with

6

the contents of each of the portfolios, exclusive of the first—the one whose contents had been so barren of interest to the king, and which contents would never now arrive at their destination in spite of his Majesty's remark about their being forwarded on. For, since the seals and thread had necessarily to be broken ere those contents could be perused, it would be impossible to send them on to those to whom they were addressed. But what became of them instead, probably Louvois only knew. It may be that they were put away carefully, to be brought out years afterward, if needed, and when their present harmless contents might, in the movement of time, have altered their nature and have become, if not damning, at least compromising.

Taking up the second portfolio, marked " Conduct of Princes and Lords," Louvois extracted one paper and read out briefly: "The young Count de Quincé has eloped with Mademoiselle le Brun, daughter of a rich mercer in Guise. Her brother, attempting to stop the carriage in which they were setting out for Paris, was slain by the count's body-servant." After reading which, Louvois looked up at his master.

"Write," said Louis in reply, "that De Quincé is not to enter Paris. He is to be arrested at the gate and taken to the Bastille. There he will be judged. Proceed."

Selecting from the third portfolio two papers, Louvois went on: "The Bishop of Beauvais referred in a sermon, delivered three weeks ago, to the birth of Madame de Maintenon in the prison of Niort, and pointed a moral as to how——"

"One may rise by good works," interrupted the king. "The bishop is indiscreet, but truthful. Let it pass. Proceed."

"The Grand Prior of Chavagnac entertains daily in Paris many courtesans at his table."

"Write that he retires at once to his priory. If he refuses, arrest him and bring him before me. Above all, the Church must be kept pure. Continue."

The work was done, however, since Louvois informed the king that the contents of the fourth and fifth portfolios scarcely needed his attention. Yet, since he knew that Louis would not be satisfied without himself seeing the reports which they contained, he rose, and, bringing each in its turn to the king, placed it before him.

"So," his Majesty said, when he had glanced at them, "our morning's work is done and easily done. The reports are meagre, and, in the latter cases, deal with persons better left to the magistrates. Now," as a clock above the mantelpiece struck eleven, "I am expected," and he rose from the table as though to depart.

"There are a few papers requiring your Majesty's signature," the minister said, "though none of great importance. Will your Majesty please to sign?"

"Let me see them," and, as before, the papers were placed before the king for him to read ere affixing his signature.

He glanced at each ere he did so, but, since he already knew their purport, made no remark as he signed, until, at last, he came to one addressed to "Monsieur Georges St. Georges, Lieutenant des Chevaux-Légers de Nivernois, en garnison à Pontarlier," when he stopped and began to read it all through; while Louvois, pretending to be busy at some other papers, watched him stealthily from under his eyebrows.

"Georges St. Georges," he said at last—"Georges St. Georges—I recall the name and that I ordered this letter to be prepared last week. Repeat the circumstances."

"Your Majesty will remember that this gentleman's commission was obtained from you by the late Duc de Vannes, and that you ordered me to watch his career, and, when the time came, to recommend him to you for promotion, should he have proved himself worthy of it."

"I remember, although it was some time ago. And also that a month or so ago you told me the time had come for such promotion, and that, therefore, he should be ordered to come to Paris. But, my good Louvois, you have here given orders to Monsieur St. Georges to particularly quarter himself upon the Bishop of Lodève, now at Dijon, upon the Marquise de Roquemaure at Troyes, and, at Melun, upon Monsieur de Riverac. I remember no instructions of that nature, nor do I see any necessity for them. Why should not this officer stay at any inn? Others have had to do so. Why not he?"

"Again," replied Louvois, once more glancing furtively at his master, "I have to remind your Majesty that, by issuing these orders to Monsieur St. Georges, we are utilizing him as a special courier on behalf of your Majesty, and that he is one who can be trusted—since he has no opportunity of betraying us. We desire to know from Phélypeaux—the bishop—whether the riots in Languedoc are to be feared or not; whether, indeed, it is necessary quietly to put into that neighbourhood any more regiments. St. Georges will bring the word, 'Yes,' or 'No.' Far better that, your Majesty, than any letter. Also we desire to know whether in Champagne, and especially in Troyes, the capital of the department, the Flemings from the north and the Lorrainers from the east are still endeavouring to stir them to revolt. And who better than the Marquise de Roque-

maure to send us the word, the one word, 'Yes' or
'No'? A fervent loyalist, your Majesty, and devoted to
your royal interests."

"Ay," the king said, "a fervent loyalist." Then,
after musing a moment, he said : "'Twas strange she
never married De Vannes; all thought she loved him in
those far-off days. And, *ciel!* Hortense de Foy was
handsome enough to suit any man's taste. I see her
now as she was then, beautiful as the morning. Why,
I wonder, did she marry De Vannes's cousin and friend,
Roquemaure, instead of him?"

Louvois shrugged his shoulders—though as respectfully as a man must perform such an action before a superior—then he said with a slight and also respectful
smile, the smile of the dependent:

"Your Majesty's royal ancestor said, '*Souvent femme
varie.*' That may explain why Mademoiselle de Foy
married one man, when the world, when even your
Majesty," with subtle flattery, "thought she loved another."

"My ancestor knew what he was talking about when
he discussed womankind," Louis remarked. "Well,
perhaps his saying explains the caprices of Hortense.
I have not seen her for years. She rests ever in her provincial manoir. It may be she has changed much—her
beauty vanished."

"If so, your Majesty, at least she has transmitted it
to her daughter. I have seen Mademoiselle de Roquemaure, and she is beautiful as ever her mother could
have been. She was the guest of Madame de Chevreuse
last summer."

"I would I had seen her, too. She would have recalled Hortense de Foy as she was in her youth; perhaps," with what seemed to the wily minister something

like a sigh, "my own youth, too." Then changing his
tone back to his ordinary one, he asked : " There is a son,
the present Marquis de Roquemaure; why does he so
rarely come to court?"

" He thinks, your Majesty, of but two things : first,
the inheritance of the Duc de Vannes, of which, through
his father, he is the heir on arriving at his thirtieth
year; and, secondly, of his horses and hounds. But when
he has attained his majority and has the duke's fortune, he proposes to present himself to your Majesty.
And——"

The speaker was interrupted by a scratching at the
door, which brought a smile to both their faces, while
Louis, starting up from his chair, exclaimed :

" *Ciel!* It is the half hour, and Malice is hungry ";
and, thrusting his hand into the pocket of his velvet
coat, he produced come crumbs of cake, which he presented to a little spaniel that rushed in and leaped about
him as Louvois opened the door.* Then, turning to
the minister, he said :

" Write to the Marquis de Roquemaure that the
king desires his company at court for the *fêtes* of the
Epiphany. Also write that he desires that Mademoiselle de Roquemaure shall accompany her brother, as the
king's guests. I would see this beautiful offshoot of so
fair a woman as her mother was," and, bending his head,
he advanced toward the door, followed by Malice. But
as he was about to leave the room, Louvois observed
with great humility that " doubtless his Majesty had
omitted, forgotten in his royal recollections of other
days, that the letter to Monsieur St. Georges, the trust-

---

* " Le roi donner à manger à ses chiens toujours soi-meme."—
La Fare, St. Simon, and others.

worthy officer who would bring the word from the
Bishop of Lodève, and from the Marquise de Roquemaure, was still unsigned."

"Ah! Monsieur St. Georges," exclaimed the king;
and taking up the pen he wrote his name at the bottom
of the last sheet, leaving roôm only for Louvois to un-
dersign it. Then, with many bows from the minister
and amid the salutes of the two sentinels outside in the
corridor, he passed to Madame de Maintenon's rooms,
accompanied by the little spaniel.

Left alone by himself, Louvois worked at his papers
for two hours unceasingly, reading some that were already written, signing and undersigning others—among
the latter the one to the Lieutenant St. Georges—and
destroying some. Also, he directed much correspondence with the marshals and generals commanding in
various parts of France—working at this with two sec-
retaries whom he summoned. But at last all his volu-
minous despatches were finished, closed up, and directed
to the different persons for whom they were intended,
some to go by the king's couriers and some by the royal
post. And among all the correspondence which went
forth that night from the minister were two letters, one
of which was addressed to the officer commanding the
Régiment de Nivernois at Pontarlier, and containing
those instructions for St. Georges which bade him repair
forthwith to Paris. The other was directed to the Marquis de Roquemaure, at his manoir near Troyes, and was
as follows :

" He sets out for Paris the last day of the year or the
first of the new one. He may take his child with him.
He is ordered to rest at Phélypeaux's, at madame your
mother's, and at De Riverac's."

That was all, the letter containing neither date nor signature.

CHAPTER X.

MADAME LA MARQUISE.

"A MANOIR!" exclaimed St. Georges, as he halted his horse in front of the place. "More like a fort! *Mon Dieu!* Madame is well installed."

She was, indeed, judging by the building which now rose before him from the side of the road along which he had come. Unapproached by any path, unsurrounded by any out-towers or fortalices, the Manoir of Roque-maure raised a great stone wall or rampart to the road; a wall almost blank on this side of windows with the exception of some arrow-slits, and at either end of it— one looking south, the other north—two tourelles, pene-trated also with *oillets* at regular distances from each other; and by each tourelle, on its outer side, a small, high door of antique, François Premier style, or even older, through which a mounted man might ride. Doors shut fast on this wintry night, and with no sign of life at either doorways or loopholes, except in so far as a great lantern, swinging on a rope above one of the for-mer and emitting its dull rays, might be said to testify to the place being inhabited.

"More like a fort!" again exclaimed St. Georges as he regarded the almost blank wall, "far more; yet, un-less I am spied on and watched from within, not over-well guarded, though I presume my lady has no foes to guard against. Well, here's for it," and advancing his horse to the doorway he reached out his hand, took the horn that hung on a chain close by, and sounded some notes. Then, while waiting for an answer to his summons, he backed his horse into the middle of the road which bulged out semicircularly in front of the long building, and observed it carefully. "A grim, hard place," he said to himself, regarding it under the rays of the young moon that was now stronger and clearer than when it had shed its feeble rays over the hamlet of Aignay-le-Duc, "and my enemy's stronghold, or I am mistaken. A place in which a man when once entrapped might find it difficult to fight his way out of. No exit but those doors at either side—a cat could hardly slip through the arrow-slits!—and all along beyond either side a wide moat, with palisades on the inner bank. Humph! Well, let us see. If my friend in the burganet, or volant-piece, or whatever he terms his rusty headdress, is here, the fight will be inside. So, so! May the end of it be as the other was! I am at least forearmed."

As he mused thus—firm, determined, and cool, and fearing not to enter this grim abode, since she whom he loved more than his life was safe in the city half a league away—he heard the locks being turned in the doorway and saw the door open, doubtless after he had been regarded from the grille high up in it. Then a man appeared in the open space and, shading his eyes with his hands, looked out at the cavalier sitting there on his horse—a man dressed as a servitor in some dark material, elderly, and with upon his head the serving-man's wig known as *la brigadière.* Behind him there stood another—almost a boy, and also evidently a servant.

"What," he asked, "may monsieur desire? He summons the house somewhat late."

"To obey the order of his Majesty the king—to wait

upon Madame la Marquise de Roquemaure.   Say to her,
if she be in her house, that Monsieur St. Georges, of the
Chevaux-Légers of Nivernois, has come by order of the
king to attend upon madame as he passes on his way to
Paris from Pontarlier."

The man bowed as he heard the words "by order of
the king"; then he said he would carry his message.
Would monsieur·be so good as to wait until he returned?   And monsieur answering that he would do so,
the other withdrew, leaving the door open, and the
younger servant standing in it, regarding St. Georges,
who still continued to cast his eyes over the ancient pile.

Presently the man came back and said:

"Madame la marquise bids me say that any one
ordered to visit her by his Majesty is welcome.   Will
monsieur be good enough to enter?   Monsieur doubtless stops the night—a room shall be at his service.
Madame and her daughter sup half an hour later; she
trusts monsieur will honour her by joining the repast."

"Her daughter!" exclaimed St. Georges; "she has
a daughter!   Indeed!"   Then remembering himself,
he replied: "Make my compliments to madame and say
that I will join her.   Yet, my friend, excuse me to her,
too, for the manner in which I shall appear before her.
I have ridden far in rough weather; I am scarce presentable."

"Madame will understand," the servitor answered
respectfully.   "As will Mademoiselle Aurélie.—Gaston," to the younger servant, "take monsieur's horse."

"And," said St. Georges, "be very attentive to it, I
pray you.   No soldier ever had a better or a truer one."
He would have liked to see it fed and littered down
himself, but could hardly insist on doing so; therefore—
though he feared he was in the house of a deadly

enemy!—he was forced to let the trusty creature, the animal on whose fleetness and strength not only his journey, but maybe his life depended—be taken away to some unknown stable.

"Have no fear, monsieur," said the old man. "Gaston loves animals better than his own kind. Even though you were his most hated foe, your beast would be sacred to him."

"I am glad to hear it," replied St. Georges, as the youth, with a smile, led the horse away. Then to himself he said, "I only hope that, should he know I am his master's enemy, he will be equally good to it!"

And now, as he followed the old man it was revealed to him how inappropriate was the name of manoir to this place, it having indeed been, if it was no longer altogether so, a strongly fortified residence, and doubtless had served as such in bygone ages. An outer court led into a second or inner one, which seemed to constitute a hall, since it was roofed and more or less furnished. On the walls hung arms of all kinds, both ancient and of the period of the day, and ranging from battle-axes, maces and two-handled swords, boar-spears, halberds, and crossbows to more modern rapiers, pikes, musketoons, pistols, and blunderbusses. Also about this court or hall there was much armour, plate, mail, both gambeson and chain, and many headpieces, gantlets, shields, etc.

"Doubtless," thought St. Georges as he followed the old man past all these and up a broad staircase leading to the first floor; "it was from this choice armoury that my friend of the burganet drew his protection. Faith! he had enough to choose from!"

Escorted along a passage on this flight, the old man showed him into a room comfortably furnished as a

sleeping apartment—vastly different from that of Phélypeaux at Dijon—and informed him that he would return later, in a quarter of an hour, to escort him to the
presence of madame la marquise, who would receive
him for supper—after which and having proffered his
services as valet, which St. Georges said he had no need
for, he left the room.

The toilet made by the cavalier was necessarily short,
since a soldier *en route* in those days had to depend
upon any attentions to his appearance which he might
be able to pay by whatever opportunities came in his
way. There were, however, in this room all the articles
generally to be found in a country house of the time—a
large metal basin and ewer of fresh water, some brushes,
and a mirror—and with these he was able to attend to
his hands, face, and hair, to remove some of the stains
of travel from his clothes and long brown boots, and to
make himself sufficiently presentable. At first, because
he was a gentleman and could not suppose that treachery
might be intended him, at least before ladies, he had
thought to leave his sword behind, but a second reflection prompted him to take it with him. It was true no
attack was likely to be made while he sat at meat with
the woman whose hospitality he was receiving, but a
sword, he reflected, was part of a soldier's dress and
therefore not out of place, and—it was, perhaps, not
safe to leave it behind!

Having decided thus and the servitor not being yet
returned, he made a slight inspection of his room, as
became one who was in a stranger's house, and that
stranger a person whose friendliness toward him might
—if he knew as much as he suspected of his history—
be doubtful. The room itself was a fairly large one,
hung with tapestry representing, as he supposed, scenes

from the ancient romancists, and lit by a window let into the upper part of the wall, so high up that no one could see out of it except by standing on the table. Of doors he could perceive no other but the one by which he had entered; nor on the floor, which was of polished wood or *parquet*, was there any sign that entrance could be made thereby—such entrance being a not uncommon thing in ancient houses of the type of this manoir. On the walls, let in between the tapestry and either lightly fastened to the panelling or painted thereon, were two full-length pictures—one of a man in full armour with his visor up and showing a stern, heavily mustached face; the other of a young woman in antique costume.

Satisfied by this inspection—made as best might be by the feeble rays of the lamp which the old man had left behind for his use—St. Georges sat down upon the chair by the bed and waited for the servitor to come and escort him to his hostess, and meditated—a little anxiously, perhaps—on what his interview with her and her daughter might bring forth.

"Is she, I wonder," he thought, "the she-wolf I have pictured her to myself as being? Does she know, for truth, who and what I am—who and what I believe myself to be? She may! It may indeed be so. If all reports are true that I have been able to gather and piece together in my remote life, far away from Paris and the world, she loved De Vannes once—was his affianced wife. What may she not therefore have known of his past? May know that I stand between this son of her husband and his desire, his succession; may stand, indeed, between her and the enjoyment for her lifetime of what her husband would have enjoyed had he lived. And more—far more—does she know of the attack on me three nights ago? Did she encourage—

perhaps prompt—that attack? I must watch her, study her for myself! The time is at hand, surely."

It was, indeed, for at that moment a knocking at the door told him that the old man had come back for him. And so he went forth, prepared to meet his hostess.

His conductor led him down the great stairs and back into the great hall; then he knocked at a door on the left, and, on being bidden to enter, opened the door and ushered St. Georges into the room.

A room large and vast, hung with great tapestries—representing here battle and hunting scenes—with, at the end, a great oriel window over which more tapestry was drawn, but beneath which could be seen the brackets, or corbels, supporting it. Near this was the great marble chimney-piece, the jambs richly carved with figures, the mantel six feet from the floor, and in the grate a huge wood fire burning. And by a table in front of this there sat, as he saw by the light of a large clear lamp, two women, one almost old and the other young.

Coming in out of the sombre hall, the light of the fire and lamp dazzled him so that at first he could see nothing beyond the fact that they were two female forms which rose at his entrance; then, while he advanced to meet them as they came forward, he heard a soft voice say:

"Monsieur St. Georges visits on behalf of his Majesty. He is very welcome.—Monsieur, let me present you to my daughter, Mademoiselle de Roquemaure."

In the instant that he was bowing with easy grace before them, and while they in their turn observed the tall, gallant form of the soldier, his long, curling hair, long mustaches, and somewhat weather-worn riding dress, there flashed through his mind the thought: "Can this be the she-wolf who sends her whelp forth to midnight murder? Can she have had a hand in that foul attack?" Then, aloud, he murmured his thanks for her reception, and looking his hostess straight in the face, observed the features of the woman who, as he believed, his father had once loved.

Her hair was almost white now, yet rich and beautiful, and still with some of the original brown left in it, her eyes soft and clear, her features delicate and telling plainly of the beauty that had been. And as he gazed at the daughter standing by her side—a girl but just entering womanhood, a girl whose hazel eyes looked out at him from under her dark lashes, and whose colour came and went as she returned his bow with stately courtesy—he knew what her mother had once been like.

"Monsieur has ridden far," the marquise said, as she motioned him to a seat by the fire where they had been sitting, and regarded him with interest; "has come a long, perhaps perilous, voyage from Pontarlier? The roads at this season are none too safe, they say, in spite of the *Maréchausse*. Yet, monsieur is a soldier."

St. Georges bowed in reply—though swift as lightning there flashed through his mind the thought that the words "perilous voyage" showed that she knew, doubtless, of one great danger to which he had been exposed. Then he replied:

"As madame remarks, it was long and has been somewhat eventful. Yet, as I have said, I ride in the king's service. It may be that you know that, madame?"

"I know," she replied, "that you were to call at the Bishop of Lodève's—ce *Phélypeaux!*—and take from him one word to the king, or to Louvois. Also that you are charged to take another word, perhaps a similar one, from me. Is it not so?"

Remembering what the bishop had said, recalling his utterance—"There is no need of secrecy; you may frankly tell her"—he answered: "It is so, madame. The bishop has sent the word. It may be that you will send the same by me when I ride forth to-morrow."

Her glance rested on him ere she answered. It seemed as if her reply depended on some unknown, subtle something pertaining to his mind or face which she was endeavouring to decipher or understand. Then she let her eyes fall upon the logs burning in the grate, and said:

"How can I say? You do not as yet tell me the word the bishop has sent."

Again he recalled Phélypeaux's remark that there was no need of secrecy. Therefore he answered, "The word that the bishop has sent, madame, is 'Yes.'"

"Ah!" she said, and again her glance scanned his face half eagerly, half wistfully, while now he noticed that Mademoiselle de Roquemaure's hand stole into hers as she sat by her side.

"Ah! It is as I thought: the word is 'Yes.'"

"That is it, madame."

"Come," she said, moving from her seat as the old servitor appeared in the shadows far down the room— "come; supper is served. Monsieur St. Georges, I pray you give me your arm"; and she placed her hand on it, and, her daughter following, went with him to the door. Then, ere they reached the corridor, she, looking up into his face, said quietly:

"It would be best—I—I—have not the same word to send as Phélypeaux. The one that I shall ask you to carry will be 'No.'"

CHAPTER XI.

THE MARQUISE TELLS A STORY.

It was a vastly different repast from that of the Bishop of Lodève's which was offered to St. Georges, although the difference consisted more, perhaps, in the manner of cooking and serving than in aught else. The wine, which was excellent—though no better than that last bottle from the old Clos—did not come in at the end, but cheered the fasting and wayworn man from the commencement; the viands were in good condition and properly prepared; the soup was not dishwater, but of a good, sufficient quality. Moreover, here, as in the great *salon*, a cheerful fire blazed on the hearth, instead of the spluttering, snow-soaked logs that had hissed and smoked in Phélypeaux's house. Also, he had for company two women, each beautiful according to her time of life—women soft, gentle, and well bred—instead of the cynical bishop of whom all France told strange tales.

Sitting there, his eyes resting sometimes on the budding loveliness of Aurélie de Roquemaure, sometimes on the mellowed sweetness of the face of the marquise, St. Georges forced himself to discard from his mind the thought which he had now come to deem unworthy—the thought that treachery lurked in their bosoms against him—that, though the present marquis might be the man who had led the foul and despicable attack on him in the graveyard at Aignay-le-Duc, they had had part or share in it. For, he told himself, to believe this was to believe that there was no faith nor honesty in womankind.

Yet one thing, at the commencement of the meal,

7

and when the old servant and another had withdrawn
from the room, had almost served to keep his suspicions
alive. The marquise—as far as a woman of rank and
high breeding might do so—had asked him many questions about himself, while Aurélie, following the rigid-
ness which prevailed in French life of the time, sat
by, a silent listener, scarce joining in the conversation
at all.

And St. Georges, moved perhaps by the company in
which he found himself, and, soldier-like, scorning to
conceal any part of his history except that which he
deemed absolutely necessary—he making no reference
whatever to the name of De Vannes—told them much of
his existence. His career in Holland until the peace;
his lonely life in garrison; his marriage with a young
girl, a daughter of the middle classes; her death, and
the little child she had left to his care, were all touched
upon by him and listened to attentively—indeed, ab-
sorbingly. And so, at last, he came to the summons to
Paris, to his setting forth, to his stay at Dijon, and the
attack made upon him and Boussac.

To both women this portion of his narrative caused
great excitement. For, stately as the marquise was, en-
vironed, so to speak, by all the dignity of the *haute
noblesse* of the days of the Great King, she could not
prevent her agitation from being apparent to him. Her
white, jewelled hand quivered as she raised it to her
breast; her eyes sparkled as they might have sparkled
when she was her daughter's age; while, as for that
daughter, her bosom rose and fell with her rapid breathing, her colour came and went—once she was as pale
as death, the next moment her face suffused.

"The cowards!" exclaimed the marquise; "the
base, cowardly dogs, to attack two men thus, and one

hampered with a defenceless child! *Quel tour de lâche!* Oh! sir, I would to God your brand or that of your brave companion had struck the poltroon, the craven who sheltered himself behind his visor, his death blow! I would to God one of your swords had found out his heart as they found out the hearts of his mercenaries!"

The sympathy of this graceful woman—sympathy that roused her from the well-bred calmness which was her natural state, to one of almost fury—earned the deepest respect and gratitude of St. Georges; yet he looked at her almost with amazement as he bowed and murmured some words of appreciation. For there was no acting here, he knew; yet she was De Roquemaure's stepmother, the kinswoman of the man whom he believed to be his and his child's attempted assassin!

And Aurélie de Roquemaure, too—what of her? A glance from under his eyes showed him that still the beauteous face was agitated as it had been before, that all which her mother had said was re-echoed by her.

Again the marquise spoke, though now she rose from the table as she did so.

"Sir," she said, "never rest until that man and you stand face to face, point to point; since, until that happens, your child's life will not be safe. For you, a man, a soldier, it matters not—is best, indeed, that you should meet him and end his miserable existence forever. I pray you may do ere long. And, when you do meet him, slay him like a dog! It is the only way."

Still astonished, almost appalled, by her vehemence, St. Georges took the hand she extended him and bent over it, and next, that of her daughter, ere the two passed out of the room.

"Forgive," said the marquise, "that I should feel so

strongly. I—I—have a child myself." Then, after a
pause, and turning round as she reached the corridor,
she added : " If we do not meet to-morrow ere you
return to the city to fetch your child, remember, sir,
I pray you, that my answer to the king or his minister
is precisely different from that of the bishop. It is
' No.' "

" I will remember, madame."

Then, with a last glance from each, both were gone.
And St. Georges, standing in front of the great fireplace waiting for the old servitor to come and escort
him to his room, was more overwhelmed with amazement than he had been at aught which had occurred
since he set out from Pontarlier.

" What does it mean ? " he whispered to himself.
" What does it mean ? "

.   .   .   .

In a room at the opposite end of the corridor from
that where the apartment was situated which had been
bestowed on St. Georges, the mother and daughter sat.
It was the sleeping-room of madame la marquise, large,
vast, and sombre—save that here, too, a fire burnt in
the grate, and that there were many candles alight in
the sconces set about the room.

And the marquise, lying back in her deep fauteuil
before the fire, her face white and drawn, and with tears
upon her cheeks, was speaking to her daughter who
knelt by her side.

" The wolf ! " she said, " the wolf ! How know it?
How find out? God ! I thought that I alone, of all
living people, knew, until I divulged my story to you, ·
until I wrote to Louis asking him to do justice to
a much-wronged man. Who—who has betrayed my
confidence ? Not the king, surely. Oh ! not he, not

he! Nay, more, I doubt if the letter ever reached his hands."

"Mother," Aurélie said, as she stroked her hand, "there must be some other who knows."

"There was no living soul on earth. Listen, even you do not know all."

The girl seated herself against her mother's knee and gazed up into her face. Then she whispered: "Tell me all now, mother. From to-night let me understand exactly with what he is encompassed. Tell me, I beg."

"You know," the marquise said, "for I have told you often, that the Duc de Vannes and I loved each other when we were young—yet that we never married. No matter for the reason now—it was my fault! Let that suffice. And we parted—he to go his way, I mine. Then, some years later, not many it is true, but still long enough for us to have forgotten what had separated us, we met again, and once more he asked me to be his wife, to renew the love vows we once had made. But it was then impossible. I was affianced to your father— the day was fixed, and I had come to admire him, to respect him; in no case would I have gone back from my plighted word. So again we parted to meet only once more in life."

The girl touched her hand—perhaps—who knows? —in admiration of her mother's strength in keeping her vow to the man who was not her first love and in discarding the man who was. And the marquise continued:

"It was one night a few weeks before he set out to join Turenne in the Palatinate. A great *fête* was given by Louis to celebrate his birthday at St.-Germain-en-Laye, his birthplace, and it was there we met again. Presently, when both of us were able to escape from the

great crowd of courtiers, marshals, and ministers who
surrounded the king, he told me that he was glad he
had met me once more—that he wished to confide a
secret to me if I would hear it, a charge if I would
accept it. At first I hesitated, then—when I found
it would not thrust against your father's honour"
—again the girl stroked her mother's hand—"I told
him he might confide in me. Aurélie, he told me that,
embittered by having lost me, he had married in private
an English lady, daughter of a refugee, that he had
learned to love her, and that death had parted them after
a few years of marriage. Also, he told me, she left him
a son, whom he had brought up in ignorance of the
position that must be his, but that—should he return
from the Palatinate—he meant to acknowledge him.
He never did return, and his son has never been ac-
knowledged."

"Why, my mother?" asked Aurélie, with an upward
glance. "Why?"

"Nay, child," the marquise replied. "Think no
evil of me. No base thoughts entered my mind. No
remembrance that his son stood in the way of your half-
brother's inheritance—he and your father being ostensibly De Vannes's heir. No! no! no! But in that
hurried interval both he and I had made one fatal slip
—had committed one hideous act of forgetfulness. He
had forgotten to tell me—I to ask—where this son was,
and in what name he was known."

The girl dropped her hands with a despairing action into her lap; then a moment later she turned
the soft hazel eyes up again toward her mother's face
and said: "Yet now you know! You have found
out!"

"Yes, I have found out. That son is the man

who sleeps beneath our roof to-night—Lieutenant St.
Georges."

"But how? How? How?"

"Again, listen. For years I sought to find him,
made inquiries in every quarter I could think of, asked
—quietly and cautiously—of all who might by chance
possess any information. Then, at last, it came—from
the quarter least to be imagined. From your half-
brother."

"Raoul?"

"Ay, Raoul, your father's heir—also heir to the
fortune of the Duc de Vannes, as all the world thought
and still thinks. He came to me one day—three
months ago—when he had been privately to Paris; for
what reason I know not, although I know that his visit
was a secret one, since he had not been presented to the
king. He came in, I say, and standing before me, he
said, 'Madame, who is Monsieur St. Georges?' I answered that I had never heard of the gentleman before, to which he replied: ''Tis strange, madame. He
is an officer of the Régiment de Nivernois. And his
commission was given him by the king at the request of your late—friend, shall I say?—the Duc de
Vannes!'

"Aurélie, I fell to trembling then, for I thought to
myself, 'I have found his son.' De Vannes had told
me that son was being educated for his own profession
of arms—nay, more, that he sought for him a commission from the king. Meanwhile, Raoul was watching
me carefully, so that I disguised as best I could my
agitation, while I replied: 'It seems to me you need
not to demand information of me. You know of
Monsieur St. Georges's existence—of the calling he
follows. On my part, I have never heard of him be-

fore!' 'Nor perhaps,' he replied, 'ever will again!' and with that he left me."

"It must be the man," Mademoiselle de Roquemaure murmured. "It must be he."

"It is he," the marquise replied emphatically. "It is he. As he stood before me to-night I saw his father in his eyes, in his glance—nay, in his bearing. That man is the son of De Vannes—is the De Vannes himself. And if more proof was wanted, is it not forthcoming when we have learned that not only his life, but the life of his child, is thrust against? His father died without a will, without naming him; *your* father was therefore the heir, and—after him—your brother Raoul. In another year, when he is thirty, De Vannes's wealth is his, if—if," and her eyes glistened as she spoke, "no direct heir bars the way. You understand?"

"Yes," the girl said slowly. "Yes, I understand."

CHAPTER XII.

LOST.

A CONSIDERABLE hubbub outside the manoir—the crying of a woman, and the voices of various men all talking together—aroused St. Georges from his sleep as the wintry dawn broke through the fogs and mists of the night.

"*Fichte*," he heard the old servitor say, "you are a fool, my girl, to come here and thrust your head in the lion's jaws. Better make off another way; he will kill you, I warrant, when he hears how you have kept your promise."

"Let him," he heard next a woman's voice reply, a voice all broken and rendered indistinct by her tears and sobs, "let him. O *mon Dieu!*" she wailed, "have pity on me! I would have shielded the little thing with my life. I left it but a few, nay, not ten, minutes, and then —then it was gone. Oh, pity me, pity me, *mon Dieu!*"

With a bound St. Georges had flung himself from out of his bed, and was hastily putting on his clothes. For the words of the weeping woman in the roadway, as they rose to his ears—above all, the voice which he recognised—told him the worst. The child, his child, was missing; the woman below was the one to whom he had confided Dorine overnight.

Huddling on his garments, therefore, while still he heard arising the voices from a short distance below him (for the first floor of the manoir, on which his room was situated, was not more than twelve or fourteen feet from the ground) and the girl's sobs and weeping as she exclaimed, "Not more than ten minutes did I leave it alone, not more, while I regarded the troops coming in," he descended rapidly to the great hall below. He met no one on his way as he did so—doubtless, neither the marquise nor her daughter were yet risen—and finding the door in the tourelle with little difficulty, he emerged into the roadway.

Standing in it were those two whose voices he had already heard—the old servitor and the girl from the inn in Troyes—and by them was the youth, Gaston, his arm this morning being bound up in a sling, as though he had met with some hurt. He was gazing silently at the girl as she sobbed and wept before the old man, listening evidently with interest to all she said, and with a look of sympathy on his face for the evident distress of mind she was in.

But now, as St. Georges appeared before her, his face stern and fierce—though already there was on it a look of misery and foreboding—she flung herself upon her knees before him in the hard, frost-bound road, and lifting up her clasped hands she cried:

"Oh, monsieur, forgive me, pardon me! I did but leave the child for ten moments, and——"

"And," said St. Georges, his face growing almost darker than before, "it is stolen, or dead! Is that what you have come to tell me?"

"Alas! alas!" she moaned, "that it should be so. Stolen, not dead, thank God. Oh, monsieur," and again the coarse, hard-working hands were clasped and lifted up before his face, "*ayez pitié, je*——"

"Be brief," the *chevau-léger* interrupted, taking no heed of her wailings, while the old and young man started at the misery revealed by the changed tones of his voice. "Be brief. I confided my child to you, and you have failed in your trust. Tell me how. Then I may know how to act. Proceed."

"Oh, monsieur," the poor creature said, wondering that, ere now, he had not torn her to pieces or thrust his sword through her, as would likely enough have been done by many of her own kind under a similar breach of faith—"oh, monsieur, my heart is broken, my heart——"

"No matter for your heart," St. Georges interrupted her peremptorily again; "tell your story at once. At once, I say!" And again the two standing by wondered that he could master himself so, in spite of his grief; while the girl, seeing that she had best obey him, told with many sobs, which still she could not repress, what had happened.

It was in the early morning, she said, and she and

the little thing had slept warm and peacefully together
—oh, so peacefully!—and the time had come for her to
arise; the hostler had come to knock on her door, for she
slept heavily. Then he told her, as he stood outside,
that a troop of the Vicomte d'Arpajou's regiment was
come in and seeking billets in the town; and she,
because she was *une malheureuse*, and also because she
had a cousin who rode in the ranks, got up and ran
downstairs to get news of him. For his mother had
heard nothing of him for many months; they were
anxious—oh, so anxious! But it was not his troop, and
so, gleaning no news, she had returned to her bedroom,
meaning to finish her dressing and to prepare the child.
And then, she went on, sobbing again, and with more
wringings of her hands—and then, oh! horror, she
found the bed empty and the child gone. Gone!
Gone! Gone! Oh, it was terrible! She aroused the
other servants with her screams; high and low they
sought for it—it might have crept even from the bed—
but, no! it was gone. And after half an hour's further
search, she, feeling demented, had told her master all
and how she had taken charge of the child, and had
begged him to let her come to the manoir to see its
father. Perhaps, it might yet be found, might, because
God was good, have been found since she had come away.
Who knew? Oh! she prayed it might be so—on her
knees she prayed——

"My horse!" exclaimed St. Georges, turning to the
younger man, Gaston, still standing close by, "my
horse, I beg of you! Lose no time in saddling it. I
must go back to the city at once." And turning his
head away from them he murmured: "My child! My
little lonely child! Oh, my child!"

They heard his moan, those three standing there—

for now the woman had risen to her feet—and they
pitied him. The old man shook his head sadly; he was
a father and a grandfather himself; the girl sobbed
afresh, and Gaston moved off at once to obey his behest.
"My arm is injured," he stammered, seeing that the
soldier's eye was on it now; "one of the horses kicked it
last night in the stable; but—but—I can still saddle
your animal. In an instant, monsieur, in an instant,"
and he moved away.

Seeing that he was in pain—indeed, the lad's face
was bloodless and also drawn with suffering—and being
himself devoured with eagerness to return to the city
and seek for his child, St. Georges followed him through
the courtyard to where the stables were. And then,
noticing that Gaston could not use his wounded arm at
all, he saddled his animal with his own hands while the
young man stood by helpless, or only able to render him
the slightest assistance with his uninjured arm. And
when this was done he led the horse forth to the front
of the manoir and mounted it.

"There is no time for me to pay my respects to
madame la marquise," he said to the servitor—"she
will understand my lack of courtesy. Yet, since it is
impossible I can continue my journey to Paris—even
the king's commands must wait now!—I will endeavour
not to quit Troyes without bidding her farewell. Will
you tell her that, my friend?"

The old man said he would—that he knew madame
would understand and sympathize with him—and—and
—but ere he could finish whatever he intended to say,
St. Georges had put spurs to his horse and was speed-
ing back to Troyes, while following him along the road
on foot went the unfortunate servant from the inn, still
weeping and bemoaning.

The hostler was standing in the gateway of the auberge as he rode in, his horse already sweating and with foam about its mouth from the pace it had come; and throwing himself off it St. Georges advanced to the man and asked him if he had heard any news of his missing child.

"Nay," he replied. "Nay. No news. *Mon Dieu!* I know not who could have stolen it. 'Tis marvellous. 'Twas none of D'Arpajou's troop, to be sure. And there were no others."

"None lurking about the inn last night—none sleeping here who might have stolen into the girl's room when she quitted it? Oh! man, I tell you," he cried, almost beside himself with grief, "there are those who would have tracked it across France to get at it!" And then, overcome with remorse at having left the child in any other custody but his own, though he had thought it was for the best when he did so, he murmured: "Why, why, did I not keep it with me? My arm sheltered it when the attack was made at Aignay-le-Duc; no worse than that could have befallen it."

"None lurking about," the man repeated, looking up at the great soldier while he chewed a straw. "None lurking about. *Mon Dieu!* why did I not think of that before?"

"There *was* one!" St. Georges exclaimed, "there was one, then? You saw some man—I know it; I see it in your face. For God's sake, answer me! Who? Who was it?"

But the hostler was a slow man—one whose mind moved cumbrously, and again he muttered to himself: "No! No, it could not be he. It——"

"Could not be whom? Oh, do not torture me! Tell me! Tell me!"

"There was one," the other replied, "who rode in last night, seeking a bed for himself and a stall for his horse. Yet he could have neither here. We were full, and we knew too that D'Arpajou's horse were on the road. So we sent him away to the *Cheval Rouge*, yet I saw him again late at night in the yard, and, asking him his business, he said that he had lost his glove when here——"

"My God!" St. Georges exclaimed, more to himself than the man. "Was it De Roquemaure?"

"De Roquemaure!" the other exclaimed. "De Roquemaure! *Par hasard*, does monsieur mean the young marquis?"

"Yes, yes. You know him—must know him, since his mother's manoir is so near here. Answer me," and in his fervour he grasped the man's arm firmly, "*was it he?*"

The hostler wrenched his arm away from the soldier's nervous grasp; then he answered emphatically—scornfully indeed: "Was it he? He! De Roquemaure? *Mon Dieu*, no! Not he, indeed!"

"You know him?"

"*Know him?* Yes. And hate him. A wild beast, *un sauvage*. See here," and he pointed to his face, on which was a long, discoloured stain or bruise, "he gave me that a week or so ago, as he rode out of the inn, because I had not brought his horse quickly enough to please him. Know him?. Oh, yes, I know him. And some day, great and strong and powerful seigneur as he is, he shall know me. The seigneurs do not lord it over us always. We shall see!"

"Not De Roquemaure," St. Georges mused aloud. "Not De Roquemaure. Great God! have we more enemies than one? Into whose hands has my little babe

fallen, then?" And again he murmured to himself,
"Not De Roquemaure!"

"No, not De Roquemaure," the man replied, over-
hearing him. "Nor one like him. Instead, a stranger
to the town—a sour, dark-visaged man, elderly. None
too well clad nor mounted either, and both he and his
beast well spent as though with long travel." ·

"Who could it be?" St. Georges muttered. "Who?"
Yet, think as he might, no light broke in upon him.
But, if this man was indeed the one who had kidnapped
his child, he felt sure of one thing: he was an agent of
De Roquemaure's. It was in the latter's light alone
that he and Dorine stood!

Again he questioned the hostler, but all that he
could glean was that the lurking traveller, the fellow
who, after being refused the hospitality of the inn, was
yet prowling about the stables at midnight, in search—
if his story were true—of a worthless glove, was undoubtedly a stranger in the city. Than that the hostler
could tell him no more.

"But," said the latter, "why not inquire at the
Cheval Rouge?—there, if anywhere, monsieur may glean
tidings of him."

Clutching at the suggestion he went toward that
inn, which was but in the next street—a place that
turned out to be a frowsy, dirty house, frequented by
the humblest travellers only. And here, after describ-
ing the man he sought, he gathered the following facts,
the stranger's actions since he had put up at the *Cheval
Rouge* being indeed enough to set the tongues of the
landlord and landlady wagging directly they were questioned about him:

For, strange circumstances in connection with a
traveller who appeared to be, as he stated he was, dead

beaten with a long journey—whence he had not said—
he had not been in all night. His bed was still unslept
in, his horse still in the stable. He had supped at the
ordinary with one or two others, and the landlady noticed he had eaten ravenously, as one might who had
fasted long; had drunk copiously, too, of *petite Bourgogne*, and had then gone out, saying he would be back
shortly. Also, one thing was curious. "*Mon Dieu!*"
the woman said, " it was remarkable!" He had given
orders that, after his horse was rubbed down and
fed, it was to be kept saddled. He might, he said,
·have to set forth again at any moment; he was on
important business. Yet now, the woman stated, the
horse was still in its stall and the man had never returned.

" And his necessaries?" St. Georges asked, after he
had told the people of the house as much as he deemed
fit. " What of them? His bags, his holsters, where
are they? Were they taken to his room or left with
his horse? "

" Necessaries! bags!" the landlord replied, " he had
none. And as for pistols—well—the holsters were empty;
doubtless he had them about him. Perhaps monsieur
would like to see the horse? "

Yes, monsieur would like to see the horse, and was
consequently taken to the stable to do so. It was a poor
beast, not groomed properly for some days; at least, it
looked poor and overstrained now, though perhaps a
good enough animal when fresh. It showed signs, too,
of having been hard ridden. For the rest, it was an
ordinary animal of the most usual colour—a dark
chestnut.

As to the holsters, they were empty, and in none
of the horse's trappings was there aught to give any

hint as to who its owner was or whence he had
come. .

CHAPTER XIII.

DE ROQUEMAURE'S WORK.

THE weather had changed, the frost was gone, and
the night was hot and murky, while rain was falling, as
alone, now, alas! St. Georges mounted the summit of a
hill that rose close above Troyes on the road to Paris.

He had commenced his journey again.

It was a gruesome spot to which he had arrived on
this night—an elevation that surmounted a billowy
country, over all of which, in the summer time, the
vines and corn grew in rich profusion, but which now
looked bare and melancholy as the southwest wind
swept the rain clouds over it beneath a watery moon.
To the left of him there swung, upon the exact crest of
the hill, a corpse in chains, with, perched upon its
mouldering head, a crow—looking for the eyes long
since pecked out by others of its brood! To the right
there rose a little wood, through which the wind moaned
and sighed onto his face, bringing with it warm drops
of rain.

Involuntarily he glanced up at the thing swinging
above his head—heartbroken as he was at having had
to leave Troyes with his child still unfound, he could
not refrain from doing that!—and wondered who and
what the malefactor had been who was thus exalted.
And as he lowered his eyes from the ghastly mass of
corruption, he saw against the gibbet a thicker, darker
thing than the gallows tree itself—a thing surmounted

8

by a white, corpselike face, from which stared a pair of
large gray eyes at him—eyes in which, as the clouds
scurried by beneath the moon, the moon itself shone
dazzlingly, lighting them up and showing their large
pupils.

The horse saw them too, and started forward a pace
or so until reined in by his master's hand, and then
whimpered and quivered all over, while its rider, with
his own flesh creeping, bent over his saddle and peered
toward the dark form surmounted by the pallid face
and glaring eyes.

"Who in Heaven's name are you?" St. Georges
whispered, "and why select this ghastly spot to stand
in and affright passers-by? What are you, man or
woman?" and he leaned still further over his demi-
pique to gaze at the figure, though as he did so his right
hand stole to his sword hilt.

"A woman," a voice answered. "A woman who
comes here to weep her husband's death. He"—and she
cast the staring gray eyes upward to the object swinging with each gust of the wind in its chains—"was my
husband. Pass on, and leave me with his murdered
remains."

"Murdered! Rather, poor soul, say executed. Murderers slay not thus."

Slowly the figure left the foot of the gibbet as he
spoke, so that he saw she was a tall young woman of the
peasant class, clad in dark, poor clothes, and slowly she
advanced the few yards that separated them, whereby
he could observe her features and notice more plainly
the awful whiteness of her face.

"Murdered, I say!" she replied, still with the glare
in her eyes. "Murdered! Wrongfully accused, foully
tried, falsely condemned. Done to death wickedly as a

braconnier. But he was none—yet there he swings. O God! that life can be so easily torn from us by the powerful!"

"Who, then, has done this deed?" St. Georges asked, deeply stirred by the woman's wild sorrow, perhaps also by the gloomy surroundings. "Who can do such things as this, even though powerful?"

"Who?" she replied. "Who? Who but one in these parts? The hound, De Roquemaure!"

"De Roquemaure!" St. Georges exclaimed with a start that caused his trembling horse to move forward, thinking that he had pressed its flanks to urge it on, which start was perfectly perceptible to the unhappy woman. "De Roquemaure!"

"You know him?" she asked eagerly, bending her face toward and up to him so that he could see her pale lips—lips, indeed, almost as pale as her cheeks—"you know him?"

"I know of him," St. Georges replied.

"And hate him, perhaps, as I do. It may be, would kill him as I would. Is it so? Answer me?"

Carried away by this strange encounter, and with so strange a third thing near them as *that* above, which once had life as they had still; carried away, too, by the woman's vehemence—a vehemence which caused her, a peasant, to speak on equal terms with one whose dress and accoutrements showed the difference between them —he answered almost in a whisper:

"It may be," he said, bending down still further to her, "that I shall be doomed to kill him some day. May be that he has merited death at my hands."

"You hate him?"

"I fear I have but too just cause to hate him."

"As all do! As all! He lives," she went on, "but

to slay and injure others as he slew and injured him,"
and she half turned her head and cast up her eyes at
the miserable relic above her. Then she continued:
"Listen. *He* was no poacher, no thief. But I—I—his
wife—was unfortunate enough to fall under the other's
notice—he sought me—you understand?—and *he*"—
with again the upward glance—"resisted his desires.
You see the end!"

Looking into her eyes, observing her well-defined
features, noticing that, except for her awful pallor, she
might well be a handsome woman, especially when bright
and happy instead of, as now, grief-stained, St. Georges
could understand. Then, while also he meditated as
to whether this De Roquemaure was a fiend that had
taken human shape, the woman went on:

"Daily almost some fall under his bane. But a
week ago a stranger here—one carrying a helpless babe
—was set upon——"

"What!" and now he felt as though the universe
was spinning round.

—"was set upon," she continued, "struck to death—
he is dying now, or dead——"

"And the babe?" St. Georges interposed.

"Carried off by those who did his bidding."

"O God! Lost again!" and the moan he uttered
startled the woman out of her own grief.

"Who are you?" she asked, her great eyes piercing
him.

"As I believe, that child's unhappy father."

Aroused by this to forget her own sufferings, even
to forget for the moment the dreadful burden borne by
the gallows tree, she thrust out her hand and seized his
sleeve.

"Who, then, is the dying man?" she whispered.

" I know not—but—but—for mercy's sake, in memory of the misery you have suffered, in pity for mine, lead me to this man! You know where he is; you can do so?"

"Come," she said. "Come. He is in my hut close by. We were very poor, we had no better. Come. Tie your horse to a tree and follow me."

Dazed, scarce knowing whether he was awake or asleep and dreaming, he obeyed her, leading the horse away some paces so that it should be no more frightened by the horrible burden of the gibbet, and following her through a thicket. In other circumstances he might have feared an ambush; now, a thousand hidden enemies would not have held him back.

She wound her way along a trodden track leading down into the valley below, but went only a few score yards when she stopped outside what was indeed no better than a hut, a wooden building thatched with turf, from a window in which there gleamed a ray of light. And she, placing her ears to the door ere she pushed it open, said to him : " He lives still. ·You can ar his breathing. Hark!"

" Thank God!" St. Georges said fervently. " Whoever he may be, he will be able to tell me of the child. Open, I beg you ; open in the name of mercy!"

She obeyed him at once, thrusting the door open and drawing him in, and then by the light of a miserable, small oil lamp that flickered on a rude wooden table he saw stretched upon a pallet in a corner of the place the dying man. Also he noticed that the room reeked and was fetid with his hot breath and with another hot, dry odour that he knew was the odour of blood.

In the shadow of the room St. Georges could see a white face, could also perceive two great staring eyes

turned up to the rafters; he could hear, too, the drawn,
labouring breath as it rattled through his throat and
chest, accompanied by a moan as it came forth.

"Quick!" he exclaimed, "quick! The light! He
lives still, but his minutes are numbered. He is dying,
dying fast. Where is his wound?"

"In the lower part of his body, through him. A
sword thrust. I have tried to stanch it, but it flows
always. I marvel he has lived so long."

She brought the oil lamp forward as she spoke and
held it near the man, and St. Georges, kneeling down,
looked at him. Then with a bound he sprang up
again, exclaiming: "He here! Heaven and earth! what
brings him here? How comes he in this mystery?
What—what does it mean, what portend?"

"You know him?"

"Yes, I know him."

The man stretched upon the pallet was Pierre, the
Bishop of Lodève's man-servant!"

"Speak!" said St. Georges to him a moment later,
smothering for the time his wonder and astonishment.
"Speak if you can. One word from you may alter my
whole life, my child's life. Speak ere you die."

It seemed, however, that he would never speak
again. But, also, it seemed as if all consciousness was
not gone from him yet—as if he recognised the man
kneeling once more at his side, while again the woman
held the lamp above them. As far as he was able with
his failing strength, he endeavoured to shrink from St.
Georges while as he did so his eyes, distended either
with fear or horror, glared at him. But from his mouth
there came no sound but the laboured breathing.

Again St. Georges besought him to speak; plied

him with questions. Was the child taken from him
Dorine; by whom had it been taken; how had he whom
St. Georges had never seen until he slept at the bishop's,
and whom he had left at Dijon, found his way here
only to be murdered? And still no answer came, while
once the dying man tried with his feeble hand to push
St. Georges away, and still stared in ghastly horror at
him.

At last the end arrived. The breathing grew faster
and faster and more laboured; it rattled more horribly
in his chest; a spasm convulsed him, and he sank back
exhausted, while from his face and throat which were
all uncovered a heavy sweat poured. Then suddenly he
raised himself to almost a sitting posture with his hands,
and, with a rolling glance that seemed to take in all the
hut, he sank back slowly again. Yet as he did so his
lips moved, and a whisper came from them—a whisper
that seemed to frame the words " De Roquemaure." A
moment after he was dead.

"Tell me all you know," St. Georges said to the
woman a few moments later. " How he came here,
how he was set upon and done to death? I must ride
on and on to-night, yet ere long, if I can compass it, I
will return to Troyes and never leave it until I have
found my child and know all. Tell me."

"He came here," she said, "five days ago—was
brought here by me, for I saw him attacked and
wounded to the death, as you know now. I was up
there by—by him who swings upon that hellish gibbet;
the dawn was at hand."

"The dawn," St. Georges whispered to himself.
" The dawn of five days ago, when D'Arpajou's horse
rode into the town. The day Dorine was lost."

"Then," the woman continued, "through the coming day I saw him advancing from the town upon this road, carrying a bundle under his arm."

"Ah!"

"Yet not so fast but that two others who had left the gate behind him came swifter than he. One, a man, young and supple, clad in the De Roquemaure russet—no need of that to tell me that devil had a hand in what was to be done; the other, a woman, all in sombre black, a mask upon her face."

"A woman in it!"

"Ho!" said the peasant, "doubt not! He has his women, too, at his beck and call. Easy enough to find one of the scourings of Troyes—perhaps an innocent girl once, before she knew him!—to do his bidding."

"Go on."

"Swiftly they came behind him, yet silently, too, the man ahead of the woman, each on different sides of the way, the former outstripping the latter, so fast did he come. Then, at last, the hunted one, this dead one here, knew that it was so; he turned and saw he was pursued. At first he made as though about to run for it; then, because, may be, the burden he bore was heavy, he paused. Next he placed the child upon the ground—for now I knew, I saw, what it was as he did so—and he drew his sword with one hand, took a pistol from his belt and held it in the other, and so awaited his pursuer."

Again St. Georges said beneath his breath, "Go on."

"The other came swiftly up, paused once himself—perhaps he feared the doubly armed man—then looked round at the masked woman, who seemed to say something. Doubtless she urged him on, and again he came forward until he and the fugitives were face to face."

"Yes," came from St. Georges's close-set lips.

"What they said I know not; I was too far away. But their action was swift. De Roquemaure's man made as though he would seize upon the child lying at the roadside—the disguised woman creeping ever nearer —when the other fired his pistol at him, and missed. I saw that as the smoke cleared away, for when it had done so they were closely engaged with their swords. Some passes they made; once it seemed as if the fugitive won upon the other, for I saw his blade go through his left sleeve; then, ere he could recover himself, the other had thrust his sword through his body—I heard him shriek; I saw him fall! A moment later the woman had snatched up the child and was hurrying back to the city, the man following after her, his left arm hanging straight by his side, as though still from pain. And I ran to this one here and saw that he had got his death. 'Tis strange he died not sooner than to-night. Strange he should linger so long."

"How got you him here?"

"My brother, who hates the De Roquemaures as I do—as God knows I have cause to do—works near here on his farm. I dragged that dead creature, all insensible as he was, into the copse, then fetched Jean, and so, together, we brought him. Say," the woman continued, leaning forward under the lamp to regard the soldier fixedly, "you are a gentleman, an officer of some regiment. You can tell me. Is not so foul a crime as this enough to doom De Roquemaure, if brought home to him?"

"If brought home to him, perhaps. But the nobles are powerful. You say that he is so, especially in this neighbourhood."

"Curse him, yes!" she replied, her livid lips drawn

tight together. "Yet not forever. There are those who will set the snare and trap him yet."

"I pray God!" St. Georges replied. "He has wronged many; surely justice will yet be done."

CHAPTER XIV.

"I MUST SPEAK!"

THE Epiphany—called in old France, under the Bourbons, *la Fête des Rois*—was drawing to a close, as St. Georges, his handsome face looking very dejected and his heart heavy as lead within him, rode into Paris by the Charenton gate.

Not so entirely over, however, but that the streets were still crowded with holiday makers of all kinds, with those who were there solely to enjoy and amuse themselves, and also with those who sought to make profit out of the others. Moreover, still from all the towers and steeples the bells rang in honour of those who had died during the past year, so that, as Boileau sneeringly remarked, "*Pour honorer les morts ils font mourir les vivants,*" while from the dark, sombre-looking houses—of which the same writer observed that they must have been built by philosophers instead of architects, so filthy were they without and so brilliant within—were still hung paper lanterns, flags, banners, and all kinds of devices and decorations.

St. Georges had found it difficult to pick his way through the many obstacles with which the streets were encumbered from the time he left the Bastille and the Rue St. Antoine, and began to approach the more fashionable part of Paris, the vicinity of the Pont Neuf. Richly gilt carriages of the *noblesse* and the *nouveaux riches* passed each other frequently, the inmates of the former disdaining to notice the inmates of the other—human nature was the same then as now—and threw the January mud upon an extraordinary crowd of foot passengers—a crowd composed of ladies with mirrors in their hands; men with huge blonde or white wigs, who would stop suddenly to take a comb from their servants' hands and arrange their false locks; others of the commoner sort selling coffee and chocolate on the footway, another drawing teeth in the open street, two men fighting a duel with short swords, a woman and a child picking pockets.*

Because it was the Epiphany—the King's Fête—Louis and the court were at the Louvre this year, occupying the vast and stately palace on which the Grande Monarque had spent since 1664 the sum of ten million seven hundred thousand francs; and high festival was being kept. All the court had come with him, including the wife who was still suspected by some of being the mistress; the duchesses and countesses who had been mistresses if they were so no longer; the bishops who were not in disgrace and under the displeasure of De Maintenon; the numerous offspring by various mothers; the ministers and officials—including Louvois. And it was to present himself to the latter first, and afterward to seek audience with Louis, that St. Georges now rode toward the palace.

"Surely," he thought to himself as he directed his course through the heterogeneous mass in the streets,

---

* See engravings of Della Bella, done at the time and representing such scenes.

"surely when I relate my tale, tell of the terrible blow
that has fallen upon me, I shall be forgiven for having halted on my route. I am more than a week behind, have lagged on my road, yet for what a cause—
what a cause! Oh, my child, my little Dorine, that I
should have had to come away and leave you behind!
My child! My child!"

Never for a moment since he had left the peasant's
hut had his thoughts been absent from that child, never
had they ceased to dwell upon the conspiracy that ex-
isted without doubt against both him and her. Moreover, so intricate, so entangled did all appear that the
mesh seemed incapable of being unravelled, and his
brain whirled as he endeavoured to pierce the darkness
of it all.

"Let me reflect," he had pondered to himself, as day
by day he drew nearer to the capital, "let me try to
think it all out, see it clearly. God give me power to
do so!"

Then he had endeavoured, by going over his life
from the commencement, to reduce matters to something short of chaos.

"That I am De Vannes's son—his heir—must be!"
he thought; "it gives the cause, the reason for what
follows. This is clear. Also the attack on me, the
stealing of Dorine, proceeds from a like cause. And if
all that was the duke's—his title, his wealth—is mine,
and, after me, hers, in whose light can we stand, against
whose interest thrust, but De Roquemaure's? All this
is as clear as day; it is here the mystery begins. For,
first, how does he know this? Next—which is more
strange—how know that on a certain night I should be
on the road between two such remote places as Pontarlier and Paris? How know, too, that I have my child

with me, as he must have known, since he mentioned it
to the myrmidons he enlisted at Recey? If I could discover this—should ever discover it, a light might break
in upon what followed—more mysterious still."

When he had turned this over and over again in his
thoughts as mile by mile and league by league he drew
nearer the end of his journey, he endeavoured to arrange and piece together the further, the newer, and
fresher mystery of all that had happened since the
night he rested under the roof of the De Roquemaures'
house. And here his perplexity was even greater than
before.

" He acts alone," he reflected; " at least without assistance from his kinswomen—his stepmother and half-
sister. For if such is not the case, then viler wretches
than they never bore the shape of womanhood. The
excitement of the marquise, the noble sympathy of that
girl expressed in every glance of those pure eyes, were
not, could not have been assumed—false! If so, perish
all my belief in woman's truth and honour! Yet from
that very manoir over which she, his mother, rules more
than he, for the present at least, came forth two—one a
man in his garb, the dress of his house—the other a
woman. For her, though, it is not so difficult of explanation! The murdered peasant's wife spoke of him
as having female instruments at his beck and call, and
although her companion wore his livery she might be
any creature in the city over whom he possessed influence."

And now, as he reflected, he knew that he had come
to the most difficult of all knots to untie, the hardest
of all the mystery to be solved. For, arrived so far in
his endeavours to unwind the plot with which he was
surrounded, he found himself at fault, groping help-

lessly in the dark, when he stood face to face with the
memory of the man who had been assassinated by De
Roquemaure's vassal—face to face with Pierre, the
Bishop of Lodève's servant, who at the time he was set
upon was in possession of Dorine!

One thought alone rose to his mind at first, one only
which would have explained his presence on the scene,
his possession of the child—the thought that the cynical Bishop of Lodève, the man of whom the whole of
France spoke so ill, might in truth have known of some
deep-laid scheme for kidnapping that child and have
sent Pierre forward—or after him—to rescue it at all
costs, thinking, perhaps, that if abstracted by him, it
could be better kept in safety than even by its own
father.   A wild and visionary idea, in truth, to have
entered St. Georges's mind, yet, perhaps, not too remote
to suggest itself to an unhappy parent so bereft as he
was.   But, in a moment, another reflection chased it
away.

"No!" he exclaimed to himself as the second
thought arose.   "No! no!   More like that the fellow
Pierre was the messenger from Dijon who put the
ruffians on their guard; who warned them that I was
accompanied by the Mousquetaire Noir; that they
would have two soldiers to contend against instead of
one.   The fellow who had tracked us all day, then passed
us, and who, masked like the others, had stood out of
the fight in the graveyard.   So! so!   That vile bishop
is in it, too.   Fool that I am to have thought that that
sneering, evil priest had ever a kindly thought in his
heart.   Yet why in it also?   Why? why?"

He could follow his chain of reasoning no more—
against all his thoughts a blacker wall of impenetrable
mystery rose than ever.   He was forced to desist from

thinking, or go mad in doing so. For if this man Pierre was De Roquemaure's auxiliary—if, as was undoubted from the peasant woman's story, he had possessed himself of Dorine on behalf of De Roquemaure— why had two other of that villain's myrmidons slain him and possessed themselves of her? His mind could find no answer to this; his reasoning ceased; he could go no further through the maze.

"God, he knows," he muttered reverently. "In his good time, in his infinite mercy, it may be he will let me know all, too."

But even as he rode through the crowded streets and drew near the great courtyard of the Louvre he was still thinking—thinking always—of the web in which he was entangled and of his helpless little child alone, unhappy—perhaps ill treated—perhaps dead! There was that day no more heartbroken man in Paris than he.

As he drew rein at the courtyard door, vast as a cathedral's, there issued from it a great emblazoned carriage, with arms and crests upon its panels, the four horses drawing it being also richly apparelled with velvet and nodding plumes, and with at the back three footmen who, as was the custom of the time, stood each behind the other on a platform instead of side by side.

His eye, glancing into the interior of the vast fabric, saw within a woman, young and beautiful, yet with her fair face disfigured—as was indeed obligatory on all women who attended the court of Louis—with powder and paint, and with *mouches*, or patches, cut into the various forms of stars, half moons, and so forth. Her dress, too, was gorgeous, being of rich velvet of the colour then known as "pigeon breast," faced with silver brocade and slashed with seams to show the red and silver lace, while the whole was enriched with plain satin and watered ribbons, and deep full point lace at breast and sleeves. On her head, though not hiding her much-curled hair, was a rich *escoffion* of ruby velvet surmounted by pearls, and tied beneath her chin.

She saw him in a moment, the soft hazel eyes resting full on him—saw, too, that he hesitated as though about to draw his horse away out of her range of vision; then with a look she beckoned him to draw near her carriage door, while through the window at the back of the vehicle she made a sign to the first of the three footmen to have it stopped against the *chaussée*.

And he, scarce knowing what to do—whether, indeed, to content himself with coldly taking off his hat and avoiding her, or to obey her glance, yet instinctively did the latter, and drew up to the window. And in another moment the embroidered glove had been withdrawn from her white hand, which was resting in his, while her eyes scanned his sorrow-stricken face.

"Monsieur St. Georges honoured our poor house no more," she said, "ere he quitted Troyes. Yet, considering all, it was not strange he should not do so."

On his guard, since—believing though he did in her honour and in her mother's—he could not forget she was a De Roquemaure, the kinswoman of the devil who had already worked him so much ill, and might—nay, would, if not thwarted—work so much more, he replied cautiously : "' Considering all,'. mademoiselle ; you doubtless refer to——"

"Oh, monsieur," she said, "let there be no more cross purposes. I know—I know as though I could see deep into your heart, beneath your gorget, that—that— you couple us with my brother. And you know," while as she spoke she leaned forward so that her fair—yet, alas! painted—face almost bent over his sleeve, and her

clear, starlike eyes gazed into his, "that he is your
enemy; at least, you fear so."

"I know nothing," he replied, "except that all—all
—in one case suspicion in the other certainty—points
to him. I know that when one, whose part in the affair
I cannot yet unravel, had my child"—he said "my
child" with a sob in his voice—"in his keeping, a
vassal of De Roquemaure's, clad in the russet livery of
your house, and accompanied by one of his master's
lemans, slew him and stole her. I know that."

"One of his lemans!" she whispered, while over
her face there crept a blush deeper than the court-
ordained paint — "one of his lemans! You know
that?"

"I know it," he replied. "Masked, too, as though,
foul as she might be, she still had some shame, dreaded'
to show her face in such proceeding."

She seemed to be endeavouring to tame some emotion
within her; perhaps, as he thought, to prevent any sign
of knowledge on her part escaping from her by accident.
Then she said, in a faint voice:

"Since you know that, you must know more. Oh,
my God!" she exclaimed suddenly—so suddenly that
he started at her excitement. "I must speak! Yet,
Monsieur St. Georges, remember; it is the man's sister, the child of the same father as himself, who
speaks to you. Remember that, I say, and listen.
Though he stole your child, though his vassal slew the
man who had it in his keeping, though his *leman*—
that I should pronounce the word!—assisted that vassal,
yet De Roquemaure has not harmed it—will not harm
it. Do you believe?"

"Tell me more. Where is it? It is mine, mine,
mine!"

9

"Do you believe me, Monsieur St. Georges?—me, though I am his sister, a De Roquemaure myself?"

His eyes looked back into hers now—looked deep into those pure, clear, gray eyes; he hesitated no longer. She was his sister, was a De Roquemaure, yet he believed.

"Yes," he said, "mademoiselle, I believe. I do believe."

Beneath the hateful, necessary carmine he saw the true blood show itself as he spoke. He saw the honest, truthful eyes glisten—at least no rococo monarch could cause them to be made vile!—he knew that his words had satisfied her. He had an ally, a friend, here. And how powerful such an ally might be! Yet he continued, his anxiety overmastering all:

"But in pity, mademoiselle, not so much for me, her father, as her own innocent, helpless little self— think of her, poor little babe, in that man's—in any man's power!—tell me all you know. Tell me, I implore."

What she would have said, what answered, he could not know. At that moment there came forth from the inner court a troop of the mounted gendarmerie, followed by an enormous carriage, three times the size of that in which sat Mademoiselle de Roquemaure, covered with gilding. It was the carriage of Louis Quatorze, who was about to proceed to Marly for the night. Naturally, therefore, the vehicle in which Aurélie sat was forced to go forward; naturally, also, St. Georges had to back his horse to the side of the huge gateway, since no obstruction was allowed to impede the gracious sovereign's progress. With a bow they parted, therefore, she giving him one glance that might mean that later on they would meet again, while her carriage proceeded as fast as was possible in the direction of the already fashionable quarter of St.-Germain.

And he, drawing aside, witnessed the passage of Louis ere he himself proceeded to present himself to Louvois. He saw the king with his great carriage full of ladies, saw the table inside it covered with sweetmeats and fruit, saw the greatest monarch in Europe lolling back alone on one seat, a dog upon his knees. And, as he bowed low before his master, it seemed to him almost as if the king had distinguished him from among the heterogeneous mass of people who thronged the filthy footpath, and had looked at him an instant as though either gazing on a familiar face or wondering where he had seen one like it before.

CHAPTER XV.

THE MINISTER OF WAR.

"You come a little late, Monsieur St. Georges," the harsh, raucous, and underbred voice of Louvois said—"a little late. Too late by far for an officer selected by his Majesty for special service."

He turned his back upon his visitor as he spoke, changing the position he had assumed in front of the great fireplace in the room set apart as his cabinet in the Louvre, and seemed now only intent on watching the logs burning in the grate, and of dismissing—or insulting—the *chevau-léger.*

" Perhaps when M. de Louvois has heard my explanation of the reason why I am late, have tarried on my road, he may be disposed to overlook my dilitoriness,"

St. Georges replied, regarding the back of the *roturier* minister as he spoke; and the well-bred tones in which he uttered the words caused Louvois to turn around and face him again.

They made a strange contrast as they stood there. Both men were more than ordinarily tall, yet both carried their height differently. Louvois's was decreased in appearance by. the heaviness of his shoulders, his head being deep set between them. St. Georges was as erect as a dart; while, as he faced the man whom, by some innate perception, he regarded as an enemy—or, at least, not a friend—his head was thrown back, so that his height and uprightness seemed somehow increased. Moreover, the whole appearance of each was in extreme contrast, and that not a contrast in favour of the minister. The stained military jacket of the soldier, the long, brown leather boots, the large cavalry spurs, the great bowl-hilted sword, all gave him an appearance of advantage over the sombre, velvet-clad Louvois; the long, curling hair falling on his shoulders in a thick mass was more becoming than the wig *à trois marteaux* which Louvois wore outside state functions. And for the rest, the pale yet weather-exposed face of the one, with its long, deep, chestnut mustache, caused the cadaverous and coarse-cut features of the other—the thick, bulbous nose and full, sensual lips—to appear insignificant, if not ignoble.

Louvois had kept him waiting three hours in the anteroom—a thing which, however, he would have done in any case and to any one seeking an interview with him, excepting only some scion of royalty, legitimate or illegitimate, one of the king's marshals, or a relative of one of the king's mistresses—for he understood as well as any vulgar, important *parvenu* of to-day, or thought he understood, the value of administering such snubs. And, now that the visitor was admitted, his manner was as insulting and as would-be humiliating as he knew how to fashion it. Moreover, with another trait of vulgarity as common in those days as these, he had bidden him to no seat.

His behaviour was the ignoble spite of the man who believed he saw in the other the son of him who had consistently ignored his existence—the late Duc de Vannes.

" The explanation," he said, in answer to St Georges's remark, and speaking in a voice which he endeavoured to render cold and haughty, but which was, in truth, an angry, bitter one, " will have to be very full, very complete, to satisfy his Majesty. You quitted the garrison of Pontarlier on the last night of the last year, riding on special service in the king's name, and you have tarried long on the road in, I imagine, your own service. Beyond bringing one message—that from the Bishop of Lodève—you have failed in your duty, sir; indeed, failed so much that the Marquise de Roquemaure, from whom you were ordered to bring another message, has actually preceded your arrival here. Has passed you on the read and entered Paris before you, though you quitted her manoir before she did; has, indeed, been able to give an interesting account of you and your supposed adventures."

" Supposed!" exclaimed St. Georges quietly—" supposed! Does madame la marquise stigmatize them as 'supposed,' or does monsieur le ministre, Monsieur de Louvois, apply that epithet to them?" and as he spoke, with still his head thrown back and his left hand resting lightly in the cup of his sword hilt, he looked very straight into the eyes of Louvois.

"Madame la marquise is a woman; she believes—and tells—a story as she hears it."

St. Georges bent his head for a moment, then as quietly as he asked the previous question, but equally as clearly and distinctly as he had previously spoken, he said:

"Monsieur Louvois will remember he is speaking to a soldier."

"*Et puis?*"

"Who permits no one, not even the minister of the army, who is his superior, to question his veracity. What he told madame he told as it happened."

Louvois laughed somewhat sinisterly and wholly insultingly, yet for him quietly, after which he said: .

"Monsieur St. Georges is also something else besides a soldier—as, indeed, his present manner proclaims. A little of—if I may say it without fear of being done to death on my own hearth—a bully."

"A bully!"

"I fear so, disguised in the uniform of the king. It was bully's work which you performed in the graveyard of Aignay-le-Duc—work which if done by others than soldiers would lead to the halter; work which, when done by soldiers, leads generally to a file of their brethren—to a platoon."

If St. Georges could have had his way, followed his own bent, it would have been his right hand instead of left which would have grasped his sword, and he would have bidden the minister unsheath his own weapon and answer for his words. Yet, since he was no fool, he saw at once that for some purpose of his own Louvois was endeavouring to anger him, to lead him into an outbreak of irritation, and he refused to be so led, so trapped. Instead, he replied, therefore:

" Monsieur is, I think, the father of children himself. A few words will, therefore, show him, prove to him, my excuse. I bore with me my child; I was set upon by hired ruffians, and in the defence of that child—by the aid of another stalwart arm—I resisted them, slew some, drove some away, disarmed others. Yet, monsieur, this was not the worst, not quite the worst, against which I had to contend."

The piercing eyes of the minister of war were resting fixedly on him as he spoke—almost, it seemed, as though he feared what might come next.

St. Georges proceeded:

"Not quite the worst. This gang of hired ruffians was led by one, a cowardly hound, who feared to show his face! by one who—so accurately had he been notified, forewarned, of my approach—must have received his intelligence from Paris, from some one who knew what my movements would be at the time. Strange, was it not, monsieur le ministre?"

Louvois's face seemed less empurpled than before— to have turned white; then, brusquely, as always, he said:

"You are here, sir, to answer questions, not to ask them. Proceed."

"From Paris alone," St. Georges continued, "could that intelligence have come, since he was there with his ruffians to meet and intercept me—though I should not omit to state that, from the time I left Dijon, there followed ever in my course another knave, who took to this craven assassin the news that I was not alone. Certain it is, he would have been of no avail, nor have been sent, had not the others known well of my intended journey. Monsieur le ministre, are you sure, do you think, that in your *bureau* here"—the words fell clear and distinct as he spoke—"there is any foul, crawling creature, say, a low-born clerk, say, some ignoble menial—it could have been none with the iustincts of a true-born gentleman of France!—who would have set so deep and foul a plot as this to waylay an innocent man?"

He saw—and, seeing, knew where one of his enemies, at least, was—the slight wince which Louvois gave—above all, the minister hated to have it known that his origin had but one or two generations of gentility to it! —and he knew also that he had laid his finger on one knot in the net. Then Louvois spoke:

"It is impossible that such can be the case. And accusations against persons who have no existence will not save you. You have failed in your duty. Is this all the explanation you have to offer me?"

"It is all I have to offer you, monsieur. If it is not sufficient, I must address myself to the head of the army —to the king himself."

"I am afraid you will have little opportunity." Then turning like a tiger toward him, he said: "Your case has been considered during your procrastination; your easily made journey by extremely short and comfortable stages. Monsieur St. Georges, you are no longer in the army. The king has no further need of your valuable services."

"What! Dismissed without appeal—without——"

"Your appeal is heard and disapproved of—by me. Had it been made differently—your explanation couched in more respectful terms, had carried with it more conviction to my mind—this," and he handed him a paper, "would have been destroyed instead of being given to you. As it is, read it, and act on it. Otherwise the results will be unfortunate. Observe also the signatures to it. They are neither those of 'low-born clerks' nor 'ignoble menials';" and he stepped back to the fire and stood regarding his victim.

Certainly one signature came not under the category of the above terms, it being that of Louis himself; the other was that of Louvois, and, perhaps, was open to cavil. But St. Georges was immersed in the document itself: beyond the (to him) fatal signature of the king, the other was of scant importance for the moment.

The paper ran as follows:

"MONSIEUR ST. GEORGES: Being extremely displeased with you for the manner in which you have tarried on your road from Pontarlier to Paris and have failed in the secret mission on which I employed you— namely, to bring me (without more delay than such which might by *force majeure* arrive) messages from two of my subjects—I write you this to say, first, you are no longer an officer in my regiment of the Chevaux-Légers of Nivernosi; secondly, you are at once to quit my kingdom of France and the dependencies thereof, wheresoever situated. In which, desiring that you fail not at once to obey my second behest, I pray that God will have you, Monsieur St. Georges, in his holy keeping.

" Written at Paris the 15th January, 1688.

" *Signé* Louis. *Soussigné* Louvois."

Briefly St. Georges said to Louvois:

" And if I fail in this second behest, what then? What if I refuse to quit France?"

" That I leave you to imagine. Sir, our interview is at an end;" and he rang a bell as he spoke, and when it was answered by a gorgeous footman, said: .

" Escort this gentleman to the courtyard."

St. Georges, however, made no sign of following the
servant, but, instead, advanced a step closer to Louvois,
so that when he stood nearer to him than he had hitherto done, the latter gave unmistakable signs of apprehension. Yet, seeing that there was no threatening
appearance on the other's face and that his sword hung
idle and untouched by his side, he said :

" You do not hear me, sir, it would seem. Our
interview is at an end."

" Not yet," replied St. Georges, very calmly. " You
have delivered your decision—I refuse to believe it is
the king's. And until I receive it from his own lips, I
shall neither quit Paris nor France."

" You will not? "

" I will not."

" So," replied Louvois in a harsh tone, " that is *your*
decision." Then changing his tone to one which, perhaps, he thought more effective—a gentler, more subtle
tone—he said : " You are, I think, unwise. The king
will not see you; and—meanwhile—he can find means
to exercise his authority, to have his orders executed."

" The king *will* see me, I think. Monsieur Louvois,
I have a petition to present to his Majesty."

" A petition ! "

" Against three of his subjects, all of whom, as I do
believe before God, have been engaged in a most foul
attempt against me and my child. Monsieur le ministre, shall I mention the names of those subjects of the
king? " and his eye glanced at the servant as he spoke.

" No, be silent," replied Louvois; " also I bid you
beware what you say, what do. Monsieur St. Georges,"
he continued, breaking out into one of those heats of
rage which were usual with him, while, even as he did
so, he roughly motioned the servant at the door to quit

the room.—" Monsieur St. Georges, do you know the
deadly peril in which you stand? Do you know, I say?
If it pleases me I have enough authority to commit you
to the Bastille to-night, to Vincennes, to Bicêtre—the
power to arrest you here in this room. If I summon
that servant again, a file of mousquetaires will be sent
for; if I touch this bell "—and he pointed to another
than the one which he had already rung—" they will
appear. Monsieur St. Georges, will you quit Paris to-
night and France directly afterward, or shall I call in
the soldiers ? "

" Call in the soldiers," the other replied, now thoroughly desperate, " or the servant, or as many of your
following as you choose! Only—ere you do so hear
me," and he raised his hand in so authoritative a manner that Louvois, who had made a step toward the bell,
paused in astonishment. Then St. Georges continued :
" I am resolved to obtain an audience of the king to-
night, and can do so if not thwarted. My charger is
fleeter than the horses of his state carriage ; I can reach
Marly as soon as he. To-day is Thursday, *le jour des
audiences iconnues;* it is my chance. Now, monsieur,
shall I see the king to-night unmolested, unprevented
by you, or shall I be dragged before him an assassin to
plead my cause? A murderer, but a righteous one?"

" An assassin—a murderer!" exclaimed Louvois,
stepping back, while his face blanched. " Explain yourself."

" Then listen—and—abstain from that bell till you
have heard me "—seeing that the other's eye roved toward it. " I intend," speaking rapidly, " to see the
king to-night or in the morning at latest, and to tell
him of the foul plot of which an officer of his *chevaux-
légers* has been the victim; to ask him if, bearing this

about me "—and he produced from his breast the letter
ordering him to leave Pontarlier and travel to Paris "—
he approves of the manner in which I have been spied
upon, tracked, nigh done to death, and robbed of my
most precious treasure, my child.; to sue for permission to seek out those who have done this thing and
bring them at last to justice.   And, M. de Louvois, I
tell you face to face and man to man that, if you approach that bell, summon your soldiers until I am outside this door, they shall find you a dead man when
they open it!   Once outside I can answer for myself.
Now choose!"

And as he spoke his right hand went round to his
sword-hilt, while his left raised the scabbard, so that the
blade could easily be drawn.

CHAPTER XVI.

PASQUEDIEU!

St. Georges was not, however, destined to arrive at
Marly on that night, nor to see Louis and lay his story
before him.

On quitting Louvois he made his way swiftly along
the corridor leading from the chamber on the ground
floor in which he had been received to the courtyard, no
interruption being attempted, as was natural enough,
considering that he was leaving instead of seeking to
enter the building.   The soldiers, gendarmerie and the
Suisses as well as the Mousquetaires Gris—whose turn
it was at the present moment to be in attendance at the
Louvre—were lounging about the guard room and the

great gateway, and they not only did not offer any oppo-
sition to his passage, but, instead, seeing about him the
signs of a cavalry officer—the gorget, long cut-and-
thrust sword, great boots, and gantlets—saluted him.

Therefore he passed out into the street—since known
in the present century as the Rue de Rivoli—and regained his horse from the *guet* in whose custody he had
left it.

That he recognised the danger—the awful danger
—in which he had now placed himself, who can doubt?
He was a soldier, and he had threatened the assassination of the chief—under the king—of the army. Moreover, he was a soldier who had just been dismissed from
that army for failing in his duty, for allowing private
affairs—harrowing as they were!—to come between him
and that duty. Now he was cooler; he became more
clear sighted; he knew that he had done a thing which
would destroy any claim that he might make for the
king's sympathy with him.

"I am ruined," he murmured, looking up and down
the street, not knowing which way to direct his horse's
steps; "have ruined myself. Louis will never forgive
this when he hears Louvois's story—never see me nor
hear me. Fool, fool that I am! I have destroyed
everything—above all, my one chance of regaining
'Dorine!"

What was he to do? That was the question he
asked himself. He had, it was true, avoided instant
arrest within the precincts of the palace, but how long
could he avoid arrest in whatever part of Paris he might
endeavour to shelter himself now?

"What have other men done," he pondered, "placed
as I am—as I have placed myself? What shall I, a broken, ruined soldier, do? What? what? Turn bully,

as he 'accused me of being, and cutthroat, bravo, or
thief—haunter of gambling hells and tripots? No! no!
no! I am a gentleman, have always lived like one; so
let me continue to the end. Yet, what to do now?"

He threaded his way through the streets, still filled
with their crowds of saltimbanques and quacks, though
the fashionable world, having seen *Le Roi Soleil*, had
gone or was going home, for the wintry evening was
setting in. And as he rode slowly, for his poor beast
was now quite spent, he tried to think of what he should
do—go to Marly at once, that evening, as he had said to
Louvois (although with scarcely the intention of doing
so, since he doubted seeing the king without preparation), or find a roof for himself and a stall for his horse
for the night.

Then he decided suddenly, promptly, that the former was what he would do. If he could get the king's
ear first, before Louvois, he might save himself. Louis
was great of heart, in spite of his childish belief in his
kingly attributes, of his love of splendour, and his van-
ity. Who could tell? A word with him—above all, a
word breathed as to whom St. Georges believed himself
to be—and he was safe. His father had been Louis's
companion; he would not slay the son. Safe—even
though dismissed the army and stripped of his commission—able to stay in France, to return to Troyes, to
seek and find his darling again!

He was resolved; he would go to Marly that night.

Only—how to get there. Marly lay beyond Versailles, four leagues from Paris, and his horse could go
no further. The marvel was that it had done so much,
and it was only by the most assiduous care and merciful treatment—by sometimes walking mile after mile by
its side, and by resting it hourly—that St. Georges had

been able to assist it to reach Paris. Now it could do no more.

However, ere long he espied an *écurie* and found that the owner had horses for hire, while one, a red roan with a shifty eye and bright-blooded nostril, took St. Georges's fancy. He knew a good horse the moment he saw one, and read by this creature's points that it would be troublesome for the first mile, and then carry him swiftly for the remainder of his journey. So, leaving his own horse—though not before he had seen it attended to, fed, and rubbed down, and taken into a comfortable, fresh-littered stall—he set out once more, tired, worn, and travel-sore as he was, for his fresh destination. Yet he knew his object, if he could attain it, would be worth a hundred times the extra fatigue. And when it was attained he could rest. Time enough then.

The red roan behaved exactly as he expected it would: it first of all bounded half across the road when once he was in the saddle, knocking down a scaramouche and a toothdrawer in doing so—the latter, fortunately, having no customer in his hands at the moment; it next proceeded sideways up the street, and then, finding it had a master to deal with, danced along in a canter until the West Gate of Paris was reached, after which, and being now sure that its exuberance was useless, it settled down into a long, easy stride, and bore its rider as smoothly as a carriage might toward his goal.

The moon, which a few nights back had shown beneath its young rays the corpse hanging on the gibbet outside the city of Troyes, lit up now the road along which he passed, disturbing on his way sometimes a deer in a thicket, sometimes a scurrying rabbit—they disturbing, too, the fiery creature he bestrode, and

frightening it into a swifter pace. Still, each moment
brought him nearer to his destination, to the arbiter in
whose hands his destiny was held; and, for the rest, he
sat like a rock upon its back. Its gambades could not
unseat him.

So the twelve English miles were nearly passed; he
was on the new road that branched off to Marly—the
strangest route that any man living in those days ever,
perhaps, rode along. On either side it was bordered by
small forests of enormous trees, mostly covered with
dead branches, since these trees had died unnaturally
long months ago, when transported from Compiègne to
where they now stood. Also he saw beneath the moon's
gleams fountains from which no water could be forced
to flow—great basins to which water could not be
brought, or only brought by depriving Versailles of its
natural supply. Louis had thought that he could force
Nature—uproot trees from one spot, where they had
flourished for a hundred years and cause them to flour-
ish equally well in another; had imagined that even
the waters on which his gondolas, brought from Venice,
might float, could be forced into existence at his command. It was a monstrous impertinence offered to
Nature, and it cost him four million and a half of livres,
with but little profit to any but the frogs and toads.

There rose now before his eyes—where the road
branched off in different directions, on the right to
Versailles, and, a little to the left, to Marly—the whitewashed walls of an auberge known as *Le Bon Pasteur*,
a place soon to be pulled down, since Louis had bought
out the owner, and was about to build a pavilion upon
it. But it stood up to this time untouched, as it had
done since the days of Henri III—long, low, thatched,
and weather-beaten, three old poplar trees in front of it,

a mounting-block also, and, of course, the usual heap of filth by its side where the stables were.

Approaching it, he felt the roan stagger beneath him, halt in its strides, then falter; and, shrewd horseman as he was, knew that it had either cast a shoe, or had got a stone in one. And as he dismounted close by the inn, though still some twoscore yards from the mounting-block, he heard behind him the clatter of other hoofs coming on, and the light laugh of a woman, also the deeper tones of a man.

"*Pasquedieu!*" he heard the latter say—and started both at the exclamation and the voice—"you may laugh, *ma mie*, yet I tell you 'tis so. He will marry her, spend her money on other women as I spend mine on you— *Morbleu!* whom have we here?" and the man riding along the road with his female companion pulled up his own horse, as the woman did hers, on seeing another traveller dismounted by the side of, and examining, his animal.

"Whom?" exclaimed that traveller, looking up— "whom? One perhaps whom you know. One whose name is Georges St. Georges." Then, vaulting back into his saddle—not meaning to be taken at a disadvantage—he bent forward and looked into the newcomer's face. "Did you ever hear that name before, monsieur?" he asked.

The face into which he gazed was that of a young, good-looking man, close shaven and with gray eyes that looked at him, as he thought, with terror. He was well dressed, too, in a riding costume of the period, while the woman who sat her horse, peering at him out of the eyelets of her mask, was also smartly arrayed in a female riding coat of the day, her head covered with a hood.

"Answer, monsieur," said St. Georges.

10

"Never," the other replied. "How should I know the name of every—person—I meet on the road?"

St. Georges bent forward over his saddle so that his own face was now nearer by a foot to the man with the gray eyes; then he said:

"Monsieur de Roquemaure, you are a liar! And more, a thief, a kidnapper; also, a would-be assassin. I know you and this, your wanton, here. You have to answer to me to-night for all you have done against me and mine in the past two weeks."

"*Mon Dieu!*" he heard the woman hiss beneath her mask. "Kill him, ·Raoul, kill him! God! that you should let him live and utter such things!" And as she so hissed she leaned down and struck at his face with her riding whip.

"Hound!" she exclaimed, "you apply that word to me? To me?"

"The woman speaks well," St. Georges said, warding off the blow with his arm while his eye rested on her for a moment; "it is a matter of killing. Either you or I have to be killed. To-night! Do you hear, or are you struck dumb with fear?"

"No," the other replied, at last, with amazement. "Who are you who, under a name I know not, dare to assault me thus with such opprobrious words? Nay," turning to the masked woman, who was again muttering in his ear, "have no fear. I will have his blood for it. If he is a gentleman with whom I can cross swords, we fight ere another hour passes."

"Also," St. Georges broke in, "you are, I perceive, a coward, besides the other things I have charged you with. You know who I am well enough. If not—if your memory is as treacherous as your courage seems poor, let me remind you. I am the man whom you at-

tacked with five others at Aignay-le-Duc; the man
whose child you sought to slay; the father of the child
whom your woman and your man-servant seized away
from one who had it in his possession, and whom they
slew also, you not appearing on the scene. You are
careful of yourself, Monsieur de Roquemaure! In the
first treacherous attack you shielded your head as none
other's head was shielded; in the second you employed
a woman and a man-servant to do that which, perhaps,
you feared to do yourself."

Every word he uttered was studied insult, every
word was weighed before it was delivered, substituted
for any other which rose to his lips if not deemed by
him sufficiently galling. He had sworn to kill this man
if ever he encountered him again, and he meant to kill
him to-night now he had met him. Therefore, since he
was resolved he should have no loophole of escape from
crossing swords with him, he so phrased his remarks
that he must fight or acknowledge himself the veriest
poltroon that breathed.

"But," he continued, "if you still value your hide
so much that you dare not meet me, now at once, tell
me where you and this woman—if it be the same, as I
suppose—have hidden my child; lead me to her, and
then you shall go free. Only choose, and choose at
once."

He heard the woman mutter to De Roquemaure:
"Who is the woman he speaks of, who, Raoul?" while
also he saw her eyes glisten again through the mask;
then, as he strove to catch her companion's reply, that
companion turned on him, and said:

"Monsieur St. Georges, as you term yourself, be
very sure I intend to slay you to-night. I do not know
you, but your insults to me and to—this—lady, although

the utterances of a madman, have to be wiped out at once. As to the child you mention, and its kidnapping by a servant of mine and a woman—bah!—I know not of what you speak."

" Do you deny that you are Monsieur de Roquemaure ? "

" I neither deny nor assert. Under that name you have chosen to waylay and insult me. Under that name, since you will have it, I intend to have reparation."

" Do you deny the assault at Aignay-le-Duc ? "

" I deny nothing, assert nothing."

" So be it," St. Georges said. " I have made no mistake. You *are* the man. Your voice, your expression condemn you. Your face, though you have shaved off your beard "—and he saw the other start as he mentioned this—" condemns, convicts you. Deny, therefore, these two things or draw your sword. We have wasted enough time."

" We have," the other answered, and as he spoke he dismounted from his horse, St. Georges doing the same.

CHAPTER XVII.

" KILL HIM DEAD, RAOUL ! "

THE duel was not, however, to take place in the road, since at that moment, and when both men were preparing to draw their swords, the inn door opened and two persons came forth—one evidently the landlord, the other a customer to whom he was saying " Good-night." Then, as he was about to re-enter his house, he saw

under the rays of the moon the three others in the road
—the two men close together and the woman still
mounted—and came forward toward them, peering in-
quiringly in front of him.

"Do messieurs and madame require any refresh-
ment?" he asked, noticing that two of the company
were well and handsomely dressed, while the third
looked like an officer. "My inn offers good accommodation for man and beast. Will monsieur and madame
not enter?"

"Curse you, no!" De Roquemaure said; "may we
not tarry a moment on the road without being pestered
thus? Begone, fellow, and leave us!"

But St. Georges interposed, saying:

"On the contrary, if you have a good room where
we can rest awhile and this *noble lady*," and he saw the
woman's eyes sparkle—perhaps with hate!—as he spoke,
"can be fittingly received, we will enter. My horse has
cast a shoe; have you a farrier near the house who can
reshoe it? It can be done while we drink a bottle."

"I am one myself," the innkeeper replied. "Monsieur may confide his horse to me. It is but a few
moments' job, and the fire in the forge is still alive. As
for the inn and the wine—*hein!* both are good; I have
a large room, and a bottle of Brecquiny fit for a king."

"Lead us to it," said St. Georges, "then attend to
the horse;" and as he spoke he threw the reins over the
hook fixed in the tree by the mounting-block. "Come,"
he said, addressing De Roquemaure and the woman in a
tone which would awaken no suspicion in the innkeeper's
mind. "Shall I assist madame to alight or will you?"

Madame, however, slipped off the horse by herself
lightly enough, brushing by St. Georges as she did so
and whispering in his ear, "If I could help him to kill

you, I would!" and so they entered the inn, St. Georges going last. He was a cautious man, this *chevau-léger*, and he had seen the little stiletto—or wedding-knife, as it was called then—in her girdle; he did not want the owner of those savage, glistening eyes to stab him in the back. She looked capable of doing it, he thought, judging by the sparkle they made behind the mask, and of stabbing the innkeeper afterward to hide her guilt.

The man led them into a long, low, whitewashed room at the end of a corridor—all three noticing that it was some distance from the inhabited part of the house, so that interruption was unlikely—a room in which a fire burnt low.

" Bring the wine," St. Georges said to the man after he had lit the candles in their sconces, " and be quick about it. We have no time to tarry here."

Five minutes later the bottle of Brecquiny was on the table with three long tapering glasses by its side; the man had made up the fire so that it burnt brightly, and they were alone; and St. Georges, having bidden him not interrupt them until they called, walked to the door, locked it, and, coming back to the table, placed the key upon it.

" There will be two leave this room," he said quietly. " There is the key for those who will require it.—Madame is comfortable, I trust," glancing at the woman who was seated at the table, her elbows on it, and her face in her hands, while still the eyes glanced through the holes of the mask at him.—" Now, Monsieur de Roquemaure, we have sufficient space for our sword play here. I am at your service," and he unsheathed his weapon.

The table was close to the fire, a deep chair on either side of it; two smaller chairs, in one of which the woman sat, against the table; beyond it a space of twenty square feet of coarse tiled floor—enough for any pair of duellists to kill each other in!

" You force this on me," De Roquemaure said, rising and removing the cloak he wore, and speaking between thin, almost bloodless lips; " whether your blood or mine be shed, it is upon your own head," and he drew his sword too.

" Not so," St. Georges replied. " Deny that you led the attack on me, on my child and my comrade at Aignay-le-Duc; deny that it was your servant—that it was your livery he wore—accompanied by some woman, if not this one, who slew the Bishop of Lodève's servant" —once more the other started, as he had started when accused of having removed his beard—" deny this, I say, and I break my sword across my knee—I leave myself unarmed and defenceless, at your mercy to slay me here for the words I have spoken."

Again from the now absolutely livid lips there came the same words, or almost the same, he had previously uttered.

" I deny nothing—I assert nothing," and he advanced past the table to where St. Georges stood, weapon in hand.

" So be it! Yet, for the last time, ere it is too late, answer me one question and I will not force you to this encounter to-night. Tell me where my child is, let me regain possession of her, and a month hence, on my honour as a soldier, I meet you again, and, *if you desire it*, give you satisfaction."

" I do not know where your child is," De Roquemaure muttered hoarsely. "And for your honour as a soldier—you are a broken one. A man dismissed the army has no honour left."

"Enough!" said St. Georges; "you knew that—
knew, not that I am broken, but that I was to be
broken! Now I understand who two of my enemies are
for sure. Thus I dispose of one. *En garde!*"

"Kill him!" he heard the woman hiss again as they
commenced. "Kill him dead, Raoul!"

A moment later they were engaged, each seeking the
other's life. And each knew that nothing but his death
would satisfy his adversary.

Their weapons scarcely made any noise, so quietly
the one stole upon the other, as point pressed point, and
through the swords the power of their wrists made
itself felt. Once De Roquemaure lunged savagely, but
the thrust was parried and returned—dangerously so.
The point of St. Georges's weapon slit his sleeve as, like
an adder's tongue, it darted forth. Then the other
drew back and fought more carefully, though the beads
of sweat stood on his white forehead now. And St.
Georges, observing them, knew that he held him safe.
His nerve was gone already—the nearness of that thrust
had shattered it!

The woman, looking on—her face also as white as a
corpse's—was, perhaps, the strangest figure of the three.
Her eyes shone like coals through the mask-holes now
—her figure shook all over; one hand clutched the
coarse cover on the table in a mass of folds; the other
tremblingly played with the hilt of her little dagger.
And the Brecquiny being near her, she more than once
released the table cover to pour out a glass full, drain
it a draught, throw down the glass, and glare at the
combatants again.

Once, too, she shrieked aloud as a second time St.
Georges's weapon, lunging full at the other's breast, was
just caught by the hilt of De Roquemaure's sword and

parried, though not without tearing from his breast a piece of the lace from his cravat. And she struck herself on the mouth with her clinched hand—so that her lips were bloody a moment after—as though in rage with herself for having done aught to alarm the house.

"You are doomed," St. Georges said to De Roquemaure in a low voice, driving him back toward the wall, so that now the latter faced up the room while the former's back was toward the table—"doomed! I have you fast. Acknowledge all, or by the God above us I slay you in the next pass!"

De Roquemaure made no answer; doggedly he fought—a horrible spectacle. Another thrust of St. Georges's was, however, also parried—the blade knocked nervously up by the affrighted man—tearing a piece of flesh from De Roquemaure's cheek, from which the blood ran down on to what was left of the cravat; the eyes glared like a hunted animal's; the mouth was half open.

It almost required St. Georges's memory of his lost Dorine, of the manner in which they had aimed under his arm at her—so appalled did his adversary appear—to prevent him from sparing the craven, from disarming him, and letting him go forth a whipped and beaten hound. ·But he remembered the wrong done him, the cruel, dastardly attempts on the child's life—and his blood was up. De Roquemaure should die. "The wolf was face to face with him"—at that moment he recalled the marquise's words—he would slay him.

Behind his back the other could see the woman—even as he endeavoured to shield himself from thrust after thrust, and thought: "God! when will it come? when shall I feel the steel through me?"—herself now a ghastly sight. Her upper lip was drawn back in her

frenzy so that her teeth were bare as are a dog's that
pauses ere it snaps; she was standing up trembling, as
with a palsy, and her mask had fallen off. And, in what
De Roquemaure felt were his last moments, he saw her
suddenly rush at the sconces and knock the candles out
of them on to the stone floor, where they lay guttering.
He supposed that she had thought to disturb his dooms-
man.

If she did so think she erred. St. Georges heard the
crash of her arm against the metal, but never turned
his head—to take his eye off the other's point would
have been fatal!—instead, in the light given by the fire
he crept one inch nearer the other.

"Now," he said, "now, De Roquemaure!" and as he
spoke the other felt the iron muscles in the man's wrist
forcing his blade down and down; the point was level
to his adversary's thigh; an instant more, and St.
Georges's sword would release his, would suddenly
spring up and—a moment later—be through his breast.

In his agony he shrieked, "*Au secours, au secours!*"
and in a last desperate effort leaped aside, the weapon
that at that moment sought his heart with a tremendous
lunge piercing his arm alone.

Another moment and St. Georges had disengaged it,
drawn it forth, and was about to plunge it through the
craven's heart—this time he would not fail!—when he
heard the rustle of the woman's riding robe behind him,
he felt a shock, and his arm instantly drop nerveless by
his side; the weapon fell from his hand, and he sank
back heavily on the stone floor, the room swimming before his eyes and all becoming rapidly dark.

Roused by her lover's cry and frenzied by the imme-
diate death which she saw threatening him; driven almost mad also by the look of terror and mortal appre-

hension on his face, she had sprung up the room, reached St. Georges, and buried her dagger in his back. She had aimed under his left shoulder, where she knew the region of the heart was—it seemed her aim was true! As he fell to the ground she knew that she had saved De Roquemaure. Yet her frenzy was not calmed ; in an instant she had seized the sword that still was grasped in her lover's nerveless right hand, placed it in his left, and muttered swiftly in a voice he did not recognise :

"Through his heart!—his heart, Raoul ! That way. Otherwise it will seem murder and confound us."

" I—I dare not," the scared man muttered, shaking all over. " I cannot, I——"

" *Lâche !* " and as she hurled the epithet at him she seized the weapon herself in her own white jewelled hand and drew it back to plunge it through his breast so that it should meet the wound behind.

Yet that was not to be. Even as she raised the sword the door was burst violently open, and the inn-keeper, with two other men and a waiting woman rushed into the room.

" *Grand Dieu !* " the landlord cried, shivering and shaking all over, as he saw the terrible spectacle which the place afforded—St. Georges stretched on the floor, the stones covered with blood, the other wounded man leaning against the wall, the maddened woman with the sword, which she had dropped at their entrance, lying at her feet, and the candles out—" *Grand Dieu !* what has been done in my house ? Murder ? "

At first neither De Roquemaure nor the panting creature by his side could answer; then the former found his tongue, while still the landlord and the other two men stared at them and the waiting woman hid her

face in her apron, not to see the ghastly form on the
floor, and said: "Not murder, but attempted murder.
This man drew on me—with a lady present—would
have assassinated me. You see my wound," and he
held up his pierced arm.

"Attempted murder!" exclaimed one of the men,
he looking of a very superior class to that of the landlord. "A strange attempt; you are young and strong
as he; armed, too, your weapon drawn. Yet it seems it
needed this also to aid you," and he stooped and picked
up the woman's toy dagger. "This demands explanation——"

"And shall be given to those entitled to ask. I am
the Marquis de Roquemaure, set upon and forced to de-
fend myself by this fellow who entrapped us here.—
You," turning to the landlord, "saw how he caused us
to enter this house, though I told you we wanted nothing. He it was who gave all the orders. For the rest,
he was a disgraced and ruined soldier, a common bravo
and bully, who deemed me the cause of his punishment.
I answer nothing further but to the king whom I serve,
or his representative."

"He looks not like a bravo or bully," said the man
who had spoken last, as he knelt down by St. Georges
and took his wrist between his fingers. "He scarce
seems that."

"Is he dead?" the woman asked hoarsely now, as
she bent down over her victim.

"Not yet. There is still some pulse."

And even as he spoke, St. Georges opened his eyes,
looked up at him, and muttered once, "Dorine!"

Then the eyes closed again and his head fell back on
the other's arm.

THE SECOND PERIOD.

CHAPTER XVIII.

LA GALÈRE GRANDE RÉALE.

THE July sun blazed down upon the sea which lay beneath it as unruffled as an artificial lake inland; there was no ripple on the water as far as the eye could see; above the water to the northwest there rose the chalky cliffs between Whitby and Scarborough—a white, hazy line over which a few fleecy clouds were massed together. Upon the water, three miles out from those cliffs, a dark blot, which grew larger and clearer moment by moment, and proved to be—when seen through the perspective glasses of the officers on board a French galley which was further out to sea and rapidly retreating from the English coast—one of King William's men-of-war.

A French galley rapidly retreating from the English coast, of the style known as La Grande Réale, and named L'Idole. On board of her six hundred and seventy souls, comprising a first and second captain, a lieutenant and sublieutenant, an ensign, also a major general, some standard bearers, a commissary general, one or two volunteer officers, over one hundred soldiers and seventy sailors, a number of subaltern officers and ship boys, and—three hundred and sixty galley slaves and sixty Turkish slaves.

A life of hell was this of the galley to all on board her when at sea—even to those in command! Neither first nor second captain, neither major nor commissary general, nor even volunteer officers—often members of the oldest and most aristocratic families of France—could ever lie down to sleep on board, for the sufficient reason that in the confined space there was no room for bed, cot, nor berth. Rest had to be taken by these superiors either when sitting on ordinary chairs placed on the poop cabin, or in armchairs if such were on board—their clothes on, their arms by their side. For not only was there no room for anything in the shape or nature of a bed, but also the galleys were rarely at sea except in time of open war, when at any moment they might be engaged in action. Truly, a life of hell!

Yet, if to the superiors such miseries came and had to be endured; such want of sleep, such constant necessity for watchfulness, such poor, coarse food as alone the galley could find room to carry—bacon, salt beef, salt cod, cheese, oil, and rice, with a small pot of wine daily, being their allowance—what of those wretches who propelled her when there was no wind, the galley slaves? What was their existence? Let us see!

Bound to the labouring oar—itself of enormous size and weight, being fifty feet long—seven *condamnés* to each oar, they sat at sixty benches, thirty on each side, four hundred and twenty men in all, including Turkish slaves. Naked they rowed for hours chained to these benches—sometimes for twenty-four hours at a stretch—while the *comites*, or overseers, men brutal beyond all thought and chosen for the post because of their natural ferocity, belaboured their backs with whips made of twisted and knotted cords. If they fainted under these continuous thrashings, their backs were rubbed with vinegar and salt water to revive them; if they were found to have died under their chastisement, the chains and rings round their legs were taken off and they were flung into the sea like carrion as they were. Then another man took their place, there being always a reserve of these unhappy creatures.

To see them would have wrung the hearts of all but those who dominated them. Their naked backs had upon them wheals, sores, old and new, scars and cicatrices; their faces were burnt black from the effects of the suns, the diverse winds, and the sprays under which and through which they rowed *en perpétuité*—since most were doomed for life; their hair was long and matted with their beards, when they were not old men who had grown bald in their lifelong toil and misery. Moreover, they were nearly starved, their daily food being twenty-six ounces of coarse and often weevily biscuit, and four ounces of beans a day—or rather "pigeon peas"—with water. And if any swooned from their long hours of rowing (hours only relieved by a favourable wind springing up, when the small sails could be set), in contradistinction to their fainting from the brutalities of the *comites*, then there was placed in their mouths a piece of bread moistened with salt water or vinegar, or sour and sharp wine, either of which was supposed to be an excellent reviver.

All were distinguished by numbers and none by name, though, in occasional moments that could be snatched from under the watchful eyes and ears of the *comites*, the doomed wretches could sometimes acquaint each other with their names, former positions in life, and supposed reasons for being condemned to their perpetual slavery. But not often, for a word spoken and overheard brought terrible retribution in its train, especially

as in nine times out of ten religion was both the cause
for which they suffered and by which they were punished. The galley slaves were in general Protestants
who would not embrace the Roman Catholic faith, while
the superior officers and the overseers were ardent pa-
pists. Yet there were others who, in ordinary eyes,
though not in those of their taskmasters, would have
been deemed to be sunk in crimes worse than that of
being Huguenots. No. 512 was a murderer—of his own
father; No. 497 had been caught giving information to
England, he being a fisherman, of the whereabouts of
Jean Bart's flotilla; No. 36 had cursed the king and
his family—a truly awful crime; No. 98 had robbed a
church, and so on. But in the eyes of the law, which
was the king, or rather the reformed and married wanton, De Maintenon, none were so vile, none deserved
such bitter punishment and bastinadoing, and rubbing
in of vinegar and salt in their wounds, and starvation,
as the pestilential heretics.

The black spot on the horizon grew larger to the
view of the officers standing aft on the *coursier*, or raised
fore-and-aft passage of the galley, which ran between
the larboard and starboard gangs of rowers, and across
which they were hourly stretched to be bastinadoed by
their fellow-slaves, the Turks; and those officers by no
means appreciated the increasing size of that spot. It
showed that the English frigate was overhauling the
French galley. The latter, low down in the water
though it was, and with its two sails furled, had been
seen by the former and the pursuit had begun. Fortunate for the galley, and unfortunate for the miserable
slaves whose lives were a curse to them, if she escaped
that frigate now following it so rapidly!

"Row! row!" howled the *comites*, as they rushed up

and down the gangways of the benches, striking the
bare backs of the *vogueurs*, or row-slaves, till they were
all crimson with blood. "Row! In time! in time!
Beware, all you," cried one, as bench 12 rowed wildly,
while the lash fell on all their backs in consequence;
"will you impede the galley's course? *Carogne!*" (a
common oath), "you wish the accursed English to take
us—foul Protestants like yourselves!"

"Ay," replied one slave on that bench, a man known
as 211—"ay. Pray God they take us or sink us! In
the next world we shall not be chained, nor you free.
The chances will be equal."

The lash fell on his back as he spoke, raised a new
wheal to keep company with the others already there,
and then the *comite* passed on, thrashing and belabour-
ing all the others on his side of the ship, and howling
and bawling and blaspheming at them.

Meanwhile the black spot became a large blur on the
blue water; now her royals were visible, white and
bright against the equally clear blue sky. She was sail-
ing down the galley.

"Have a care, 211," muttered the *galérien* next to
him—"have a care. If we escape the English ship with
life, your existence will be a greater hell than before for
those words!"

211 threw his matted hair back from his eyes with a
jerk of his head—his hands he could not release from
the oar—and looked at his neighbour. He was a man
burnt black with the sun, thin, emaciated, and half
starved. On his shoulders, where they caught hourly
the cords of the *comite's* whip, great scars, and livid—
as well as raw—wounds; yet still young and with handsome features.

"We shall not escape," he replied. "She gains on
11

us each moment. See!" and as their faces were naturally
directed aft of the galley, they could observe, through
the great scuttle by the poops, the frigate rising larger
each instant behind them.

" Better even this than death," said the other. " We
know where we are now, at least—who knows where we
shall be? Hist! he returns."

Again the *comite* ran along the gangway, dealing out
more blows and curses, each of these men getting their
share. Then, when the hoarse, foul voice of the overseer was heard at the other end of the hundred and
eighty feet long galère Grand Réale, No. 211 answered
him.

" No," he said, " death is better than this. It is
peace at least."

" You seek it—hope for it ? "

" Ay," No. 211 replied, " pray for it. Hourly! "

" What was your crime? " his companion asked.
They had been chained together for two days only, the
slave whose place the questioner now filled having been
beaten to death, and this, in the excitement of the
impending attack, was their first opportunity of con-
versing.

" Nothing."

The other grinned. Then he exclaimed, " We all
say that."

" Most of us say true."

" It is put about," the other went on, " that you are
English yourself, like our pursuers. Is that true? "

" Partly. Henceforth, if ever I escape, wholly so.
That or death, somehow."

On the *coursier* there arose more noise and confusion now. The English frigate was nearing them; they
could see with the perspective glasses her guns being

run out on the lower tiers, so as better to sweep the galley; the course must be altered or their whole larboard side would be raked when once the frigate was on their beam. Therefore the chief captain gave his orders for the usual tactics of the galleys in an engagement to be pursued—they were to turn and " ram " the pursuers.

. The first vessels of comparative modern warfare to utilize what is now known as the " ram " were the French galleys, they having at their prow or stern a long *éperon*, as it was termed, projecting from the deck above the water, and occupying the place of a bowsprit. Being far lower in the water than the ship, this spur was, consequently, in the exact position where it could inflict terrible damage; it struck a vessel of any size below the water line. And to add to the injury which a galley could do in thus advancing to meet an enemy " end on," there were behind this spur two huge gun forts in which were five bronze cannons of large calibre. As they rammed, therefore, propelled by hundreds of galley slaves, they fired also, and as the charge used was that known as *à mitraille*—viz., a metal case filled with balls of various sizes and pieces of iron, which exploded as it struck, the wounds inflicted in any ship were terribly effective. Moreover, the galley which advanced this presented but a small object for attack, the breadth or beam being never more than forty-eight feet at the broadest.

The order was given, the larboard side *galériens* backed water, the starboard side pulled lustily, assisted and urged on by both the whips and oaths of the *comites* and by the alteration of the helm, and slowly—for it was a long business to turn so lengthy a fabric as L'Idole— the galley wore round to meet her pursuer.

She would not have done so could she have escaped

by flight, but that was impossible. Even four hundred and twenty galley slaves, Christian and Turk, could not propel her as fast as the lightest breeze could move the great frigate. Moreover, they were caught unawares since they happened to be alone instead of, as was almost always the case, in company with half a dozen other galleys. Their companions had that morning. gone in chase of a Dutch merchantman whose mainmast had broken, so that she could only proceed slowly, and L'Idole was being sent back to Dunkirk when observed and chased by the English man-of-war. She had, therefore, to fight and beat the enemy or be sunk and every man on board of her be slain—certainly every man not a slave. For the British sailor of those days so hated the French galleys, in which he knew well enough men of his own faith were kept and tortured, that he spared none in authority in those vessels whenever the chance to slay them arose. Nor, indeed, did he always spare the Protestant slaves themselves in the heat of an engagement. They were fighting against England, and that was enough for him.

"*Saperlote!*" exclaimed the captain of the galley to the *maître-canonnier*, by whose side he now stood in the fore part of the galley, "the *cochons* will not be pierced! See how they change course with us! *Grand Dieu!* they have our beam. To your guns, at once! What will they do now?"

What they would do in the frigate was obvious. *Their* master gunner was also busy at his work; they could see his figure with the linstock in his hand, or could rather catch the gleam of the linstock itself, as he moved behind his gun ports. A moment later what he did was equally obvious. He ran along his tier, firing his cannon. Then there was a crash, followed by an-

other, and another, and another, as cannon after cannon
were discharged and the balls smashed into the galley.
Some swept the *coursier*, cutting down the captain, two
of the blaspheming and brutal *comites*, and the *aumô-
nier*, or chaplain—who was encouraging the Protestant
and Turkish slaves by reciting the Catholic service to
them. Half a dozen more balls struck the benches of
the *galériens*, wounding and killing one fifth of them,
smashing even the chains by which some were bound
to their seats, even smashing the benches themselves,
and taking off legs and arms and heads. Then by a
quick and masterly manœuvre the frigate altered course,
came round on the other side, and repeated the broad-
side with her other tier.

As that was delivered, and a moment afterward her
boats were lowered, filled with sailors to board L'Idole,
the galley heeled over and began to sink.

And No. 211 muttered, as with a jerk from the
lurching craft he was thrown into the sea, " Thank God,
the end has come ! " *

---

* The description of the galley is taken from Mémoirs d'un
Protestant condamné aux Galères de France, and written by one
Jean Marteidhe. It was published in Rotterdam in 1757, and
again in Paris, by the Société des Écoles du Dimanche, in 1865
and 1881, and is perhaps the best account in existence of the sufferings and terrible existence of French galley slaves. It is also
well known in the translations by Oliver Goldsmith, a reprint of ɪ
which, edited by W. Austin Dobson, has just appeared.

CHAPTER XIX.

"A NEW LIFE."

FROM the frigate there floated at the maintop-gallant-masthead the flag of a rear admiral; on the poop of the frigate herself there stood, surrounded by his officers, Admiral Rooke, the brilliant seaman, soon to win his knighthood and other honours.

The galley had disappeared—was gone forever—and with her had disappeared most of the sufferers from the cruelty of France, and also all those who had inflicted that suffering. Of her survivors there were but a dozen all told, who, some wounded and some untouched, were being brought on board. Among the latter was No. 211, who, in spite of the thanks he had given to God for having brought the end of all his miseries to him, now stood dripping on the deck of the Englishman.

" Send them down to the cockpit to be attended to," the admiral said, " and let them be well cared for. Poor wretches! they all seem to be galley slaves; they have suffered enough, God knows, if all accounts be true!" Then he called to his own men attending to the rescued, and asked if any were unhurt.

" Only two, sir; this man standing here," and he pointed to 211, " and one other. He has just fainted."

" Let that man come up to me; I wish to know something of the—the late galley."

To his surprise the man himself instantly turned and advanced toward the poop ladder, and slowly mounted it. Then, as he reached the poop itself he saluted Rooke, raising his hand to his dark, matted hair, and stood silent and dripping before him and the officers round.

"My man," the admiral said, while his eye roved over the torn and lacerated bare back and shoulders, saw the old and new cuts and bruises, and observed the half-starved flanks through which the bones were plainly visible—"my man, you understand English. Are you an Englishman?"

"My mother was an English woman," No. 211 replied, in a deep, hollow voice.

"That any English woman's son should suffer this!" exclaimed the other, again glancing at the worn, bruised body with warm and manly indignation. "And that!" pointing out to his officers the *fleur-de-lis* roughly branded on his shoulder; sure sign of the *forcat*. Then, continuing, he asked, "What was your fault?"

"Nothing," 211 answered, as he had answered his brother *galérien* an hour before. Only now he lifted his eyes and looked at the admiral, as though by that straight glance he would force him to believe. "No crime, no fault. I was—oh!" he broke off, "not now; not now! The story is too long to tell now."

His tone and bearing—sad and miserable as both were—told all who stood around him that this was no common man, no malefactor flung to the slave ship for an ignoble crime, no wretched printer sent to the galleys for producing Protestant pamphlets, or chapel clerk for assisting in a Protestant service.

"You are of gentle blood?" the admiral asked kindly. "Followed, doubtless, the calling of a gentleman? What are you?"

"I was a cavalry officer of King Louis. But broken and ruined for—for——" and again he broke off.

"Will you tell me your name?"

"Georges St. Georges."

The name conveyed nothing to any on board the frigate; the rank he had borne, when stated by him, stirred them all. They knew one thing, however—namely, that the cavalry officers of France were all gentlemen of birth, and many of great position. Could this be true, or if true was it possible that the man before them had not perpetrated some hideous crime? Louis had the reputation of encouraging and treating good officers well; surely no man of that position could have been condemned to this awful existence but for some great sin. Rooke, however, thought he knew the clew, and continued:

"You are, perhaps, a Protestant? The King of France still wages bitter war against them. Is that your crime?"

"I am a Protestant; but that was not my crime."

He shivered as he spoke, although he stood in the full glare of the July sun, the burnt face whitened beneath its bronze, and the lips became livid and ghastly, then he reeled and staggered against the gun tackle on the poop.

"Take him below," Rooke said, turning to one of the subaltern officers at his side; "let him be seen too and carefully tended and those sores dressed. Also find some proper apparel for him. And—treat him as a gentleman. It is more like that he has been sinned against than sinned himself."

So the fainting man was carried below in the brawny arms of the sailors, a spare cabin was found for him—it had but a few weeks before been occupied by a lieutenant who was killed in the disastrous battle off Beachy Head—and he was put into a clean, comfortable bunk. The release which he had prayed for from the galley's slavery had come, though not in the only way he had dared to hope for.

. . . .

"So!" exclaimed Rooke as he helped himself to a glass of Calcavella and passed the bottle to the man whose life had been saved—"so the wanton stabbed you in the back just as you had the fellow at your mercy. The deuce is in it that you missed his heart and could only pink him in the arm. But go on—go on. Faith! 'tis a wondrous story of wrong and cruelty."

They were seated in the admiral's cabin on another such hot July day as that on which St. Georges had been dragged out of the sea with still a portion of his chain attached to the ring round his ankle, and which was rapidly sinking him, but the latter was looking in very different case now. The burnt face was still very black and hollow, the lines of suffering still plainly marked, as they would be for many a day, but otherwise all was changed. He was dressed as a gentleman once more, in a plain but neat suit of blue clothes, guarded with white cotton lace—it had been the unfortunate lieutenant's. His hair, which was combed and brushed now, was, although still somewhat short—it being the custom in the galleys to crop it close to the head for those days once a month—no longer thick and matted.

St. Georges went on as the admiral bade him; he was telling the whole story of his life to his host.

"Yet, sir," he continued, "she was no common wanton either, as I heard afterward, but a lady of Louis's court who loved De Roquemaure. Doubtless her hate and anger were roused by the words I addressed to her. And I must have wronged her in one instance at least; it could scarce have been she who stole my— my poor little babe." And, as ever, when he mentioned

that lost one, his eyes filled with tears. She was gone
from him now, he feared, forever—he had been in that
accursed galley for two years!—how could he hope to
see her again on this earth? No wonder that the tears
sprang to his eyes!

The seaman opposite to him certainly wondered not
at their doing so; instead, he passed his own hand before
his eyes, as he had done more than once before in the
course of the narrative. Countless men had been sent
to their doom by that hand and by his orders, but that
was in battle; now, as he thought of St. Georges's little
lonely child and wondered if it still lived, his memory
wandered back to Monk's Horton, a pleasant seat in
Kent, where his own children were doubtless playing at
their mother's knee, and his brave heart became as
tender as a woman's.

"Poor babe!" he said, "poor babe! Pray God the
other woman, the one who did steal her at Troyes, has
some bowels of compassion! Surely she must have,
however base in other respects."

"I pray so night and day," St. Georges said. "O
God! how I pray so." Then again, at the admiral's
desire that he should not fret too much, but hope ever
for the best, he went on with the account of all that had
befallen him.

"When my wound was nearly healed," he said,
"there came to the room in the inn, where I was closely
guarded, a small body of exempts who carried me to
Paris to the prison of La Tournelle, a place from which, as
I shortly afterward learned, a chain of condemned galley
slaves was to set out, all winter as it was, for Marseilles."

"'But,' I cried to the man who fed us morning and
night like animals, while we lay each with an iron collar

round our necks by which we were chained to a beam
that traversed the dungeon——"

"In a Christian country!" exclaimed the admiral—
"a Christian country!"

"Ay! in a Christian country! Yet I cried, I say,
to the man who guarded us: 'But these companions of
mine *are* condemned—I am not. I have undergone no
trial!'

"'*Bah!*' he replied, 'your trial is made and done. *Bon
Dieu!* the courts cannot wait until criminals feel themselves in sufficient good health to assist at the *séances*.
Your trial is over,' and the wretch made a joke therewith.
'Your *trials* have now to commence. Keep a good
heart!' 'Show me my sentence, then,' I exclaimed,
'produce it.' '*À la bonne heure*,' he replied. 'To-
morrow I will obtain it from the governor. You shall
see.' And the next day he showed it to me. It was
not so long but that I remember every word of it now.
It ran: 'To Georges St. Georges. For that you, a
cashiered officer of his Majesty's forces, have drawn
sword upon and threatened assassination to his Majesty's
chief of the army, Monsieur de Louvois, in his Majesty's
own palace of the Louvre; for that, also, you attempted
the assassination of his Majesty's subject, le Marquis de
Roquemaure, appointed captain of his Majesty's Regiment of Picardy, and of a lady of his Majesty's court,
you are condemned to the galleys in perpetuity. Signed,
Le Marquis de Vrillière.'"

Again the admiral exclaimed, "In a Christian country!" and again St. Georges continued:

"A week afterward we were on the road, chained
together two and two by the neck, while all along the
line through our chains ran another, joining the first
couple to the last. The snow lay on the ground until

we reached Avignon, six weeks later; at night we slept
in barns, in stables, sometimes in the open air. Some—·
the old and sickly—fell down and were left by the roadside for the *communes* to bury; more than fifty were
left thus ere we reached Marseilles. There we were
distributed to the galleys that were short of their complement, though not before the bishop of the province
gave us the Roman blessing, saying that thereby the
heretic spirit of the devil could alone be driven out of
those who were Protestants. From then till now my
life has been what my appearance, as you saw me naked,
testifies."

"What," asked the admiral very gently, "can you
do now? To live is easy enough. You have been both
soldier and sailor"—though he uttered the last word
with an expression of disgust as he thought of what
manner of sailor this unhappy man had been—"your
existence is therefore easy. You can serve the king,"
and he touched his hat with his finger as he spoke.
"Many Huguenots are doing so now, and some other old
ones who followed Charles back to England. But"—and
he leaned forward across the table as he spoke earnestly
—"that will bring you no nearer to regaining your poor
little babe; will scarce enable you to thrust your sword
at last through the villain De Roquemaure's breast; to
obtain the dukedom you believe to be yours."

"Obtain the dukedom, sir!" St. Georges replied,
looking at him. "Nay, indeed, that is gone forever.
You know what befalls the man in France who has been
condemned to the galleys for life?"

"What?"

"He is as dead forever in the law's eyes as though
he were sunk to the bottom of the sea. He can never
inherit, can never dispose of aught that is his; if he is

married, his wife is not considered as a married woman,
but a mistress—every right has gone from him forever!"

"Is there no pardon?"

"Never. Unless he can by some wild chance prove
a wrongful condemnation. And for me, how that?
Louvois, the all-powerful minister, is my judge and
executioner; and, further, when once I set foot on English ground I shall become an English soldier or sailor."

"But the child! At least"—and the sailor spoke
more softly even than before—"you must know her
fate. And—De Roquemaure's punishment! How obtain these?"

"Heaven alone knows! May it, in its supreme
mercy, direct me! Yet this is what I have thought,
planned to do since you, sir, have taken pity on me.
England and France are now most happily, as I think
it, plunged in war once more. There is much to do——"

"Ay," interposed the admiral, while his handsome
face flushed and his eyes glistened, for he was smarting
over his and Torrington's recent defeat. "There is.
There is Beachy Head to be wiped out—oh, for our
next encounter with them!"

"Thereby," continued St. Georges, "my chance may
come. For I may meet De Roquemaure. The sentence on me said he was appointed captain in one of the
northern regiments; there have been stranger things
than foes to the death meeting on the field, on opposite
sides. Then for the child!"

"Ay, the child."

"For that I must go back to France, disguised it
may be; nay, must be! That will be easy. The language is mine—though because of my mother's memory
I have perfected myself in yours—in hers—there is

nothing to reveal who or what I am but one thing"—
and he made a gesture toward his shoulder where the
hateful *fleur-de-lis* was branded in forever—"and that
thing you may be sure none shall ever see again until
my body is prepared for the grave. But—which to do
first? To become a soldier or a sailor fighting for Eng-
and, or travel disguised to Troyes and find out if—if—
my child still lives. That would be my desire—only—
only——"

"Only?" repeated the admiral, looking at him.

"Only," the other said—then broke off.

And Rooke knew as well as though St. Georges had
uttered the words what he would have said. He knew
that the man before him was beggared, that he had not
a crown in the world to help him perform such a
journey.

CHAPTER XX.

"HURRY, HURRY, HURRY!"

ST. GEORGES was lodged in an old inn on Tower
Hill now, in a large room that ran from the front to the
back of the house and with, on the latter side, a look-
out upon an old churchyard, which in the swift-coming
spring of 1692—for it was now April of that year—was
green and bright with the new shooting buds. Here he
worked hard to earn a living, spending part of his day
in translating a book or so from French into English—
at beggar's wages!—another part in giving lessons in
fencing and swordsmanship—he knowing every trick
and *passade* of the French school—and a third in giving lessons in his old language. And between them he

managed to earn enough to support existence while waiting for that which through the interest of Admiral Rooke had been promised him—namely, permission to volunteer into the first vessel taking detachments of recruits to sea with it.

Meanwhile, there were many about the court who had heard his story and who knew he was a man who had once worn the red dress of the *chiourme*—when his back was not bared to the lashings of the *comites!*—that he had slaved at the galley oar in summer and been put to road-mending and road-sweeping in the winter, and that he nourished against France a deep revenge. And among them was the king himself.

Rooke had told William his history, over long clay pipes and tankards at Hampton Court, and the astute Dutchman had not hesitated a moment in promising him employment—would, indeed, have taken a hundred such into that employ if he could have found them. He had learned how the exile hated France—as he did himself, his hatred being the mainspring of his life; moreover, that exile knew more about Louis's regiments and whole military system than almost any one else whom the English king could discover. That was sufficient for him.

So St. Georges went on his way, waiting—waiting ever for one of two things to occur: either that the marine regiment should call for volunteers and be sent out again to France, or that he should be able to return disguised to that country and recommence his search for Dorine.

During the period that had elapsed, however, since he was rescued by Rooke, one thing had happened that had brought great happiness to his heart: he had heard more than once from Boussac, now a lieutenant of the

Mousquetaires Noirs, and in so hearing had gained
news of his child, who was still alive, and, as Boussac believed, well treated.

"*Mon pauvre ami*," that gallant officer had written,
in reply to a letter forwarded him by St. Georges and
addressed to Paris, where he imagined the Mousquetaires
might be, " how shall I answer yours, since, when I received it, I had long deemed you dead ? Ah! monsieur,
I was desolated when we came into Paris at the tidings
I gleaned. I sought for you at once, inquired at the
Bureau Militaire, and learned—what? That you had
threatened to murder the minister—had, indeed, almost
murdered the Marquis de Roquemaure; and that for
this you were condemned to the galley L'Idole, *en perpétuité.* Figure to yourself my dismay—nay, more, my
most touching grief—for, my friend, I had news for you
of the best, the most important. And I could not deliver
it, should never now deliver it to you in this world.
Monsieur, I had the news to give you that I had seen
your child—had seen it well, and, as I think, not unhappy."

It was St. Georges's habit to sit sometimes in the
little, old city churchyard beneath his window, and there
to muse on his past and meditate upon the future. It
had an attraction for him, this old place, more, perhaps,
for the reason that scarce any one ever came into it on
week days, except himself and a decrepit gravedigger to
occasionally open old graves or prepare new ones, than
for any other; but also because there was one tombstone
that interested him sadly. It bore upon it a child's
name, " Dorothy," and told how she had died, " aged
three," in January, " in the yeare of Oure Lorde "
1688. And below the scroll of flowers, with an angel's
head in their midst, was the quotation from Kings:

"Is it well with the child? And she answered, It is well."

To his seared and bruised heart some sad yet tender comfort seemed to be afforded by this stone, which marked and recorded the death of one whose very name partly resembled the name of her he had lost—whose little life had been taken from her almost at the very time Dorine was snatched away from him. And the question of the prophet was the question that he so often asked in his prayers. The answer was that which so often he beseeched his Maker to vouchsafe to him.

He was seated opposite to this stone on the day he first received Boussac's letter, having brought it out with him to peruse in quiet. He was seated on it now, many months later, as he reread the mousquetaire's words which told him that Dorine was well, and, he thought, not unhappy. And he raised his eyes to the words of the Shunamite woman and murmured, "It is well with the child," and whispered, "God, I thank thee!" as he had done on the day when first the letter came to him. Then he continued:

"We passed through Troyes, monsieur, three months after you, and I saw her. She was a little outside the town, with an elderly *bonne*, hand in hand. I obtained permission to quit the ranks for a moment—I was not then promoted, you will understand—and, dismounting and leading my horse toward them—you remember the good horse, monsieur?—I said to the woman, 'Whose child is that, madame?' She drew away from me, gathered the *petite* to her, and answered, 'Mine,' whereon I smiled; for I could not be harsh with her—the little creature looked so well cared for——"

Again St. Georges lifted up his eyes, again he mur-

mured, "I thank Thee!" and again went on with the
letter:

"'And the father,' I demanded, 'where may he be?'
'Dead,' she answered. 'You know that?' I asked
hurriedly, and she replied, 'Ay, I know it, monsieur.'
But," Boussac continued, "I could see that she repeated
a story she had been taught, that she was a paid *gouver-
nante*. Yet, what to do? Already the troop was out
of sight; I might not linger. Had I been alone, it may
be I would have snatched the child from her, jumped
on my horse, and carried it away as once you carried it,
guarded it as you—as *we*, monsieur—guarded it. *Helas!*
that could not be. Therefore, on your behalf, I kissed
the little thing, and I emptied my poor purse into the
woman's hand. 'Keep it well,' I said, 'keep it well,
and thereby you shall reap a reward greater by far than
any you now receive. I know—I know more than you
think.' Then the *bonne* replied to me: 'So long as I am
able it will be guarded well. No danger threatens the
child at present'—she said 'at present'—I am unhappy
that I have to mention those words. But she spoke
them. I knew not what had happened then; I know
now from your letter. But, monsieur, what does it
mean? De Roquemaure tried to slay the child when
you had her in your keeping. Now that he has her in
his own—for who can doubt it?—he treats her well.
Monsieur, again I say, what does it mean? And the
'at present'—what, too, does that mean?'"

St. Georges was no more able to answer that silent
question than the far-distant writer of it. Instead, he
repeated to himself again and again, as he had often
done, the same words, "What did it mean?" And as a
man stumbling in the dark, he could find no way that
led him to the light.

"How can I answer him?" he mused. "What answer find? The villain tried to slay her, as Boussac says, when we were there to guard her; now that he has her in his charge, now that his hate is doubled, must be doubled and intensified by my determination to slay him, as I almost succeeded in doing, he stays his hand. What does the mystery mean?" And one answer alone presented itself to him. De Roquemaure might have discovered that that which he once suspected to be the case was in reality not so. He might have found that, in truth, he, St. Georges, was *not* the Duc de Vannes.

"Thus," he reflected, "he would hesitate to murder the harmless child. His vengeance on me is glutted; he must have known, even so early as Boussac's passage through Troyes, that I was as good as dead in that vile galley; if he knew, too, that I am not really De Vannes's heir, the child no longer stands in his light. And devil though he is, even his tigerish nature may have halted at the murder of so helpless a thing."

Also he knew, by now, that both De Roquemaure and Louvois must be perfectly confident that not only was he practically dead but actually so. The galley was gone—sunk; and of the few saved none had gone back to France. And the other galleys—those which had chased the Dutch merchantman—would take the news back; none would suppose that he and a few more were still alive.

As he reflected on this month by month—while often his eyes would rest now on the words before him, "It is well with the child"—another light came at last to his mind: he saw that, almost without any danger, he might return to Troyes. He was a dead man; none would be on the watch for him.

"Return to Troyes!" he repeated. "Return to

Troyes!" And starting from his seat he walked hurriedly away after one more glance at the consoling
words. He would go at once, find the child, and then
return to England forever. Yes, he thought, he would
do that. He had money enough now to reach that city.

Excited by this determination, he strode toward his
lodging, determined to set out directly. Months had
passed, no fresh volunteers had been called for, and
although he knew that Louis was massing together a
large number of troops in the north of France—with
the intention of once more attempting to put James II
on the throne he had fled from—nothing had yet been
done. It seemed as if nothing would be done beyond
endeavouring to guard the shores of England from a
French invasion and securing suspected persons and
sending forces to the seacoast. But for himself he
heard nothing from any source. Perhaps, he mused, he
was forgotten.

Yet as he entered his room he learned that the time
had not yet come for him to take that solitary and dangerous journey to France. There was something else to
be done first.

Lying on his table were two letters: one, with a great
seal upon it, from Admiral Rooke; the other, addressed
to a firm of merchants in the city, but with—since its
arrival in London—St. Georges's name written over
theirs, from Boussac. He read the latter first; before
all else it was the child he thought of—then threw it
down almost with impatience. He looked eagerly for
these letters; they were indeed the anxiety of his life,
and now that this had come it told him nothing that he
cared to hear.

Yet there was one piece of intelligence in the letter
that once would have interested him. The mousque-

taire had seen Aurélie de Roquemaure, had spoken with her.

"I met her, *mon ami*," he wrote, "entering the gallery of audience at Versailles where I was in attendance, and she looked, although pale, for she wears no paint like the other *grandes dames*—I know not why, since his Christian Majesty expects it——"

"She wore enough when I saw her last!" St. Georges muttered.

"—most beautiful. *Mon Dieu!* what eyes, what a figure! I knew her only from seeing her pass in to audience before, while as for me she had never deigned so much as a glance. Yet now, *figurez vous, mon ami*, she spoke to me while waiting for the others to pass before her. 'I have heard,' she said, speaking very low, 'that you are Monsieur Boussac.' I answered that that was my name. Then, after a glance around to see that no eyes were upon us, she went on : 'You did a service once to an unhappy gentleman—a *chevau-léger*—now dead?' What she was going to say further I know not, since I interrupted her so by the slight start I gave that she paused in her intention, whatever it may have been, raised her eyes to mine and regarded me fixedly. Then she approached her face nearer to mine and whispered : 'Why do you start? He *is* dead—is he not?' *Mon ami*, what could I reply? She is the sister, by marriage, of your foe; if I told her you lived, who knows what evil I might work? Therefore, I answered briefly, 'Madame, the *galère* L'Idole was sunk, and he was in it.' Still she regarded me, however—*mon Dieu!* it seemed as though her eyes would tear the secret from out of my brains. Then—for now the throng was moving on and she had to go with it—she whispered again : 'If—if by any hazard—he was not sunk with the galley—if he

still lives, there is news for him that would make him
happy.' Then she passed on with the others, and
so out by the main gallery, and I have not seen her
since."

There was more in the letter, but at that time St.
Georges read no further. Once this news would have
stirred every fibre in him, for once he had believed that
Aurélie de Roquemaure was his friend—was on his
side! He had long ceased, however, to do so; had, instead, come to believe that she and her mother were as
inimical to him as their cowardly brother. And long
months of meditation had brought him to the belief
also that the marquise's scorn against the man who had
attacked him and Boussac, and endeavoured to slay the
child, was simulated; that they regarded his and
Dorine's existence with as much hatred as did De
Roquemaure himself. And now, now he felt sure that
she knew he was alive and was only eager to discover if
he was anywhere near them—near enough to work
vengeance on them. As for the news which would
"make him happy!"—well, any scheming intriguer
might endeavour to hoodwink so simple a soldier as
Boussac with such a tale as that! He was only too
thankful Boussac had had sufficient discretion not to
betray his existence to her. To have done that would
be to have put her and De Roquemaure on their
guard against that return to France which should yet
be made, against that revenge which should yet be
taken.

He opened Sir George's letter now, quietly and without excitement, for he had grown used to occasional
communications at long intervals from that gallant
sailor, telling him that at present it was not in his
power to be of service to him; but as he hastily ran his

eye over the lines he uttered an exclamation of delight. They ran:

"Namesake, if you are still of the mind you were, the time has come. There is a big muster at St. Helens, for Tourville puts to sea to invade us. A place shall be found for you, though maybe not in my ship. Hurry, hurry, hurry!"

CHAPTER XXI.

MAY, 1692.

NONE riding along the Portsmouth road that warm April night could doubt that a great crisis was at hand. Certainly St. Georges did not do so as couriers and messengers galloped past him toward London calling out the news to all who cared to hear it. As he mounted Kingston Vale two men, hastily jumping on their steeds outside "The Baldfaced Stag," cried that they must rouse the queen even, though she be a-bed,* for the Frenchman was at sea with an enormous fleet and had been seen in the morning from the coast of Dorset; and all along the route it was the same. Wherever he changed his horse he found couriers setting out for London; whomsoever he passed on the road gave him the same news. At Ripley they told him the French had landed under the command of Bellefonds and King James—but these were rustics drinking in a taproom —at Guildford the news was contradicted, but the cer-

---

* William was fighting on the Continent, and, as usual, being defeated.

tainty of the landing taking place shortly was much
believed in. Then, at Godalming, where by now the
day had come, he passed a regiment marching as fast as
might be toward the coast, and the officer in command
told him that no landing had yet been effected; at
Petersfield he heard the same; at Portsmouth laughter
and derision, scorn and contempt were hurled at all
who dared even to suppose that a French fleet would
put a French army ashore. For here, in every inn and
tavern, were men who had fought in a score of naval
engagements, and who were going out now to fight
again. And, as he stood upon the Hard, waiting for a
boat to take him off, he observed the vast fleet of sixty-
three ships under Russell's command lying at anchor
off the island, and saw from the maintop-gallant-mast
head of the Britannia (flagship) the admiral's flag flying.
Also on the main shrouds he saw another flag, showing
that a council of war was already being held. There,
too, were visible the ensigns of Rooke, Sir Cloudesley
Shovell, Sir John Ashley, Sir Ralph Delaval, and Rear
Admiral Carter, and as the noble spectacle met his view
his heart beat fast within him. The country that had
adopted him was about to help him revenge his wrongs
on the country that had sent him forth to stripes and
beatings and ignominy.

The shore boat made its way through countless
others—some filled with officers and their baggage going
off to the ships, some with sailors half drunk, who
would, nevertheless, fight to the death when once they
boarded the Frenchmen; some with provisions for the
fleet; and some with other volunteers like himself, and
with, in several cases, girls going off to say farewell to
their sweethearts, or with mothers and wives. From
most of these boats there rose the babel of scores of

different songs and ballads, all telling how when French sailors met English their doom was sealed. Yet at this time, and for about another month, the French held the supremacy of the sea. After that month was over the supremacy was gone forever!

From the Britannia there came away, as St. Georges's boat approached the lines, several barges bearing the admirals and captains who had attended the council of war, and among them St. Georges saw that of Admiral Rooke, who, as he saluted him, made signs for the other boat to follow to his ship.

"Now," said Rooke, after he had greeted St. Georges and complimented him upon his promptitude in hastening down to the fleet, and also on his improved appearance—for the two years he had passed in London had done much to restore his original good looks, and, with the exception that there rested always upon his face a melancholy expression, none would have guessed the sufferings he had once endured—"now let me understand. Therefore, speak definitely and frankly. You have thrown in your lot forever with England."

"Forever," St. Georges replied.

"Without fear of change, eh?" the admiral said. "Remember—recall before we sail to-night—all you are doing. If you fight on our side now, there will be—henceforth—no tie between you and France. That dukedom of which you told me once is gone forever, no matter how clearly you may find your title to it. Louis will never forgive the work we mean to do. If you are English to-day—for the next week, the next month—you are English for always."

"I have come down here," St. Georges replied, his voice firm, his words spoken slowly, so that Rooke knew that henceforth his resolution would never be shaken, "to fight on England's side against France. There will be no wavering! If I fall, I fall an Englishman; if I survive, I am an Englishman for the rest of my life. I renounce my father's people, whomsoever that father may have been, provided he was a Frenchman: I acknowledge only my mother's. Short of one thing—my endeavour to regain my child."

"How is that to be accomplished? If you survive this which we are about to undertake, your life will be forfeited in France."

"It is forfeited already. Remember, sir, I am still, in the eyes of the law of France, a galley slave. That alone is death, or worse than death. In the future when I go, as I intend to go if I live, upon another quest for her I have lost, I shall be in no worse case. Only, then, it will be the halter and not the galleys. So best!"

"Be it so," the admiral replied. "Henceforth you belong to us. Now, this is what I can do for you. Listen. I find there is a place for you here on this very ship. You know something of seamanship from your bitter experiences; as a soldier, also, you understand discipline. The master's mate of this ship was drowned a week ago; you can try the post if you please. And when the campaign is over, it may be that I can find you a better one."

"I accept, with thanks," St. Georges said. "I adopt from to-day your calling. Henceforth I am an English sailor."

"Come, then, and see your captain," Rooke replied; "you will find him a good one, and hating France as much as you can desire."

He followed the admiral to another cabin, where they found the captain, who was Lord Danby—Rooke's flagship being now the Windsor Castle—and here they

were made acquainted with each other, though Danby
had already heard the history of the man who was
coming into his ship.

"I am very glad to see you, sir," he said quietly. "I
know your story—at least so far as it concerns me. I
only trust you will encounter some of your late friends'
galleys and be able to repay them for some of the kind-
nesses they once testified toward you."

So St. Georges became a sailor once more—though
in a very different manner from what he had last been
—and as master's mate sailed in the Blue Squadron of
Russell's fleet against the French fleet under Tourville.

The Dutch allies were coming in rapidly ere they
left St. Helen's and Spithead on the 26th of April, and
already of the fleet of thirty-six ships under Van Al-
monde many had joined. Their first cruise was, however of no result; they simply picked up their pilots
from the Sally Rose, these men having been got from
Jersey, and observed that all along the peninsula of
Cotentin—where James and Marshal Bellefonds were
encamped—great beacons were burning by night. They
knew, therefore, that France expected the English fleet.
A little later, while once more they lay off Spithead and
St. Helen's, they knew that Tourville had put to sea to
meet them. Fishermen coming into harbour, spies sent
out in various directions, the Sally Rose herself—all
brought the news that the French admiral was on the
sea—his squadron headed by his own flagship, Le Soleil
Royal, and by Le Triumphant and L'Ambitieux, had
been seen from Portland cliffs.

The time had come.

On May 18th that great English fleet, formed into
two squadrons—the Red commanded by Russell, Delaval,
and Cloudesley Shovell, and the Blue by Sir John Ashby,

Rooke, and Carter—and followed by the Dutch, stood away from the English coast, their course south and south by west. Swiftly, too, when clear of the Isle of Wight, the line of battle was formed, the Tyger leading the starboard and the Centurion the larboard tacks. And so they sailed to meet the enemy, and to frustrate the last attack of any importance ever made by the French to invade England.

It was not long ere that frustration commenced.

Scouts coming back swiftly on the morning of the 19th reported the enemy in full force near them, and from the Britannia ran out the signal—received with cheers from thousands of throats—to "clear the ships for action!" And St. Georges, busy with his own work, knew that the time was at hand for which he longed.

To the west there loomed up swiftly the topmasts of the French flagships; soon the figurehead of Le Soleil Royal was visible—a figurehead representing Louis standing upon his favourite emblem, a great sun, and with the inhabitants of other nations lying prostrate at his feet and bound in chains.

"Behold," said Rooke, as St. Georges passed close to him, " your late king! Ah, well! that sun shall set ere long, or——"   .

His words were drowned in more cheers. From all those English seamen on board the various ships—nearly thirty thousand men exclusive of the Dutch allies—there rose hurrah after hurrah, as swiftly the opposing forces advanced to meet one another. Then the Britannia saluted the Soleil Royal—a sinister politeness—and from the French flagships there came an answer in the shape of a discharge of small shot. The battle had begun.

From the English vessels that discharge was answered by broadsides from their great guns : from the

Britannia, the Royal Sovereign—Delaval's flagship—
those broadsides were poured in with merciless precision. Moreover, the wind favoured the English foe
more than it did the French; their great ships being
enabled to form a circle round their foes and to pour in
their fire on either side of them. Already one Frenchman had blown up, hurling her contents into the air;
already, too, the Soleil Royal had had her maintopsail
shot away by the Britannia; in another moment she
had let down her mainsail and was tacking away from
her untiring foe. And following her went L'Admirable
and Le Triumphant.

"Heavens!" exclaimed St. Georges, as, black and
grimed with powder, he worked with the men under his
direction at the lower-deck tier of guns in the Windsor
Castle, "they run already! Is that the king the world
has feared so long—the king I served?"

The French flagship was not beaten yet, however—
it was too soon; and though she could not force her
way through those enemies which surrounded her, she
could still keep them off, prevent them from boarding
her. Twice the Britannia and another had endeavoured
to lay themselves alongside her for that purpose, but the
fire she vomited from her gunports was too hot; like a
gaunt dying lioness she made it death to come too near.
Yet her struggles were the struggles of despair; already
twenty of her squadron had deserted her and, pursued
by English vessels, were tearing through the Race of
Alderney as fast as their shot sails would take them, in
the hopes of reaching the lee of Cotentin. Two alone
remained with her—remained to share her fate—the
Admirable and Triumphant.

That fate was not yet, however; those three ships
had yet a few hours of existence left to them. Fighting

still, still belching forth flames and destruction, they
closed together, and so withstood the merciless broadsides of the Britannia and Royal Sovereign; then, at
last wounded and shattered—the figure of Louis, his
emblem the sun, and the downtrodden representatives
of other nations were long since shot away and floating,
or sunk, in the sea—a favourable wind sprang up and
beneath it they ran, Tourville having already transferred
his flag to L'Ambitieux. Yet, fly as they might, behind
them came their pursuers as fast as they. Delaval in
the Royal Sovereign with a small squadron never halted
in the chase. Still pouring volley upon volley from his
bow fire into their sterns, he hung upon them, and, when
they found they could not enter St. Malo, followed them
to Cherbourg.

And here their end came. They had struggled into
shoal water, forcing themselves aground in the hope the
English men-of-war could not follow them, and rapidly,
in a frenzy of fear, the men were casting themselves
over the sides and gaining the land. The ships were
doomed they knew, their own lives might still be saved.
They were none too soon even for that. The fireships
and attenders were soon among those three. Le Soleil
Royal was ablaze first, Le Triumphant next, and then
L'Admirable. As the night came on they lit up the
coast for miles around; as morning dawned they were
burnt to the water's edge. Their own magazines as
they took fire assisted in their destruction and helped
by their explosions to finish them.

Meanwhile the remainder of the great French fleet
had run for the bay of La Hogue, and behind them,
like sleuthhounds, went Russell, Shovell, and Rooke
with their squadrons.

CHAPTER XXII.

LA HOGUE.

THE sun was setting brilliantly behind the peninsula that juts out into the English Channel and forms the department of La Manche; its last rays as it fell away behind Cherbourg lit up a strange scene. On land, looking east, were thirty thousand so-called French troops; they were, indeed, mostly Irish rapparees whom Louis had thought suitable for an invasion of England under James and his own marshal, Bellefonds; among them and in command were Bellefonds, Melfort, and James himself—now a heartbroken man. Also there stood by his side one who knew that not only his heart but his life was broken too—Tourville, who had now come ashore.

What they gazed on in the bay was enough to break the hearts of any.

There, gathered together, the flames leaping from the decks to enfold and set on fire the furled sails, the magazines exploding, the great guns turned toward the land that owned them and their projectiles mowing down all on that land, were the best ships of that French fleet which had put out to sea to crush the English. Among them were Le Merveilleux, L'Ambitieux, Le Foudriant, Le Magnifique, Le St. Philip, L'Etonnant, Le Terrible, Le Fier, Le Gaillard, Le Bourbon, Le Glorieux, Le Fort, and Louis. And all were doomed to destruction, for the English fleet had blockaded them into the shallow water of La Hogue; there was no escape possible.

. . . .

Three hours ere that sun set, Rooke had sent for St.
Georges and bade the latter follow him.

"I transfer my flag at once," he said, "to the Eagle,
so as better to direct a flotilla of fireships and boats.
Come with me," and stepping into his barge he was
quickly rowed to that vessel with St. Georges alongside
him in the stern sheets.

Reaching the Eagle, Rooke, who had now the command of the attacking party, rapidly made his disposi-
tions for despatching the flotilla—the officering of the
various fireships being at his disposition.

"My Lord Danby," he said to that gallant captain,
who had refused to remain doing nothing in his own
ship, "you will attack with the Half Moon and thirty
boats; you, Lieutenant Paul, with the Lightning and
thirty more.   Mr. St. Georges, who has done well for us
to-day, and has a trifling grudge against our friends,
will take the Owner's Love."

And so he apportioned out the various commands,
until, in all, two hundred fireships and attenders were
ready to go into the doomed fleet.

At first things were not favourable.   The Half
Moon ran ashore, blown thereto by the breeze from
off the sea, but in an instant Lord Danby's plans were
formed.   He and his crew destroyed her, so that she
could not be used against their own fleet, then swiftly
put off in their boats and rejoined the others.   Meanwhile those others were rapidly creeping in toward the
French.

Already two fireships had set Le Foudriant and
L'Etonnant on fire, the boats were getting under the
bows of all the others, the boarders were swarming up
the sides, cutlasses in hand and *mouths*, and hurling
grenades on to the French decks.

"Follow!" called St. Georges, as, his foot upon a quarter-gallery breast rail, his hand grasping the chain, he leaped into the huge square port of Le Terrible. "Follow, follow!" and as he cried out, the sailors jumped in behind him.

Yet, when they had entered the great French ship, there was no resistance offered. She was deserted! As they had come up the starboard side, her crew, officers and men, had fled over the larboard—as hard as they could swim or wade they were making for the shore. Yet her guns on the lower tier forward were firing slowly, one by one as the boats reached them. A grenade had been hurled in as St. Georges's party passed under her bows and had set the ship alight forward, and the flames were spreading rapidly.

"Quick!" St. Georges exclaimed, "ignite her more in the waist and here in the stern. Cut up some chips, set this after cabin on fire. As it burns, the flames will fall and explode the magazine. Some men also to the guns, draw the charges of those giving on us; leave charged those pointing toward the shore."

All worked with a will—if they could not get at the Frenchmen themselves, they had, at least, the ships to vent their passions upon—some tore up fittings, some chopped wood, some ignited tow and oakum; soon the stern of the Terrible was in flames. Meanwhile, from Le Fier hard by—so near, indeed, that her bows almost touched the rudder of the ship they were in—there came an awful explosion. Her magazine was gone, and as it blew up it hurled half the vessel into the air, while great burning beams fell on to the deck of the Terrible and helped to set her more alight.

"To the boats!" ordered St. Georges, "to the boats! There is more work yet, more to be destroyed." And

13

again, followed by his men, they descended to their attenders and barges.

But now the tide was retreating, they could do no more that night. They must wait until the morrow when the tide would come back. Then there would be, indeed, more work to do. There were still some transports unharmed; they, too, must be annihilated!

.   .   .   .

They called the roll that night in the British fleet. There were many men wounded, but *not one* killed. So, amid the noise of powder rooms and magazines exploding, and under a glare from the burning French ships which made the night as clear as day they lay down and rested. And in the morning they began again.

"The work," the admiral said, " is not done yet. It is now to be completed."

Back went, therefore, the fireships and attenders—this time it was the turn of the transports.

"Hotter this than yesterday," called out Lord Danby to St. Georges from one boat to the other, as, propelled by hundreds of oars, all swept in toward the transports. His lordship's face was raw and bleeding now, for on the previous day he had burned and nearly blinded himself by blowing up tow and oakum to set on fire a vessel which he and his men were engaged in destroying. "Hotter now. See, there are some soldiers in the transport, and the forts on shore are firing on us. On, on, my men!" and he directed those under his charge to one transport, while St. Georges did the same as he selected another.

There were more than a dozen of those transports, and against them went the two hundred boats, Rooke in chief command. As they neared the great vessels, however, on that bright May morning, they found that the work of last night had only to be repeated. They poured into the ships from the starboard side, the French poured out on the larboard; those who could not escape were slaughtered where they stood. And if to St. Georges any further impetus was needed—though none was, for his blood was up now to boiling heat and France was the most hated word he knew—it was given him as he approached the vessel he meant to board; for, from it, out of a stern port, there glared a pair of eyes in a ghastly face—a face that looked as though transfixed with horror!—the eyes and face of De Roquemaure! With a cry that made the rowers before him think he had been struck by a bullet, so harsh and bitter it was, he steered the barge alongside the vessel; in a moment he had clambered on the deck, followed by man after man; had cut down a French soldier who opposed him, and was seeking his way toward the cabin where the other was.

"There is an officer below," he muttered hoarsely to those who followed him. "He is mine—remember, mine—none others. My hand alone must have his life, my sword alone take it. Remember!"

As his followers scattered—some to slay the few remaining on board who had not escaped, some to rush forward and ignite the fore part of the transport, others to fire the great guns laid toward the shore, and still others to find and burst open the powder room—he rushed down to where that cabin was, his sword in hand, his brain on fire at the revenge before him.

"Now! now! now!" he murmured. "At last!"

Under the poop he went, down the aftermost companion ladder, through a large cabin—the officers' living room—and then to a smaller one beyond, opening

out of the other on the starboard side—the cabin from
which he had seen the livid, horror-stricken face of his
enemy. But it was closed tight and would not give to
his hand.

"Open," he called; "open, you hound, open! You
cannot escape me now. Open, I say!"

There came no word in answer. All was silent
within, though, above, the roars and callings of the
sailors made a terrible din.

"You hear?" again cried St. Georges, "you hear
those men? Open, I say, and meet your death like a
man! Otherwise you die like a dog! One way you
must die. They are setting fire to the magazine. Cur,
open!"

The bolt grated from within as he spoke, and the
door was thrown aside. De Roquemaure stood before
him.

Yet his appearance caused St. Georges to almost stagger back, alarmed. Was this the man he had dreamed
so long of meeting once again, this creature before
him! De Roquemaure was without coat, vest, or shirt;
his body was bare; through his right shoulder a terrible
wound, around which the blood was caked and nearly
dry. His face, too, was as white as when he had first
seen it from the boat, his eyes as staring.

"So," he said, "it is you, *alive!* Well, you have
come too late. I have got my death. What think you
I care for the sailors or the powder room? I was struck
yesterday by some of the Englishmen who passed here
as the tide turned, who fired into this ship ere the tide—
the tide—the——"

"Yet will I make that death sure!" St. Georges
cried, springing at him. "Wounds do not always kill.
You may recover this—from my thrust you shall never

recover!"—and he shortened his sword to thrust it through his bare body.

"I am unarmed," the other wailed. "Mercy! I cannot live!"

"Ay, the mercy you showed me! The attempted murder of my child—the theft of her, the murder perhaps done by now—the galleys! Quick, your last prayer!"

Yet even as he spoke he knew that he was thwarted again. He could not strike, not slay, the thing before him. The villain was so weakened by his wound that he could scarce stand, even though grasping a bulkhead with his two hands; was—must be—dying. Why take his death, therefore, upon his soul when Fate itself was claiming him? It would be murder now, not righteous execution!

Moreover, he had another task to execute ere it was too late.

"Wretch," he exclaimed, "die as you are—find hell at last without my intervention! Yet, if you value a few more minutes of existence, gain them thus. Tell me, ere you go, where you have hidden my child—what done with——"

Before he could finish there came another roar from an exploding transport, the sound of beams and spars falling in the water round; a darkness over the cabin produced by the volumes of smoke; the screams of wounded and burnt Frenchmen hurled into the sea; the loud huzzas and yells of the British sailors. Then, as that roar and shock died away, there rose in the air another sound—a pæan of triumph that must have reached the ears of those on shore as it also reached the ears of those two men face to face in that cabin. From hundreds of throats it pealed forth, rising over all else—

crackling wood, guns firing, the swish of oars, orders bawled, and shrieks of dead and dying.

It was the English sailors singing Henry Carey's song, almost new then, now known over all the world :

> " God save our gracious king !
> Long live our noble king !
> God save the king ! "

" Answer," St. Georges cried, " ere your master, the devil, gets you ! ere I send you to him before even he requires you ! "

The man had sunk down upon a locker outside the bunk, his two hands flattened out upon the lid, his face turned up in agony. From either side of his mouth there trickled down a small streak of blood looking like the horns of the new moon; the lips were drawn back from the teeth, as though in agony unspeakable. And did he grin mockingly in this his hour—or was it the pangs of approaching death that caused the grin?

Then he gasped forth :

" You are deceived. The woman who stole—your child—was Aurélie——"

" What ! " from St. Georges.

" Aided by—servant—Gaston. Her—servant—not mine——"

" My God ! " In that moment there came back to him a memory. The lad, Gaston, had his arm in a sling the morning he learned the child was missing; the woman, who lived in the hut and saw the child taken from Pierre, had said, " His arm hung straight by his side, as though stiff with pain."

Had he found the truth at last?

" Go on," he said.

" The bishop's man—had—got it safe. Aurélie and

Gaston—caught—slew him—took the child. She—
knew—your birth—and—hated you—and would gain—
as much as—as I. Seek her—if you—would—
know——"

He fell prone on the lid and spoke no more.

And St. Georges, reeling back against the opposite
bulkhead, stared down at him, forgetting all that was
taking place around the burning transport in his misery
at that revelation.

"Aurélie," he whispered, "Aurélie! Hated me, too,
and hated her. O God, pity me!"

And again above all else there rose the triumphant
shout:

"Send him victorious,
Happy and glorious,
God save the king!"

NOTE.—The description of the battle of La Hogue is taken
from many sources, but principally from the narrative of the
chaplain on board the Centurion. It is the most full and complete, especially as regards the ships engaged, which I know of.
The worthy divine was a Fellow of Corpus Christi College, Oxford, and this seems to have been his first cruise. He returned
"home" afterward, viz., to Oxford, and has left very fervent
expressions of gratitude at having been able to do so.

CHAPTER XXIII.

THE BITTERNESS OF DEATH.

As he staggered back after that revelation, St.
Georges noticed that the great chant sounded less
strongly and more distantly in his ears, and, seized with
a sudden apprehension, he rushed to the cabin port-hole.

Then he knew that what he had dreaded, that the idea which had sprung into his mind a second before, as the sturdy English voices became more hushed and subdued, was indeed an absolute fact—the flotilla was retiring. It had finished its work of destruction—it was returning to the man-of-war.

And he was left behind!

Behind! to fall into the hands of the French, who, he knew very well, would come forth from the fort and batteries directly the conquerors had withdrawn. He was in a trap from which there was no escape. He would be found there, and his doom be swift.

Yet, in a moment, even as he glanced down at his enemy at his feet and noted the set features—handsome as in life—the white face, the blood at either side of the mouth, looking as before like two small down-turned horns, he asked himself if he was indeed doomed? Also, why stay there to be taken like a rat in a trap? The sea was beneath him; a mile off was the English fleet. If he could swim to that, even halfway to it, he could· make signs and, perhaps, be seen and rescued; at the worst it would but be death. And a more fearful death than any the sea could bring awaited him if he remained here.

He cast one more look at De Roquemaure lying with his head upon the locker. At last he was done for! He would never cross his path again. If he himself could live, if he could escape out of this burning pandemonium, could again stand a free man on an English deck, he would have to contend with him no more. There would be but one thing further to do then—to stand face to face with Aurélie de Roquemaure, to ask her if this charge against her was true—as St. Georges never doubted!—to demand his child, and, if she would not

restore it to him, to—to—what? His mind was full of
deeds of savagery now; the last few days, filled with
slaughter and spent amid the arousal of men's fiercest
passions, had made him fierce too. At this moment if
Aurélie could appear before him he knew that he should
slay her—send her to join her brother and all the other
victims of his own aroused passions. It would be dangerous for her if she were face to face with him at this
moment and refused to acknowledge where she had
hidden Dorine.

She was not there, however; at the present moment
he had to take steps to free himself, to escape from the
burning transport. "'Twill be time enough," he muttered, "to tax her with her perfidy when I stand once
more before her to punish her for it. And my own hour
is too near, may be too close at hand, for me to think
of that. But when it comes, then——"

He heard an explosion in another part of the vessel
—he knew another tier of guns had been reached by the
flames; he was tarrying too long. The magazine must
be close to the cabin in which he was, might be, indeed,
beneath the cabin floor—at any moment he risked being
blown to atoms. He must lose no time. To be caught
there was death, instant and certain!

Lying at the door of the main cabin where he had
been slain was one of the officers of the transport; near
him another man of lower rank, the one shot through
the back the other cut down by Rooke's sailors as he
fled into the cabin; and as his eye rested on them a
thought struck him. None of Bellefonds and James's
forces on land could say who were or were not officers
of the transports—what was there to prevent him from
being one for the time being? All was fair in war!—
and he was as much French as any who might come out

from the forts or batteries to the sinking and exploding ships—if any dared to come at all. Once in the garb of either of these lying here, officer or petty officer, and he would be able to get safely ashore, and could avoid question by disappearing a moment afterward, or as soon as might be.

And he would be in France—would be so much nearer to the reckoning with Aurélie de Roquemaure!

He drew on the jacket of the officer as the thoughts of all this chased one another through his mind, threw his own sword down and took up that of the dead man, placed on his head the hat he had worn—bearing in it a gold cockade on which a glittering sun was stamped—and then, glancing through the square porthole that gave on the shore, he looked to see if, yet, any of the French were coming out to save some of their vessels from the conflagration. But the wind was blowing off the sea to the land and carrying with it the smoke from the burning ships; between those ships and the shore all was obscured. And still, as he looked, the explosions—though fainter now—took place at every moment; he could hear the crackling of the flames in the vessel in which he was.

He knew that he must go—must not tarry another instant. Those flames were gaining round him; they would reach the magazine before long—and—then! He must go at once.

He cast one more hurried glance at De Roquemaure, who seemed quite dead now. But, dead or alive, what mattered it? If dead, so much the better; if alive, he would be blown to atoms in a few more moments—as he would himself if he tarried longer. He must go at once.

"Farewell, dog!" he muttered, with one look downward at his enemy. "Farewell. Your account is made!" And without wasting another moment—for his fear of being hurled into eternity himself the next moment had gained terrible hold on him—he rushed to the main cabin door and seized the handle.

An awful sweat of fear—a cold, clammy sweat—broke out all over him as he did so; he knew now how dear life was to him—dearer than he had ever dreamed before that it would be; or was it rather the fear of an awful death than death itself? Was it that which caused him to almost faint with horror as he recognised that the door was either locked or jammed, so that it would not open?

He was doomed—the fire was spreading—he heard one great gun explode by itself—a gun on the lower deck near where the powder room must be—*beneath* him—he was doomed! In another few moments—perhaps not more than four or five at most—the bulkheads would fly asunder, the deck split like matchwood, he and the dead bodies of De Roquemaure and the others be flung to the elements, be blown into portions of the elements themselves.

Drenched with sweat, paralyzed with terror—it *was* the terror of an awful death and not of death itself; livid with horror—though he was not aware such was the case; his lips parched and glued together; not knowing whether his limbs were shaking beneath him or the deck of the cabin quivering before its impending upheaval, his starting eyes glared round the prison he was in. And as he so glared he saw—if God gave him a moment more—his opportunity. The great square ports—an invention of but the last few years and superseding the old small round ones—furnished that opportunity.

With a gasp—nay, almost a cry—he clambered on the locker beneath the nearest one—again it seemed as though the ship was quivering with the impending explosion! —thrust his head and shoulders through, dragged the sword by his side carefully after him, seized a top chain hanging down into the water, and was himself in the water a moment later.   Then a nervous, hurried thrust of one foot against the hull, with an impetus obtained thereby which propelled him a dozen feet from the vessel, a few masterful strokes made boldly, all trembling with fear and horror as he was, and he plunged into a puff of black smoke, the cinders among which hissed on his face as he struck it, and he was saved—saved from that most awful death, even though countless other deaths surrounded and loomed up before him; saved, at least, from being dismembered and flung piecemeal in a million atoms on the bosom of the ocean.

The smoke drifting in his face recalled to him that he was swimming toward the English fleet; the current still making toward the shore told him that he could never reach that fleet.   Even as he swam away from the doomed transport he knew that the powerful tide beneath was carrying him back; he must change his course, or another moment would carry his body against the after part of the ship he had but now escaped from, the ship which must now ere long be hurled out of the sea!   It was easy to do so, however; to turn himself away from her so that, even though borne back to the coast of Cotentin, he would pass far astern of her. He had enough strength for that, enough left to haul himself far out from where she lay—but not much more.   He was sore spent now with all he had gone through, and was borne down also with the double weight of clothes upon him; as he glided by, or was carried back—though some forty yards adrift of the transport—he could do nothing more than tread water and so manage to keep himself afloat.

Borne through the murky grime, along that water there came now the swish of oars and the voices of men speaking in French—French strongly accentuated and in the Manche *patois*. What were they doing, he wondered. Had they come out to save some of the burning transports and boats, to endeavour to stop the flames and also the firing of the guns by the heat—their own guns that, as they fired, hurled their charges on their own shore? Were they going to meet their dooms unknowingly by venturing on that very place of death which he had just escaped from?

It might be—might well be so; and though he had fought against them—though they were Frenchmen and his enemies, too, he must warn them, save them, if he could: they were men, human beings; he could not let them go unwittingly to such an awful end as this, could not let them board that ship and meet the fate he had avoided. Therefore he hailed them as loudly as he was able, screamed to them, besought them to enter no vessel near; above all to avoid the burning transport. But whether they understood him, even if they heard, he could not guess; he caught still the beat of the oars upon the waves, heard their chattering voices, even one or two of their expressions; and then, as the tide took him nearer and nearer to the shore, he lost sound of those voices altogether.

"Strange," he muttered, "strange she blows not up— many minutes have elapsed since I quitted her—twenty at the least, and yet the explosion has not come. They may have boarded her, those men, have extinguished the

flames: there may have been no powder left in the
mag— Ah!"

There came an awful roar as he so muttered, a roar
such as he had heard twenty times in as many hours; a
hundred feet above and behind him, as he turned swiftly
in the water, he saw a fan-shaped mass of flame ascend-
ing to the skies; he saw black objects amid that mass of
flame—what were they, beams, masts, or human
bodies?—he saw the smoke rent open, and great pieces
of the transport floating or falling on to the waters with
terrific crashes.   Then there rushed down on him a
fresh mountain of blood-coloured smoke, with blazing
cinders and pieces of burning wood, and smouldering
sails all borne along in its midst, and it enveloped him
and choked him, while the burning matter fell on him
and hissed on his wet hair and skin, so that he was fain
to let himself sink below the waves for some few seconds
to escape the *débris* and those suffocating fumes.   And
even as he did so, and when he arose to the surface once
more, cooled and refreshed by the immersion of his face,
his first thought was to utter a heartfelt prayer for his
escape from the awful fate that, but half an hour ago,
had threatened him and been so near.

Scarce had he done so than, as he swam a little now,
being eased by having floated and trod water for some
time, he saw beneath the smoke, which dispersed as it
neared the shore and drifted inland, that he himself was
close in shore.   He could perceive quite clearly the yel-
low beach of Cotentin on which the incoming tide was
rippling, and could see also several bodies lying about on
that beach—soldiers doubtless killed by the fire from
the English war vessels, or, perhaps, by the discharge of
the French guns when turned upon them by the parties
which had boarded their own ships.   But that was all,

except one or two figures moving about and bending over them—no doubt the ghouls who are to be found wherever a dead body is after a battle.

And as he glanced at these last relics of the great battle of La Hogue, his foot touched the bottom; a moment later he was wading ashore.

He stood once more in France, the land in which he would find his child—if she was still alive.

CHAPTER XXIV.

ON THE ROAD.

HE stood once more upon French ground—then fell half fainting on the wet, shining shingle, struggling to get his breath back, panting and gasping painfully.

Then came toward him a figure terrible to behold, a creature in the garb of a woman, a knife at her girdle, her pockets, which were outside her dress, bulging, and from their openings pieces of gold lace, a silver-hilted pistol, and other things protruding. But besides her and the dead bodies lying further inland upon the beach nothing else was to be seen. The thirty thousand men —some, and most of them, those rapparees whom Louis had thought good enough to send against England— some forming part of the regiments of Picardy, Verdelin, Le Calvados, and others, were not visible, although he could see on the roofs and turrets of the forts that they were still there and lined the coast for many miles. Also he saw with dimmed eyes that the English fleet was moving. It had done its work !

The creature prowling about came nearer, and St. Georges sprang to his feet and drew from the wet scabbard which had remained by his side during his swim ashore, his sword.

"Wretch," he said, "put down that knife and come no nearer, or I will run you through, woman though you seem to be! Begone, vulture!"

The robber of the dead and wounded paused and stared at him; then she assumed a whining tone, and exclaimed in her northern accent:

"Oh, good gentleman, you mistake. I am no slayer of injured men, but a comforter thereof. Will you not take a sup of good Nantz to ease you?"

"No, begone! Away. Yet stay. Where is the nearest village where I can procure food? Answer me, quickly."

"A mile off, good gentleman; there is an auberge there. It is very good. *I* keep it."

"You!"

"Yes, I. Yes, an excellent inn. But," with a suspicious glance at him, "why not go to the fort, good gentleman? The marshal is there and that king who has been ruined by his own subjects to-day."

"I do not wish to go to the fort. I am not a soldier, but a sailor—saved from one of the transports. Direct me."

"Ha!" she said, with a grunt. "You are not the first. There are many like you who do not want to go to the fort. A many poltroons who are deserting from the army, now defeat has come to France. Are you deserting too, friend?"

"No. But I have nothing to do with the forts nor the army. Direct me, I say."

"There is the road," the hag said, pointing to the north across the sandhills. "Follow that a mile and you will come to my house. But," and she came a step nearer, "give me some money, or you will, perhaps, be followed. The others have given me some. Give me a piece, and I will be silent."

"Away, wretch!" St. Georges said. "If the soldiers come forth again you will flee from them, not wait a moment. I do not fear you," and pushing past her he made toward the road she had indicated, while she stood there muttering curses after him. Then she returned to her work of prowling among the dead and dying, and rifling their pockets.

He made his way among those dead and dying, most of whom were wounded French seamen who had managed to get ashore only to fall down and expire where they fell, and a few of whom were soldiers on land who had been struck by the projectiles from the French vessels while standing gazing at the sea fight. In all, there were lying about the dunes some hundred men, who were in different states of approaching death. One thing he noticed as he went on—several wore the colours of the Picardy Regiment, which he knew well, from having once been quartered with it. Therefore, he understood why De Roquemaure had been on board the transport. They had doubtless been shipped ready for the projected invasion, and these wretched soldiers had been more fortunate than he in one way—they had at least escaped ashore to die, instead of being blown to pieces in the explosions of the transports.

He made his way through the sand, stopping once or twice to endeavour to help some dying wretch whom he came across, and then going on again when he found his efforts useless; and so he came at last to what he sup-

14

posed must be the auberge spoken of by the woman, a
miserable wooden structure with a seat and a bench out-
.side the door.

Two horsemen were drawn up in front of this, and
were speaking to some stragglers standing before them,
all of whom St. Georges noticed stood cap in hand. One,
a tall thin man with a hatchet face, dressed in gray, was
questioning them; the other, who sat his horse by his
side, was an elderly man of dark, swarthy features, who
was, however, deathly pale. His eye—a wandering one—
lighted on St. Georges's the instant he approached the
front of the inn, and turning away from his companion
he addressed him in good French, which, however,
St. Georges noticed had a strong accent.

"What uniform is yours, sir?" he asked. "I do not
know it. And you seem to have been in the water. Are
you one of his Majesty's naval officers?"

"I am," St. Georges replied, recognising at once the
danger he was in. "And the uniform is that of a transport officer."

"A transport officer!" the other exclaimed, turning
round suddenly at the words—"a transport officer! Have
any escaped?"

"I have, at any rate," St. Georges replied.

"You can then give us some information," the first
said. "How many others are there who have also
escaped?"

"Very few, I imagine. I myself did so only by swimming ashore. And even then the transport was blown
up ere I had quitted it very long."

"And," asked the second, "have the—English—made
many prisoners?"

"A great number, I should suppose."

"God help me!" the dark, pale man exclaimed.

"Louis will do no more. This is our last chance, Melfort."

As he spoke St. Georges knew in whose presence he was—the presence of the unhappy James. Then, because he knew also that this place was full of danger to him—some naval officers of the French fleet might by chance have got ashore as he had done, and might also come here at any moment—he saluted James, and said he must make his way onward as fast as possible.

"Where are you going to, sir?" the late King of England asked. "You will be better in the forts. They will not refuse you succour."

"Doubtless. Yet I must go on. I have to——"

As he spoke his eyes fell on the doorway of the inn, and, brave man though he was, what he saw there appalled him.

Leaning against the doorpost, regarding him fixedly, were two French sailors whom he had last seen on board the transport—two sailors who, as he had leaped on board followed by his own men, had disputed his entrance, had then been driven back to the larboard side of the ship, and had hurled themselves into the shoalwater and so escaped.

What was there for him to do? In another moment it was possible—certain—that they would denounce him, that he would be seized by the half dozen soldiers standing or sitting about.

He had to make his plans quickly ere these men could speak—already he could perceive they were about to do so; one touched the other with his finger and called his attention to him, and looked with an inquiring glance into his companion's eyes, as though asking if by any possibility he could be mistaken? He had to act at once. But how? Then in a moment an inspiration came.

With a cry he wrenched his sword from his sheath and rushed at them, uttering exclamations that at least he hoped might confuse the others round and also drown any words of those two men.

"Villains! *Lâches!* Deserters!" he cried, as he flew at them, striking one with the flat of his sword and, with his elbows and body, forcing the other into the passage behind. "Villains! You would desert in the hour of need! Fly the ship, would you!" and other exclamations in as harsh and loud a tone as possible.

And the ruse succeeded beyond even what he dared to hope. The two sailors affrighted, perhaps not hearing his words, and only thinking that the terrible English officer meant to slay them on land, as he had almost succeeded in doing on their own deck, fled down the passage roaring; while to add to the hubbub two large dogs, sitting by the fire of a room opening out of that passage, dashed out barking and yelping. A woman too came from the kitchen and screamed for help, and meanwhile the soldiers who had been lounging about rushed in at the front door. As for James and Melfort, they shrugged their shoulders and turned their horses away. Such a scene as this, which they but half understood, had little enough interest for them. An officer punishing two deserters, as they assumed to be the case, was a trifle in comparison to the ruin which had fallen forever on their cause that day.

The sailors fled down the passage yelling "*Au secours! au secours!*" and "*Sauvez-nous!*" and after them rushed St. Georges, making as much noise as he could, and so they reached first a yard behind, and then the *potager*, or herb garden. One man dashed into an outhouse full of billets of wood and kindlings, and yelled for mercy. "The fight is over!" he screamed; "spare me, spare me!" and in a moment St. Georges had shut the door and turned the key—fortunately it was outside—on him; then he rushed after the other down the sandy path of the garden.

His object was to drive the man on as far as possible away from the inn, and then desist from the chase and escape himself. Behind the garden there ran another path that passed up to a copse of stunted, miserable, wind-blown trees; if he could get into that, he might succeed in avoiding any pursuit.

So he let the sailor gain on him as he neared this copse, and then another chance arose before him—an unhoped, undreamed-of chance! Tethered at the end of the garden, by the reins to the paling, was a horse belonging possibly to some *bourgeois* who had ridden in to the inn from a village inland and had left his horse at the back. A chance sent by Heaven in its mercy!

Still the sailor ran on swiftly, until, no longer hearing his pursuer behind him, he dared to look over his shoulder, thinking the chase was over; what he saw when he so looked caused him to renew his speed, even to yell with fresh terror.

St. Georges was mounted now, he was urging the horse to its greatest pace, he would be behind him in a moment. And then it would be death, dealt from the sword wielded by the terrible Englishman—almost the man could feel that sword through his back as he ran and the hoofs clattered behind him!

He stumbled and nearly fell in the white sandy dust, got up again with a shriek, and then, in a last, frenzied hope, plunged into the copse which he had now reached.

And the awful horseman passed on—could that dust, the poor wretch wondered, have hidden him from his view?—a moment or two more and he knew that he was safe. The clatter of the hoofs on the road grew fainter and fainter; when at last he dared to peer from the edge of the little wood, the Englishman had disappeared.

For a couple of hours St. Georges urged the poor roadster to its best speed, then slackened rein as the wayside track reached the bay of Charenton. He was safe now from any recognition—or rather exposure— the army of Bellefonds and all who might by chance have got ashore from the destroyed fleet were far behind.

Yet he had been exposed to risks, too, on that ride. Once, near the auberge he had fled from, a farmer riding along called to him to stop, yelling at him to know why he was riding Dubois's horse; but his presence of mind did not fail him, and he called back : " Ride on and see ! The French are defeated, the English have burned Barfleur and destroyed La Hogue!" and ere the man, whose terrorstricken face he long remembered, could speak again, he was far away from him.

Also he more than once passed deserters from the army—men who no sooner saw another in a uniform riding as though for life, than they fled away into woods and copses or over fields, imagining that he was in pursuit of them. And, once, he again come in contact with two together whose faces he thought he remembered as he leaped on board a French man-of-war the evening before—men who looked up at him with startled faces and oaths upon their lips—did they recognise him as he dashed by them ?

But at last he had outdistanced all who might have

escaped from La Hogue; his way lay along a sandy sea-blown road, at the sides of which were fields of millet, sanfoin, and sometimes, though not often, wheat. And ahead of him, against the bright May sky, he saw the tower and two high spire steeples of the ancient cathedral of Sainte Marie at Bayeux.

He eased his horse at a pool of fresh water, descended from it and removed the coarse saddle, and, while it drank eagerly, rubbed its sides and back.

"Good horse!" he said.—"good horse! I have been a hard taskmaster and a stranger to you to-day. Heaven knows I would not have urged you thus but for my necessity. And you have served me bravely, all rough bred as you are. Well, we will not part now, and some day, may be, I can find out your owner—that Dubois the farmer spoke of—and repay him for the friend I stole from him."

And he sat down by the animal's side for half an hour, and then, walking with the reins in his hand and carrying the saddle to ease it, he followed the road toward Bayeux.

It was the road, too, to Troyes and Aurélie de Roquemaure, the woman who had to answer to him for the theft of his child, and also for her duplicity when they had met in Paris!

CHAPTER XXV.

"I KNOW YOUR FACE."

THE deserted road along which he now walked was, in a way, a relief to him. Nothing could have better suited his present needs than to be thus outside the life of any town and free from all observation, for he had much to meditate upon—many plans to form for his safety. And of those plans, the first to be carried out was to free himself from any appearance of conspicuousness which would draw attention on him.

There was, to begin with, the officer's jacket and cap which he had assumed, and the naval sword by his side, from which he had by now removed all damp it might have received from being in the sea. Yet how to deprive himself of the latter, and still be safe, he knew not.

As for the jacket—which was, indeed, a short coat filled with pockets, outside and in—he could dispense with it very well. He had dragged it on over his own coat when quitting the burning transport, simply as a disguise, as a safeguard. It could now be discarded.

His clothes—the plain English clothes which he had worn in London, and in which he had joined Rooke's flagship and fought through Barfleur and La Hogue *— would attract no attention. They were suitable to any one in the middle class; but with the cap it was not the same thing, since he had nothing wherewith to replace it, and if he rejected that he must go bareheaded. This would not do; he had, therefore, to cast about for some headdress.

At last, however, he was obliged to retain it, altering it as well as he was able with his fingers, tearing off a strip of lace round it and throwing away the gilt cockade. As for the jacket, that was easily disposed of; he rolled up some stones in it and flung it into a pool of water among the reeds by the wayside, where it soon

---

* In those days none possessed naval uniform, and, from admiral downward, all wore what they chose.

sank beneath the surface. But the sword still remained —a good enough blade, in a leather scabbard, and with not too much to proclaim that it was a sailor's except an anchor—on, of course, the eternal sun, Louis's emblem—fastened to the top of its handle. There was also a sword knot, which followed the jacket into another pool, and he decided that he must take his chance with the weapon itself.

"At least," he thought grimly, "none will have much chance to observe it closely if I am using it against them; if I am not, I can keep my hand on the emblem. Under any circumstances it cannot be parted with."

And now he neared Bayeux, worn and spent with all he had gone through in the last twenty-four hours, since he had hardly slept at all, and that only by snatches after the battle off Barfleur had begun; also his immersion in the sea and his long ride had made him very weary.

"Rest! rest!" he muttered to himself, "a long rest I must have. And then for Troyes and my child—and for Aurélie de Roquemaure. Ay, for her!"

He trudged along by the horse's side, still carrying the saddle over his arm to ease it, and it was not until the gates and walls of Bayeux came into sight that he mounted it again. It would have a good night in a stall before long; that small addition to its day's work would not hurt it much. And he could not present himself on foot before the custodian without raising suspicion of having come a long distance, without courting remark.

"You are from the coast?" the man asked, as he rode through the gate. "How goes it with the marshal's army there? Have they invaded England yet?"

"Not yet, so far as I am aware," he answered. He knew it would be madness to appear cognizant of what had taken place at La Hogue. The whole town would clamour for news, and he would be for the time the most conspicuous man in it. "Not yet."

"We have heard strange rumours," the man said. "But this morning one came in from St. Mère Eglise who said that loud sounds of firing were heard all last night out to sea; and another, a *pêcheur de mer*, says that great fleets have been seen passing from the west. *Mon Dieu!* it cannot be that those English *chiens* would dare to attack us!"

"Impossible, *mon ami*, impossible! There can be no chance of that. Tourville's fleet would prevent that."

"*Je crois bien.* Yet why fire all through the night? One fires not on imaginary foes."

"True. Well, later, no doubt, we shall hear more. My friend, tell me a good inn, where I may rest awhile."

"Oh! as for that, there are several. The *Pomme d'Or*, among others, is good and cheap; also *Les Rochers de Calvados*. Try one of those and you will be content."

Thanking him, St. Georges passed into the old city, though without the slightest intention of going to either of those houses. His object was to remove every trace of himself as he passed onward to the goal ahead of him —to obliterate his tracks entirely.

He rode quietly through the town, therefore, observing what good and comfortable-looking inns those were which the man had mentioned, but at the same time regretfully avoiding them. For under no circumstances would he have felt justified in alighting at either —he doubted if he could have afforded to do so. When he received Rooke's hasty summons to join him he had

but forty-five guineas, saved after two years of an existence that at best had been a hard one. It had been a
task to accumulate even that sum, a task entailing careful living, abstinence, almost even a life of total depri-
vation; when he had paid scrupulously every farthing
he owed in the neighbourhood where he lodged, the
sum had dwindled down to thirty-five guineas. It
was little enough to enable him now to reach Troyes
and provide for himself and the horse he had become
possessed of on the road, to regain his child, and find
his way back to England—if he succeeded in doing so.

To find his way back to England! Would that be
possible? Could he pass through the north of France un-
discovered? Could he, the ex-galley slave, the man
whose face had become known to hundreds of persons
connected with the galleys, besides having been known
to hundreds of soldiers also, with whom he had been
quartered, hope to escape recognition?

"God only knows!" he murmured as he rode through
the empty streets of the already dead-and-gone city.
"He alone knows. Yet, ere I will be taken alive—ere
the mark upon my shoulder shall ever testify against
me—I will end it all! Yet, courage! courage! At
present I am safe."

He reached the neighbourhood of the east gate, for
he had traversed the whole of Bayeux by now, and
knew that if he would rest for a night in the old city he
must make choice of a halting place. Casting, therefore, his eyes round the wide streets, he saw an auberge
—a place, indeed, that in France is known as a *pant*—
a low-roofed, poor drinking place, yet with, inscribed
upon its walls over the door, the usual words, "*Logement à pied et à cheval.*"

Around the door several scraggy chickens were picking up anything they could find in the interstices of the stones, and two or three gaunt half-starved-looking dogs lay about basking in the sun and snapping at real or imaginary flies. The place looked none too clean. Yet it was obscure, and it would do for one night. None would molest him here.

"Can I have a room until daybreak to-morrow and a meal?" he asked of a slatternly looking woman leaning against the doorpost; "I have ridden some distance and am very fatigued."

"Without doubt," she answered. "'Tis for that we keep house. Come in."

"And my horse?"

"That also—hard by," she said. "I will call my good man," and uttering a shriek, which was answered from the back by a gruff male voice, she called out again: "Come and take the traveller's horse, *scélérat!* *Mon Dieu*, have you nothing else to do but sit drinking there all day?"

A heavy footfall sounded in the passage, and presently a large, unkempt man came along it, and, seeing the traveller standing there, put up a dirty hand to his tousled hair and said, "*Bon jour, voyageur.*" But the next moment he pushed that hair away from his eyes and, staring at St. Georges, said: "I know your face, stranger. Where have I seen it before?"

"How can I say?" St. Georges asked in reply. "I at least do not know yours."

Yet he turned pale as he answered, and regarded the man fixedly, for he had recognised the other at once. The fellow before him had been one of the *comites* of a galley in which St. Georges had rowed before being transferred to L'Idole—had thrashed and belaboured him often. Of all the brutal overseers this man had been, perhaps, the most cruel! He was in a trap if he should recall where he had seen him before, a trap from which escape would be difficult. For at a word from him he would never be allowed to pass the gates of Bayeux, but would be arrested at once, taken before the president of the city, and—sent back to the galleys if not executed, as he would undoubtedly be if it leaked out that he had fought against France!

"All the same, I know you," the man replied. "I must reflect. I must think. In my time I have known——"

"*Dinde!*" shrieked the woman at him, "will you keep the traveller standing all day in the passage while you indulge in your accursed recollections? *Mon Dieu!* are we so overrun with customers that you have naught else to do but gape at them? *Sot!* take his horse to the forge outside."

The fellow—who seemed bemused by frequent drinkings in the back place whence the termagant had called him forth—did as he was bid, and, seizing the nag's head, led it down an alley running at a left angle to the house, and so to a forge—in which, however, there was no sign of any work being done. And St. Georges, whose old soldier instincts never deserted him, followed by his side, intent on seeing where the animal was taken. The horse was to him—as once, four years ago, another and a dearly loved horse had been—his one chance of reaching Troyes easily, of finding his child, and—Aurélie de Roquemaure!

"A poor place," he said, speaking in as unnatural a tone as possible, while all the time he wondered if the fellow recognised him. And he took heart in recollecting that while he had been subject to this man's brutalities, with scores of other victims, his head had always

been either shaved or cropped close and his mustache
absent from his face. Now, both hair and mustache
were grown again; it might be that the ex-*comite* could
not recall where he had known him. "A poor place for
a good horse! And none too secure, I imagine. It has
no door. On a winter night a horse stabled here would
be chilled to the bone."

"It is not winter now," the man replied. "Your
horse will come to no hurt. And we have no thieves in
Bayeux. We send them to the galleys!" and his eye
roved over St. Georges as he spoke.

The latter was, however, too wary to start at the
hateful word; moreover, since this man had been an
overseer of the galleys, it was not strange, perhaps, that
the name of the system by which he had once sub-
sisted should rise to his mind. Therefore he replied
quietly:

"That is well. Now for my room; but, first, a
meal."

As he sat over that meal, a plain enough one as be-
fitted the cabaret in which he was, and partook of it in
a squalid room which represented the combined functions of living room for the man and his wife, drinking place for those who patronized the house, and general common room, he saw the fellow still casting
long glances at him and regarding him from under his
eyelids.

And over and over again he asked himself: "Does
he recognise me; and, if so, what will he do?"

Presently the woman—who had been knitting behind a counter at which she sat, superintending the
bringing in of his sparse meal, and ordering her husband, whom she addressed as André, to call to the serving maid for one thing after another—left the room to

see to "monsieur's appartement." He had said to her he was very tired; he would go to it at once if it was ready, early in the evening as it was.

Then he rose as she disappeared and requested the man to show him where it was, and, when he too rose, followed him upstairs.

It was a poor enough place when he got there, in keeping with the whole of the house—a room in which there was a bed in one corner and a chair in another, and with some washing utensils in a third, but nothing more.

"Call me at daybreak," he said to the man André. "I shall sleep until then if I can. Then I must be on my way to—Paris."

"Si, si," the other replied. "You shall be called," and he went toward the door, though, both there and before, he did not cease to glance furtively at him. These glances had not been unobserved, however, by St. Georges, who in his turn had been equally watching him to see if any absolute recognition appeared to dawn upon him. And now, as the man prepared to depart and leave him alone, he said, speaking as carelessly as possible:

"Well! you thought you knew my face, friend. Have you been able to recall yet where you saw it last?" and he looked him straight in the eyes.

But the other only shook his head, and grumbled out:

"No, no. I cannot remember. Perhaps—it may be —I am mistaken."

CHAPTER XXVI.

IN THE SNARE.

HAD St. Georges followed the impulse that first occurred to him when he recognised the man André, he would have made some excuse for not remaining a night in Bayeux, but would have proceeded at once on his journey to Troyes—though not to Paris as he had said, only with a desire to throw dust in his late oppressor's eyes. For to Paris he had no intention of going under any circumstances, deeming it likely to be full of danger to him. There he would be known to countless military men; he might be seen at any moment and recognised; and the result would, in all likelihood, be ruinous. He meant, however, to proceed some distance toward it and then to strike into another road, and so, leaving the capital a little to the north of him, reach Troyes. He thought he could do this by branching off at Evreux and passing through Fontainebleau, but at present he was not even sure that this would be the direction to take—was, indeed, uncertain if such a course would lead him to the goal he sought, though he believed it would.

But the impulse to quit André's auberge had to be resisted at once as soon as it arose—to follow it would be fraught with, possibly, as much danger as remaining there for a night. For if André really suspected who he was, he would not permit him to quit Bayeux—not at least without extorting something from him for his silence—while, if he could not absolutely remember him, his suspicions would be so much aroused by St. Georges's suddenly altered plans as, perhaps, to absolutely verify them, or to cause him to have the stranger denied exit from the city. Therefore, at all hazards, he must remain the intended night. It was the only way in which to avoid aiding the fellow's hazy recollections, which, after all, might not have taken actual form by the next day's dawn. And there was another thing : however much he might overmaster Nature sufficiently to be able to proceed without rest, the horse could not do so. He must, he decided, remain, and trust to chance.

" What a miserable, what an untoward fate is mine!" he murmured; " could Fortune play me worse? Of all men to light on, that it must be this brute—whom, if I could do so in safety, I would slay for his countless cruelties to me and others! It is hard, hard, hard! There are thousands of inns in France to which I might have gone without meeting any who could recognise me, yet at the very first I stumble on I encounter one who knows me, and knows what I have been. A galley slave!—a man doomed for life, while there, to that brutal work; a man who, since he has escaped, is doomed to death. Ah! well! I am in God's hands. As he has protected me before, may he do so again!"

He threw himself upon the bed as he uttered his little prayer—he must sleep at all cost. Even though André should denounce him to-morrow ere he could quit Bayeux—even though he should have to join *la chaine* again on its road to the galleys—ay! even though the scaffold was to witness his death in the morning, his wornout frame must rest. He had been without sleep for now almost the whole time that had elapsed since Tourville's fleet had first loomed up before the English; it seemed to him that he could scarce recall when he

15

slept last. And what terrible events he had gone
through since that time!

Had he tried to keep awake, he could scarce have done
so; as it was he made no such effort. Wrapped in the
coverlet, the sword unbuckled but grasped in his hand,
he stretched his body out and gave himself up to slumber—slumber deep and heavy as that of a drugged man.

He would not have awakened when he did, would
have slept on, perhaps, for hours longer, had not a continued deep, droning, noise—interrupted now and again
by a shriller one—at last succeeded in thoroughly rous-
ing him—a noise that came as it seemed from below
the bed he lay on, and was only interrupted and drowned
once by the booming of the cathedral clock striking
three. Three! and he had lain down in early evening,
had slept for hours. Yet how weary he still felt! It
was as yet quite dark—the dawn would not come for
another hour, he knew—what could those sounds below
mean? He raised himself on his elbow to listen and
hear more plainly.

At first he could distinguish nothing but the deep
hum, broken now and again by the sharper, more me-
tallic sound; but as he bent over the bed—being now
quite wide awake and with his senses naturally very
acute—he recognised what those sounds were. And
more especially was he enabled to do so from the fact
that the planks of the floor were not joined very closely
together—or had come apart since they were first laid
down—as he had observed when he entered the room
the day before.

The sounds were André and his wife talking. At
this hour of the night, or morning! And gradually,
with his senses strained to the utmost, he was enabled
to catch almost every word that they uttered.

"But," said the woman, "I like it not. It is treachery—*bassesse*. And he is *beau*. *Mon Dieu! mais il est beau*——"

"*Peste!*" the man replied. "It is always of *les beaux* you think. Once 'twas the fisher from Havre, then Le Bic, of the *maréchausse*, now this one. And why base? The king pays a hundred gold pistoles for such as he. And if not to us, then others will get it. Why not we?"

"You are sure? You are not mistaken?"

"Sure! From the first moment. Though I held my peace. Ho! why frighten the bird away from the nest? At first the hair and mustache puzzled me— then——"

St. Georges started as he heard this. *Now* he knew of whom they talked.

"—it came back to me. A *galérien* in the Raquin, a surly dog—one of the worst; one of those who had been gentlemen. Gentlemen! *Ma foi!* I have made their backs tingle often, often!"

"Ay!" muttered St. Georges between his teeth, "you have! 'Tis true."

"You are certain?" the woman asked again. "A mistake would be terrible—would send you back to the galleys yourself, only as beaten slave—not overseer."

"Certain! So will the others be when he is taken— alive or dead. There on his shoulder, *ma belle*, they will see proof—the *fleur-de-lis*. Fortunate for him he was not a religious prisoner, a victim of our holy Church. Otherwise it would have been burnt into his cheek, and he would have been so marked he could not have escaped a day!"

"Will it be alive—*or dead?*"

"Dead, if he resists, at daybreak, in an hour. Then

they will come for him; it is arranged. And take him —doubtless slay him. What matter? The reward is the same. 'Alive or dead,' says the paper—they showed it me at La Poste—'one hundred gold pistoles.' And the horse will be ours, too."

"How will they do it?"

"Hist! Listen. And get you to bed before they come. You need not be in it. I have arranged it, *je te dis.*"

"But how—how—how?"

"I will awake him, bid him hurry; tell him he is discovered, lost, unless he flies. Then, doubtless, he will rush to the door, and, poof! they will cut him down as he rushes out. I have told them he is violent. They must strike at once. *Tu comprends?*"

" Yes," and it seemed to the listener as if the woman had answered with a shudder.

" And," the man said again, " the horse will be ours, too. I have not told them of that. No! we shall have that and the pistoles. Now, get you to bed. They will be here ere long. The day is coming. His last on earth if he runs out suddenly or resists."

The listener heard a moment or two later a stealthy tread upon the stairs outside—a tread that passed his door and went on upstairs and was then no more apparent. It was the woman withdrawing from the place where he was to be slain.

To be slain! Possibly. Yet, he determined, not as the man had arranged it. To be slain it might be, but not without a struggle, an attempt for life; without himself slaying others.

He crept to the window after finding that the door had been locked from the outside—no doubt during his long slumber!—and gazed out. It was not yet near daybreak; the miserable street was still in darkness; in no window was there any light—but above in the heavens there was, however, a gray tinge that told of the coming day. Then he looked around.

Beneath the window, which was a common dormer one, as is almost always the case in northern France and the Netherlands, there was nothing but the rain pipe running beneath it along the length of the house. Below was the street full of cobble and other stones—a good thirty feet below! To drop that height, even though hanging by his hands to the rain pipe and thereby diminishing the distance some eight feet would, however, be impossible; it would mean broken ankles and legs and dislocated thigh bones. Yet, what else to do? Behind him was the locked door; in front, through the window, an escape that would leave him mangled and at the mercy of those who were coming to slay him.

Still peering out into the darkness—that was now not *all* darkness—he saw about six feet to the left of him the mouth of the perpendicular pipe into which the horizontal one emptied itself and which must run down the side of the house. His chance, he thought, was here. Yet if he would avail himself of it he must be quick; the day would come ere long; at any moment those who had been summoned by the landlord must be approaching; he would be discovered.

He fastened his sword to his back with his sash—he could not drag it by his side—then head first he crept out of the window, testing with his right hand the water pipe—for six feet he would have to rely upon that to fend him from destruction, to prevent him from rolling off the roof to death below on the cobblestones! With that right hand pressed against it he could—if it did not give way under the pressure—reach the spout of the upright pipe. As he tried it it seemed strong, securely fastened to the lip of the roof; he might venture.

Face downward, his chest to the sloping roof, of which there was three feet between the sill of the window and the pipe at the edge, he lowered himself—his right hand on the pipe, his left, until obliged to loose it, clinging to the window frame. And at last he was on the roof itself, with the right hand still firmly pressed against that pipe, and the top joints of his left-hand fingers, and even his nails, dug into the rough edges of the tiles. That frail pipe and those tiles were all there was now to save him—nothing else but them between him and destruction! Slowly he thus propelled himself along, feeling every inch of the pipe carefully ere he bore any weight on it, feeling also each tile he touched to see if it was loose or tight. For he knew that one slip—one detached tile, one inch of yielding of the pipe —and he would go with a sudden rush over the sloping precipice to the stones below. And as he dragged himself along, hearing the grating of his body and the scraping of the buttons on his clothes against the roof, he prayed that the man watching below might not hear them also. At last he reached the mouth of the upright pipe, grasped it, and, as before, pressed against it to discover if it was firm—as it proved to be—then drew his body up over it, and gradually prepared to descend by it, feeling with his feet for the continuance of it below.

But, to his horror, there was no such continuance! His legs, hanging down from his groin over the roof —while his body was supported on the wide mouth of the pipe and by his hands being dug into the sides of the tiles, where they were joined to each other—touched nothing but the bare space of the wall. There was no pipe! It was broken off short a foot below the horizontal one, and the wall, he could feel, was damp from the water which had escaped and flowed down from where it was so broken.

He was doomed now, he knew; which doom should he select—to fall below and be crushed and mangled, or return to the room and, refusing to come out, be either done to death or taken prisoner? As he pondered thus in agony, away down the street he heard voices breaking on the morning air, he heard the clank of loosely fastened sabres on the stones—they were coming to take him—to, as André had said, "cut him down." And, scarce knowing what he did, or why in his frenzy he decided thus, he let his body further down into space, and, with his hands grasping the pipe's mouth, swung over that space. And once, ere he let go, which he must do in another moment, for the sides of the spout were cutting into his palms, he twisted his head and glanced down beneath him.

Then as he did so he gave a gasp—almost a cry of relief unspeakable. Beneath him, not two yards below his dangling feet, was the stone roof of the porch or doorway of the inn. The fall to that could not break his legs surely!—he prayed God the sound of it might not disturb the man within, who must be on the alert.

Closing his feet so that both should alight as nearly as possible on the same spot, pressing his body as near to the wall as he could, he let go the spout and dropped.

CHAPTER XXVII.

ANOTHER ESCAPE.

He alighted in the exact middle of the porch roof and fell with his ankles against the foot-high raised parapet. Then he paused a moment ere deciding what he should do next.

The sound of voices and clanking sabres were coming nearer—also it would soon now be light. And he wondered that he heard no noise from the man watching within; wondered that he was not staring about for those who were coming; almost wondered that he was not standing at the door with it open, ready to go out and meet them.

One thing St. Georges recognised as necessary to be done at once, viz., to quit the roof of the porch. There was no safety for him there; the instant André entered his room he would perceive he was flown, would rush to the window, and, looking out, would doubtless perceive him crouching and huddled up. He must quit that, and at once. But where? Then suddenly he bethought him of the stable that ran off at left angles from the house, close by the porch itself. That would be his best place of safety; moreover, he would have the horse to his hand; on it he might yet escape. And also from the open door of the stable he could reconnoitre, observe what happened, what must happen, in the next few moments. For now the voices of those who were approaching sounded very near. A little while, and his fate now trembling in the balance would be decided.

He lowered himself quickly over the side of the doorway roof—having but a distance of four or five feet to drop when hanging down—and observed that still the door was fast and that there was no sign of André about—doubtless he was waiting for the men to come, ere opening it! Immediately afterward he touched the ground and turned his steps to the alley leading to the stable and swiftly passed up to it, keeping under the shelter of a low wall. So far he was safe!

The horse whinnied a little as he entered—already the creature had come to know him well, perhaps because of his kindly treatment—but he silenced it at once by placing his arm over its mouth and nostrils, then seized the bridle and saddle and prepared it ready for mounting, doing so very quietly, for now the men were close at hand! This he did very rapidly, yet determinately, for, the animal once saddled, his chance would be still better. He had made his plans: if, when he was discovered missing, any should advance down the alley to seek for him, or to search if the horse was gone, he had resolved to mount as they advanced and to charge through them. Then, when he had done all that was necessary, he removed his sword from his back, drew it from the sheath and affixed the latter to his side. He was ready now.

And not too soon! In the now gathering light, sombre and lead-coloured, with, above, some clouds from which a misty rain was falling slightly, he saw three men belonging to the Garde de la Poste arrive in front of the door. One, a sergeant, struck lightly with his finger on the door and bent his ear against it.

"*Si, si!*" he heard this man say, a second after, evidently in reply to André from within, "quite ready. Send him forth." And still he kept his ear to the side post. A moment later he spoke again, also doubtless in answer to a question from within.

"Nay, have no fear," he said; "once outside ho is ours," and he turned to the other two and gave them some orders which St. Georges could not overhear. He could see, however; and what he saw was, that under their superior's directions each of the others drew their heavy dragoon sabres—for to that branch of the army the Gardo de la Poste belonged—and placed themselves one on either side of the porch.

Then all listened attentively.

A moment later, from the first and top floor, through the open window from which St. Georges had escaped, they heard the shouts of the man André; and St. Georges heard them, too, and grasped his sword more firmly, and with them came from the other side of the house a cry from the woman.

"*Carogne!*" exclaimed the sergeant, "the galley boy is giving trouble—André cannot induce him to descend. Yet, hark! he comes! listen to his tread on the stairs— he is rushing down. Be ready!" and as he spoke the two men raised their swords.

Again all heard the voice of André shouting within, the woman screaming, too; the door was fumbled at, and in the still, dim, misty light St. Georges saw a form rush out, and a minute later fall shrieking heavily to the ground, cut down by both sabres of the dragoons.

"We have him! we have him!" the sergeant shouted. "Come forth, man; he is ours!"

And as he spoke St. Georges leaped into the saddle, knowing that the time had almost come.

Another moment, and he heard one of the dragoons, who had been bending over the fallen man, exclaim:

"*Mon dieu!* What have we done? This is no *galé-rien*, but André himself!"

"What!" bawled the sergeant. "What! *Mon dieu!*

it is." Then he said in a horrorstricken hoarse voice, " Is he dead ? "

" *Ma foi!* I fear so. His head is in half," the man replied. And with a look of terror he addressed his comrade : " That was your stroke, not mine. I struck him on the shoulder. Thank God, his blood is on your head ! "

" *Fichte!* " exclaimed the second, a man of harder mettle. " What matters? It is our duty. And the *piége* was his, not ours. He was a fool. But where— where is the *galérien?* We must have him ! "

" Into the house," exclaimed the sergeant, " into the house ! The woman screams no more—doubtless he has murdered her. In, I say, and seek for him; scour cellar and garret. In, in ! " and together they rushed into the cabaret, finding, as they pushed the door further open, André's wife lying fainting in the passage. She had followed her husband down the stairs and witnessed his end.

That husband's greed—his withholding from the others the fact that the escaped galley slave had a good horse—led to that galley slave's escape. For, all unknowing that, not twenty paces off, the horse was there ready saddled to bear him away, they never thought of the stable, but, instead, plunged into the inn and commenced at once roaming from room to room searching for him.

As they did so, his opportunity came. Swiftly he led the animal down the alley to the door—it had no other exit, or he would have escaped by it—equally swiftly he led it some distance down the street, praying to God all the time that its hoofs striking on the stones might not reach their ears, and sweating with fear and apprehension as he heard their shouts and calls

to one another. Then, when he was fifty yards away
from the house, he jumped into the saddle, patted
his horse on the neck, and rode swiftly for the East
Gate.

Whether he would get through before the whole
east part of the city was alarmed—as he knew it soon
must be—he could not tell yet. If the gates were not
open, he was as much lost as before; he must be taken.
But would they be so open? Would they? As he
prayed they might, the cathedral clock rang out again,
struck four.

"O God!" he murmured, "grant this may be the
hour. Grant it! grant it!"

It seemed to him as though his prayer was heard.
Nearing the East Gate, placed on the west side of a
branch of the river Eure, he saw the bascule descending; he knew that four o'clock *was* the hour. Also he
saw several peasants standing by, ready to pass over it
into the country beyond, doubtless either to fetch in
produce for the city or going to their work. He was
safe now, he felt; if none came behind, there would be
no hindrance to his exit.

"You ride early, monsieur," the keeper said, glancing up at him from his occupation of throwing down
some grain to his fowls, which he had just released for
the day. Then, taking out a pocketbook, "Your name,
monsieur, and destination?" he asked.

"Destination, Paris. Name——" and he paused.
He had not anticipated this. Yet he must give a name
and at once; at any moment from the city might appear
a crowd, or the dragoons shouting to the man to bar his
egress. "Name, Dubois. And I ride in haste. You
have heard the news?"

"News! no," exclaimed the man, while even the

peasants going to their toil pricked up their ears. "What news?"

"Tourville's fleet is ruined—burned—by the English! Stop me not. I ride to carry it. By orders!"

"*Mon Dieu!*" the man exclaimed, "by the English. Tourville defeated by them? It is impossible!"

"It is true," while as he spoke—still moving across the now lowered drawbridge as he did so—one of the peasants, an old woman, wailed: "My boy was there—in the Ambitieux! Is that burnt?"

"I do not know, good woman," he replied, unwilling to tell the poor old creature the worst. "I must not tarry."

And in a moment he had put the horse to the gallop. He had left Bayeux behind. Out of the jaws of death he had escaped once more. "But," he asked himself, "for how long? How long?"

.   .   .   .

That danger which he had escaped so soon after setting foot in France was not again equalled on the road, and a week later he neared the old fortified town of Rambouillet. He had progressed by obscure ways to reach it, avoiding every large city or town to which he had approached, and skirting, either on the north or south, Caen, Evreux, and Bernay. He was drawing nearer to Troyes now, nearer to where his child was, if still alive, nearer to the satisfaction he meant to have by his denunciation of the treachery of Aurélie de Roquemaure.

Yet, as he so progressed, he asked himself of what use would such denunciation be—of what importance in comparison with the regaining of Dorine? That was all in all to him; the supreme desire of his life now—to regain her, to escape out of France once

more; to earn subsistence sufficient for them both in
England. Beyond that, the satisfaction of taxing
Mademoiselle de Roquemaure with her treachery—the
treachery of, with her mother, appearing to sympathize
with him when they first met at the manoir, of expressing that sympathy again in Paris during their brief encounter outside the Louvre, of her false and lying words
to Boussac—would be little worth. Yet, small as that
satisfaction would be, something within told him he
must obtain it; must stand face to face with her and
look into those clear gray eyes that had the appearance
of being so honest and were so false; must ask her why,
since she so coveted all that his and his child's life
might deprive her of, she had stooped to the duplicity
of pretending to sympathize with him; to the baseness
of stealing his child from the man who had himself
stolen it—he knew not why; to the foul meanness of
accompanying her menial—herself masked to prevent
detection—and urging him on to murder; herself, by
complicity, a murderess! And as he so pondered, he
reflected also with what eager, cruel pleasure—for he
knew now, and almost shuddered at knowing, that the
wrongs inflicted on him had turned him toward cruelty
—he would tell her of how her vile brother had died
before his eyes.

So, determinately, he rode on, nearing Rambouillet,
yet feeling as though sometimes he could go no further,
must drop from his horse into the road. In the week
since he escaped from Bayeux he had been feeling that
day by day he was becoming ill, that all he had gone
through—the immersion in the sea, the intensity of his
excitement at Bayeux, his long rides and exposure to
the weather—was like ere long to overwhelm him.
Sometimes for hours he rode almost unconscious of what

was passing around him; he burned with a consuming fever, his limbs and head ached and his thirst was terrible.

Yet, urged on and on by the object he had in view, he still went forward until, at last, he halted outside the town he had now come to, beneath the walls of the old castle of Rambouillet.

CHAPTER XXVIII.

THE FLEUR-DE-LIS.

THE hot sun of those last days of May beat down on the white roads and the orchards and the pastures surrounding the town of Rambouillet, and shone also with unpleasant strength upon La Baronne de Louvigny, being driven back to her house within the walls. And madame's aristocratic countenance, handsome as she was, showed signs of irritation—perhaps from the effects of the heat, perhaps from other things—while her dark eyes, glancing out from under the hood of the summer *calèche* in which she was lying back, looked as though they belonged to a woman who was not, at the present moment at least, in the best of humours.

She was still a very young woman and was also a widow, the baron having been killed in a duel some few years ago, which had not grieved her in the least, since he was an old man who had married her for her good looks and, possibly, her more aristocratic connections than he himself possessed; yet, in spite of these advantages, there were things in her existence which annoyed her. Among these things was, for instance, one which was extremely irritating—namely, that for four years

now she had been required to abstain from visiting Paris
or the court, either at Versailles, Marley, or St. Germains, and this notwithstanding that her blood was of
the most blue and that she claimed connection with the
most aristocratic families in France.

Truly it was an annoying thing to be young, handsome, and very well to do—owing to her not *too* aristocratic husband, the late baron—and to be of the blue
blood owing to her own family, and yet to be under a
cloud in consequence of a scandal—of being mixed up in
an affair, a scene, or tragedy, which it was impossible to
altogether hush up. At least she found it annoying,
and, so finding it, revolted a good deal at the ban laid
on her. Still, revolt or repine as she might, Louis's
word was law in all matters of social importance, and
she was forced to bow to it, in the hopes that, as time
passed on, the ban might be removed. But it was not
strange, perhaps, that in so bowing, her temper, always
a hot, passionate one, had grown a little uncertain.

It did not serve to improve that temper on this hot
day that, at a moment when the *calèche* emerged into a
particularly sunny portion of the road, unsheltered by
either tree or bank, it should suddenly come to a stop and
expose her to the full glare of the sun itself. Moreover,
the jerk with which the horses were pulled up gave her
a jar which did not tend to better matters.

"What are you stopping for?" she asked angrily of
one of the lackeys who had by now jumped down from
behind. "I bade you take me back as soon as possible.
And why in this broad glare? *Animal!*" and she
drew her upper lip back, showing her small white teeth.

"Pardon, my lady," the man said—he knowing the
look well, and remembering also that, before to-day, it
had boded punishment for him and his fellows—"but

there is a man lying in the road, almost under the hoofs of the horses. And his own stands by his side."

" Well! What of that? Thrust them aside and drive on. Am I to be broiled here?"

" Pardon, my lady," the man again ventured to say submissively, " but it is not a peasant. He looks of a better class than that."

" What is he, then, a gentleman of the *seigneurie?*" And she deigned to lean out of the *calèche* somewhat, as though to obtain a glance of the person who had barred her way. " Has he been drinking?"

" I do not know, my lady. But his head is hurt. He may have been attacked or injured by his fall. He is plainly dressed, but carries a sword. He is young, too, and wears a mustache like an officer."

" I will see him. Open the door."

The lackey did as he was bidden, his fellow jumping down also from behind, and each of them offering an arm to their imperious mistress to aid her descent from the high vehicle; then madame la baronne advanced to the front of her horses' heads and gazed down at the unconscious man lying in the dust.

" Turn his face up," she said, " and let me see it." The servants doing as she bade them, and parting also the long hair that fell over the face, the woman gave a start and muttered under her lips, " My God!" And at the same time, beneath her patches and powder, she turned very pale. " Is he dead?" she asked a moment later, in a constrained voice, while still she gazed at him.

" I think not, my lady," one of the men said who was kneeling beside the man in the road. " His heart beats. It may be a vertigo or the heat of the sun. Certainly he is not dead."

" Take him up," she said, " and carry him, you two,
16

into the town. Attach his horse, also, to the carriage
and lead it in. Follow at once;" and she re-entered
the *calèche*.

"Where, madame, shall we place him?" the lackey
asked, who had first spoken. With the *corps-de-garde*,
my lady?"

"No; bring him to my house. He shall be attended
to there. He—he may be a gentleman, and the *corps-
de-garde* are rough. We will attend to him. Now bid
the coachman drive on, and follow at once; do not lag
with him, or you shall be punished."

Slowly the carriage proceeded, therefore, into Rambouillet, and Madame la Baronne de Louvigny, lying
back in it, white to her lips, pondered over the face that
a few minutes before had been turned up to her gaze.

"Alive," she said to herself. "De Vannes, and
alive! And in my power; another half hour and he
will be in my house. So—he was not lost in the galley
that those vile English sunk! And Raoul is no nearer
to the wealth he needs than ever—no nearer. And, my
God! the man lives who called me ' wanton ' in the
road that night, the man whom I tried to slay, the man
through whom came my exposure. And in my house!
In my house!" And she laughed to herself and showed
her teeth again. Then she muttered to herself: "But for
how long! Oh, that Raoul was here to advise with!"

Late that night St. Georges opened his eyes and
glanced around him, wondering where he was and endeavouring to recall what had befallen him. Yet, at
first, no recollection came; he could not recall any of
the events of the day—nothing. All was a blank. He
had sufficient sensibility, however—a sensibility that
momentarily increased—to be able to notice his sur-

roundings and to observe that he lay in a large-capacious bed in a commodious room, well furnished and hung with handsome tapestry representing hunting scenes; also that at the further end of the room by a hugh fireplace—now, of course, empty—there stood a lamp with, by it, a deep chair in which a female figure sat sleeping—a female whose dress betokened her a waiting maid.

"Where am I?" he asked feebly, trying to send his voice to where she sat. "And why am I here?"

The woman arose and came toward the bed and stood beside him; then she said:

"You were found lying in the road outside the town."

"What town?"

"Rambouillet."

"Ah!—I remember. Yes."

"By my mistress, La Baronne de Louvigny. She had you brought here."

"She is very merciful to me, a stranger. A Christian woman."

To this the waiting maid made no reply; in her own heart she had no belief in her mistress's mercy or Christianity—she had served her a long while. Then she said:

"You had best sleep now. You are bruised and cut about the head. But the doctor has bled you, and says you will soon be well. Where are you going to?"

"To—I do not know. I cannot remember."

"Sleep now," the woman said, "sleep. It is best for you," and she left the bedside and went back to the chair she had been sitting in when he called to her.

The comfort of the bed combined with the feeling of weakness that was upon him made it not difficult to .

obey her behest; yet ere he did so he had sufficient of
his senses left to him—or returned to him—to raise his
hand and discover by doing so that his clothes were not
removed; to satisfy himself that the brand upon his
shoulder had not yet been observed. Being so satisfied,
he let himself subside into a sleep once more.

Meanwhile, in a room near where he lay, La Baronne
de Louvigny, sometimes seated in a deep fauteuil, sometimes pacing the apartment which formed her boudoir
or dressing room, was meditating deeply upon the chances
which had thrown this man into her hands.

"*Mon Dieu!*" she muttered to herself, as she had
done once before while her *calèche* had borne her back
into the town of Rambouillet, "if Raoul were but here!
What shall I do with him? What! What! After that
horrible night when the prefect examined us at Versailles, pronounced that I was an attempted murderess
—Heaven! if Louvois had not stood our friend with
Louis, what would have been the consequence!—Raoul
told me all: That this man was in truth the Duc de
Vannes; that, if he once knew it, or Louis guessed it, it
meant ruin; that all his father's vast estates would go
to him instead of to Raoul, who had long felt secure of
them; that, worse than all, Louis would never pardon
the attack upon his friend's son, would know that he had
been struck down from behind by a foul blow, not fairly
in a duel. And now he is here, alive in my house—has
crossed our path again; is doubtless on his way to the
king to tell him the truth, prove his false condemnation to the galleys, claim all that is his. God! if he
does that I shall never be Raoul's wife—never, never,
never!"

As she had once drunk feverishly of the wine standing on the inn table, while it seemed that to the man

who ought, even then, to have been her husband his
doom was approaching from St. Georges's avenging
sword, so she now went to a cabinet and took from it
a flask of strong waters and swallowed a dram. The
habit had grown on her of late, had often been resorted
to since the night when she—hitherto a woman with no
worse failings than that of lightness of manner and
with, for her greatest weakness, a mad, infatuated pas-
sion for Raoul de Roquemaure—had struck her knife
deep between his shoulders, and had become a murderess in heart and almost one in actual fact.

Then, having swallowed the liquor, she mused again.
"What best to do? I can not slay him here in my
own house—though I would do so if I could compass it.
He called me 'wanton'; read me aright! For that
alone I would do it! Yet, how? How? And if he
goes free from here 'tis not a dozen leagues to Louis;
doubtless he knows now his history, he will see him—
Louvois is dead and gone to his master, the devil—he is
a free man."

Yet as she said the words "a free man" she started,
almost gasped.

"A free man!" she repeated. "A free man! Ha!
is he free?"

Through her brain there ran a multitude of fresh
thoughts, of recollections. "A free man!" Yet he had
been condemned, she knew, to the galleys *en perpétuité;*
there was no freedom, never any pardon for those so
sentenced. Once condemned, always condemned; no
appeal possible, their rights gone forever, slaves till
their day of death; branded, marked, so that forever
they bore that about them which sent them back to
slavery. If he bore that upon him, he was lost; the galleys still yawned for him—yawned for him so long as

Louis did not know that the escaped *galérien* was the
son of his friend of early days.

"I know it all, see it all," she whispered to herself.
"The galley was lost, but he was saved—saved to come
back to France and ruin us. Yet he bears that about
him—must bear it, since all condemned *en perpétuité* are
branded—which, once seen, will send him back to his
doom. Let but the *préfet* see that, or any officer of the
garrison or citadel, and the next day he will travel again
the road which he has come; go back to Dunkirk or
Havre, back to the *chiourme* and the oar. They will
listen to nothing, hear no word or protest, grant no
trial. He is mine—mine!" and again she went to the
cabinet and drank. "Even though he has found proof
of who he is, they will not listen to nor believe him."

One fear only disturbed her frenzy now. That he
was the man who had called her "wanton," the man
who stood between her lover and his wealth, and consequently between her and that lover, she never doubted.
Those features, seen first by the lamp in the parlour of
the inn—seen, too, when apparently he lay dying from
her murderous stab—were too deeply stamped into her
memory to ever be forgotten. And as he lay there,
looking like death, so he had looked as he lay in the
dust outside Rambouillet. He was the man!—and this
was her fear! But was it certain that the galley mark
was branded into him, the mark which proclaimed him
as one doomed to those galleys forever, that would send
him back without appeal, and would make all in authority whom he might endeavour to address turn a deaf
ear to him?

She must know that, and at once. She could not
rest until she knew that upon his shoulder was the
damning evidence.

All was quiet in the house, it was near midnight, the domestics were in their beds by now: she resolved that she would satisfy herself at once. Then, if the brand was there, as it must be, she could arrange her next steps—could send for the commandant of the *château*, deliver the man into his hands, be not even seen by him. If it was there!

Leaving her room, she crept to the one to which he had been carried, and, pushing open the door, looked in. The waiting maid, who had received orders not to quit him under any pretext, was sleeping heavily in her chair; on the bed at the further end of the room lay the man.

Then swiftly and without noise she advanced toward him, carrying the taper which had been burning by the watcher's side in her hand, and gazed down upon him.

He was sleeping quietly, his coat and waistcoat off—for they had removed these in consequence of the warmth of the day, though nothing else except his shoes—his shirt was open at the neck. If she could turn it back an inch or two without awaking him, her question would be answered.

Shading the lamp with one hand, with the other she touched the collar of his discoloured shirt, her white jewelled fingers looking like snowflakes against it and his bronzed skin; lower she pressed the folds back until, revealed before her, was the mark burned deep into his neck, the fatal iris with, above it, the letter *G*.

"So," she said, "the way is clear before me;" and softly, still obscuring the light with her hand, she stole from the room quietly as she had come.

CHAPTER XXIX.

FAREWELL HOPE!

"MADAME," the waiting maid said to her the next afternoon, "the gentleman is desirous of setting forth upon his journey again. He is well now, he says, and he has far to ride."

"Well," said la baronne, glancing up from the lounge on which she lay in her *salon* and speaking in her usual cold tones, "he may go. What is there to detain him? The surgeon says he is fit to travel, does he not? His was but a fit from long riding in the sun."

"Yes, my lady—but——"

"But what?"

"My lady, he *is* a gentleman—none can doubt that. He—he is desirous to speak with you—to——"

"To speak with me?" and from her dark eyes there shot a gleam that the woman before her did not understand. Nor did she understand why her ladyship's colour left her face so suddenly. "To speak with me?"

"Yes, my lady. To, he says, thank you for your charity to him a stranger—for your hospitality."

"My hospitality!" and she drew a long breath. Then, and it seemed to the waiting maid as if her mistress had grown suddenly hoarse, "He said that?"

"He said so, madame. He begged you would not refuse to let him make the only return that lay in his power."

"I will not see him."

"Madame!"

"I will not see him—go—tell him so. No! Yet, stay, on further consideration I will. Go. Bring him."

Left alone, she threw herself back once more on the cushions of her lounge, muttering to herself: "After all," she said, "it is best. He never saw my face on that night—the mask did not fall from it until his back was turned—I remember it all well—Raoul's cry for help—this one's determination—my blow. Ah, the blow! It should never have been struck—yet—yet—otherwise he had slain Raoul. And," she continued rapidly, for she knew that the man would be here in a moment, "and I may find out if he knows who and what he is. If he guesses also the fate in store for him."

Rapidly she went to a cabinet in this great *salon*, took out from it a little dagger, and dropped it in the folds of her dress, muttering: "It may be needed again. He may recognise me even after so long and in such different surroundings," and then turned and faced the door at which a knocking was now heard. A moment later St. Georges was in the room.

Pale from the loss of blood he had sustained both from his fall and at the surgeon's hands, and looking much worn by all he had suffered of late—to say nothing of the two years of slavery he had undergone—he still presented a figure that, to an ordinary woman, would have been interesting and have earned her sympathy. His long hair was now brushed carefully and fell in graceful folds behind; his face, if worn and sad, was as handsome as it had ever been. Even his travel-stained garments, now carefully cleaned and brushed, were not unbecoming to him. And she, regarding him fixedly, felt at last a spark of compunction rise in her bosom for all that she had done against him. Yet it must be stifled, she knew. That very morning's work—a letter to the commandant at the castle—had been sufficient to make all regret unavailing now.

"Madame," he said, bending low before her with the courtesy of the period, "I could not leave your house without desiring first to thank you for the protection you have afforded me. And, poor and unknown as I am, I yet beseech you to believe that my gratitude is very great. You succoured me in my hour of need, madame; for that succour let me thank you." And stooping his knee he courteously endeavoured to take her hand.

But—none are all evil—even Nathalie de Louvigny would not suffer that. Drawing back from him, she exclaimed instead: "Sir, you have nothing to thank me for. I—I—what I did I should have done to any whom I had found as you were."

He raised his eyes and looked at her. A chord or tone in her voice seemed to recall something in the past, and she standing there divined that such was the case. Then he said, quietly:

"Madame, I can well believe it. Charity does not discriminate in its objects. Yet, since I so happened to be that object, I must thank you. Madame, it is not probable that I shall ever visit Rambouillet again, nor, indeed, France after a little while; let an——"

"Not visit France again!" she exclaimed, staring open-eyed at him. "Are you not a Frenchman?"

"Madame, I was a Frenchman. I am so no longer. I have parted with France forever. In another week, or as soon after that as possible, I intend to quit France and never to return to it."

She took a step back from him, amazed—terrified. What had she done! This man had renounced France forever—would have crossed her and Raoul's path no more—have resigned all claim to all that was his. And she had taken a step that would lead to his being de-

tained in France—that might, though his chance was
remote, lead to his true position being known. Yet,
was it too late to undo that which she had done?
Was it?

She had bidden the officer in command at the *château*, who aspired to her regard, send to her house that
night and arrest a man who, she had every reason to
believe, had escaped from the galleys. Also she had
warned him to let no man pass the gate without complete explanation as to who and what he was; and he
had sent back word thanking her, and saying that, provided the person of whom she spoke did not endeavour
to leave Rambouillet before sunset, he would have him
arrested at her house. She had done this in early morning; now the sunset was at hand. Ere long the soldiers
would be here, and he would be detained—would speak
—might be listened to. She had set the trap, and she
herself was snared in it.

Yet, she remembered, she wanted one other thing—
revenge for the opprobrious word he had applied to her
long ago. If he quitted France she must forego that.
But need she forego it? He had spoken of himself in
lowly terms—was it possible he still did not know who
he was, as De Roquemaure had told her long ago he did
not know then? The revenge might still be hers if he
knew nothing. She must find that out if she could.

"Monsieur must have very little in France that he
deems of worth," she said, "since he is so desirous of
quitting it. There are few of our countrymen who
willingly exchange the land of their birth for another."

She had seated herself as she spoke before a table on
which stood a tall, thin vase filled with roses; and she
caught now in her hands the folds of the tablecloth,
while he standing there before her saw these signs of

emotion. Also he observed that her eyes sparkled with an unnatural light, and that her upper lip, owing to some nervous contraction, was drawn back a little, so that her small white teeth were very visible. And as he so observed her and noticed these things, the certainty came to him that they had met before. But where? He could not remember at first—could not recall where he had seen a woman seated at a table as she was now seated, clutching the folds of the cloth in her hands.

"My countrymen," he said, still vainly wondering, "have not often suffered as I have suffered—have not such reasons, perhaps, for quitting their native land forever."

"What reasons?" and as she spoke her nervousness was such that she released the folds of the cloth which her left hand grasped, and with that hand toyed with the slim vase before her which contained the roses.

And this further action stirred his memory still more. When had he seen a woman seated thus, her hand trifling first with a table cover, then with some object on the table itself? When?

"Reasons so deep, so profound," he said, "that scarce any who knew of them would be surprised at my resolve: a career cruelly blighted for no fault of my own; my life attempted secretly, murderously; my little child doomed to assassination; the wrongdoer in my power, a treacherous stab from behind—" He paused amazed.

The woman's right hand—the left now gathering up the folds of the cloth again in its small palm—had dropped to the side of her dress, was thrust into a pocket in that side, was feeling for, perhaps grasping, something within that pocket. That action aided remembrance and cleared away all wonder. Swift as the lightning flashes, there flashed to his recollection the woman who had sat at the table of the inn—the woman whom, as he and De Roquemaure had once changed places as they fought, he had seen seize the flask of wine with her left hand, her right grasping her small dagger. *And this was the woman!* The drawn-back lip, the glassy stare with which she regarded him in the swift-coming darkness of the summer evening, all reproduced the scene of that night—a scene which, until now, he had almost forgotten amid the crowd of other events that had taken place since then. Advancing a step nearer to her, so that he stood towering above, he said, his voice deep and solemn:

"It is strange, madame, how we stand face to face once more—alone together. Is it not? It was your hand dealt that stab!"

She could not answer him, could only regard him fixedly, her eyes glaring as they had glared four years ago, and as they had glared not four minutes since. Only now it was with the wild stare of fear added to hate and fury, and not with hate and fury alone; also she kept still her right hand in the fold of her dress.

"When last we met, madame," St. Georges continued, his voice low and solemn as before, "you interfered between me and my vengeance on one who had deeply wronged me. You had the power to do so, bore about you a concealed weapon, and—used it! Have you one now?" and he pointed with his finger to where her hand was.

Still she maintained silence—trembling all over and affrighted; even the arm hanging down by her side with the hand in the pocket was trembling too.

"Well," St. Georges said, "it matters not! I shall

not give you a second opportunity—shall not turn my
back on you."

Then she spoke, roused by the contempt of those
last words.

"I would not have struck at you," she said, "even
though I loved De Roquemaure—am his affianced wife
when he returns from England——"

"When—he—returns—from England!" St. Georges
repeated, astonished.

"Yes. His affianced wife." In her tremor she
thought his disbelief of this was the cause of his astonishment, never dreaming of how he had last left her
lover. "Not even for that love. But you had abused,
insulted me, called me wanton, suggested it was I who
stole your child. And you were very masterful, ordered
us to follow you into the inn, carried all before you,
treated him like a dog, would have slain him——"

"I have since learned I wronged you, at least; that
it was another—woman—who stole my child. But
enough. We have met again, madame, and—and—I
must——"

"What!" she gasped, thinking he was about to slay
her. "What will you do to me?"

"Do!" he replied. "Do! What should I do?"

"God knows! Yet in mercy spare me! I am a
woman," and overcome with fear she cast herself at his
feet. "Spare me—spare me."

"I do not understand you," St. Georges said, looking down disdainfully at her. "I think, too, you do
not understand me. I wish to do only one thing now,
to quit your presence and never set eyes on you again,"
and without offering to assist her to her feet he backed
toward the door.

But now—perhaps, because of the discovery that

this man meant her no harm, intended to exact no horrible atonement from her—a revulsion of feeling took place in the woman's breast.

"No, no!" she cried, springing to her feet. "No, no! Do not go—for God's sake do not attempt to quit the town yet! You will be lost—if you are seen—lost, lost! Ah, heavens!" she screamed, for at that moment there boomed a cannon from the *château*, "the sunset gun! The sunset gun! It is too late!"

"What is too late?" he asked advancing toward her. "What?" And as he spoke he seized her wrist. "Woman, what do you mean? Is this some fresh plot, some new treachery? Answer me. Am I trapped—and by you?"

"No, no!" she wailed, afraid to tell what she had done, afraid that even now, ere the soldiers should come, he would strangle the life out of her, or thrust the sword he carried by his side through her heart. "No, no! But it is known—they know—that you have been a *galérien*—you will be arrested! The mark upon your shoulder is known to the commandant."

"How?" he said, again seizing her by the arm. "How? Who knows it? Who? Outside this house none can have seen it."

"Come!" she replied, not daring to answer him; "come, hide. They will look for you here. Yet I can secrete you till the search is over. For a week—months —if need be. Come."

"They know I am here! Through *you?*"

"No, no! The mark was seen when you lay insensible—ah!" she screamed again. "See, see! it is too late! They are in the garden. It is too late!"

It was true. Along the garden path to which the windows of her *salon* opened, six soldiers were advanc-

ing led by a young officer. Across their shoulders were
slung their muskets; the officer carried his drawn
sword. And St. Georges looking from her to them
knew that he was snared, his freedom gone. Doubtless
his life, too.

"Devil," he said to the woman as she reeled back to
the lounge and fell heavily on it—"devil, I thanked you
too soon. Had I known, dreamed of this, I would have
slain you as you dreaded!"

CHAPTER XXX.

"IT IS TRUE."

THE windows of the *salon* giving on to the crushed-
shell path of the Hôtel de Louvigny had been open all
day to let in the air, and the handsomely apparelled
young officer of the Régiment de Grancé, stationed at
Rambouillet, was enabled therefore to at once enter the
room, leaving his men outside. Yet as he did so he
seemed bewildered and astonished at the sight which
met his eyes.

Lying fainting, gasping, on her couch was Madame
de Louvigny—*la belle Louvigny* as they called her, and
toasted her nightly in the guardroom—standing over
her was a man, white to the lips, his hands clinched,
his whole form and face expressing horror and contempt.

"*Pardie!*" the young fellow muttered between his
lips, "I have interrupted a little scene, *un roman
d'amour! Bon Dieu* the lover has detected madame
in some little infidelity, and—and—has had a moment

of vivacity. Yet 'tis not my fault. *Devoir avant tout,*" aud as he muttered the motto of the noble house to which he belonged—perhaps as an aid in that *devoir*—he advanced into the room after bidding his men remain where he had stationed them.

"Madame la baronne will pardon my untimely appearance," he muttered in the most courtly manner, and with a comprehensive bow of much ease and grace which included St. Georges, "but my orders were—what—madame herself knows. Otherwise I should regret even more my presence here."

She, still on the lounge, her face buried in her Valenciennes handkerchief, was as yet unable to utter a word—*he*, standing before her, never removed his eyes from her. The officer's words had confirmed what he suspected—what he knew.

"But," continued the lieutenant, "madame will excuse. I have my orders to obey. The man she mentioned to the commandant has not yet endeavoured to pass the barrier—is it madame's desire that her house should be searched?"

She raised her head from the couch as he spoke, not daring to cast a glance at him whom she had betrayed to his doom. Then she said, her voice under no control and broken. "No. He is not here. He—has escaped."

"Escaped, madame? Impossible! Rambouillet is too small even for him to be in hiding—he——"

"Has not escaped," St. Georges said, turning suddenly on the officer. "On the contrary, he has been betrayed. I am the man."

"You! Madame's——" and he left his sentence unfinished. "You! Here alone with her, and a *galérien!*"

17

" Yes—I."

It was useless, he knew, to do aught than give himself up. Escape was impossible. It was known, must
be known in this small town, that he was the only
stranger who had entered it lately; nor did he doubt
that when the treacherous creature had informed against
him she had described him thoroughly. Even though
now she lied to save him, it would be of no avail. He
could not remain in her house, hide in it as she had
suggested, take shelter from her. From her! No!
even the galleys—or the gallows—were better than that.

" I regret to hear it," the officer said, " since monsieur appears to be a friend of madame la baronne.
Yet, under the circumstances, monsieur will not refuse
to accompany me."

" I will accompany you."

Whatever the young fellow may have thought of the
man who was now in his custody—and what he did
think was that he was some old lover of la belle
Louvigny who had either cast her off, or been cast off
by her, and had reappeared at an awkward moment, so
that she had taken an effectual manner of disposing of
him—he at least did not show it. But for her he testified his contempt in a manner that was unmistakable.
He motioned to St. Georges to precede him to the open
window where his men were, and, putting on his hat
before he had quitted the room, he strode after his
prisoner without casting a glance at the woman.

But as they neared the window, and were about to
step on to the path, St. Georges stopped and, addressing
him, said : " Sir, grant me one moment's further grace,
I beg of you. Ere I go I have a word to say to madame."

Courteous as he had been all through—to him—the

young fellow shrugged his shoulders good-naturedly, raised no objection, and lounged by the open window, while St. Georges returned to where she still crouched upon the lounge. Yet, as she heard his footsteps nearing her, she looked up with terrorstricken eye, and shrunk back even further into its ample depths. The officer had not demanded his sword, it hung still by his side; her craven heart feared that in his last moment allowed to him he might wrench it from its sheath and punish her for her treachery. But, as she learned a moment later, he had a worse punishment in store for her than that.

"You have sent me to my doom," he said, gazing down on her, "yet, ere I go, hear what has been the doom of another—as vile as you yourself——"

In an instant she had sprung to her feet, was standing panting before him, one hand upon her heart, the other by her side in the folds of her dress. "Vile as she herself," he had said. "Vile as she herself!" To whom else but De Roquemaure could such words apply when issuing from that man's lips?

"The doom of another!" she hissed, repeating those words; "the doom of another—of whom?"

And again on her face there was now the look—the *canine* look—that had been there before—the lip drawn back, the small teeth showing, the threatening glance in the eyes.

"Of whom but one! Who else but your vile partner"—the young officer, of noble race as he was, and steeped in good breeding, could scarce refrain from being startled at those words—"the man you say you love? Well, love him! Only learn this, you have nothing but his memory to love. He is dead!——"

With a scream that rang not only through the *salon,*

but the house also, and penetrated out into the cool
garden beyond—a scream that caused the lieutenant to
start toward them, and his men to peer into the room—
she sprang at him, her right hand raised now, and in it
the dagger she had so long concealed.

" Beware !" the officer cried. " Beware, she is dangerous !" And, even as he spoke, she struck full at St.
Georges's breast with the knife.

" Bah !" he exclaimed, thrusting aside her upraised
arm with the hand in which, all through the interview
with her, he had held his hat—thrusting it aside with
such force that she almost staggered and fell. " Bah !
you mistake, woman. Did you think it was my *back*
again at which you struck ?"

The room was full of servants now ; her own waiting
maid and one or two of the lackeys busy about the
house, preparing a little supper madame had intended
giving that night to a few admirers, had rushed in at
her scream ; and now the former stood behind and half
supported her while she muttered incoherent sounds
amid which the words only could be caught, " You slew
him !—at last !"

" Nay," he said, standing still in front of her, calm
and sinister ; " such satisfaction was not granted me,
nor so easy an ending to him. The English who drove
Tourville's fleet to its doom at La Hogue did their work
effectively. Each ship, each transport, found by them
was blown out of the water ; in one of those transports,
named the Vendôme, he was blown up, too. I was
there but a little while before it exploded ; I saw its
fragments and all within it hurled into space. I think,
madame, my doom is scarce worse than his."

With another shriek, as piercing as the first, she
threw her arms above her head, then fell an insensible

mass into the serving woman's arms. And St. Georges, turning to the young officer, said:

"Sir, I am at your service."

.   .   .   .

They took him that night to the Château de Rambouillet, he marching with three of the soldiers in front of and three behind him, the young officer by his side. And this scion of nobility, one of the De Mortemarts, testified by his actions that night that the French good breeding of the great monarch's day was no mere outward show. He permitted his prisoner to still retain his sword, and he walked by his side instead of ahead of his men, because he did not desire that those whom in his mind he considered the *canaille* should make any observations upon that prisoner as they passed through the streets. Moreover, wherever a knot of persons were gathered together in any corner he affected a smiling exterior, so that they should be induced to suppose that St. Georges was an ordinary acquaintance accompanying him.

"Sir," said the latter, observing all this, "you are very good to me. You make what I have to bear as light as possible."

"It is nothing, nothing," the lieutenant replied. "I only wish it had not fallen to my lot to undertake so unpleasant a duty. By the way, I suppose it is true, as she told the commandant! You have, unfortunately known—been—at the galleys?"

"It is true."

"*Tiens!* A pity. A thousand pities! Above all, that you should have encountered that she-devil. Well, I am glad you had those hard words with her. *Ma foi!* she is a tigress! I only hope you may escape from— from other things—as you did from her dagger."

The commandant—who was also the colonel of the Régiment de Grancé—was, however, a different style of man from his lieutenant—a man who from long service in the army had become rough and harsh; also, like many men commanding regiments under Louis, he had risen solely by his military qualifications, and owed nothing to birth or influence.

He listened, however, very attentively to all De Mortemart told him of the scene that had taken place, and especially as to how the Baronne de Louvigny—to whom he himself was paying court, as has been told—had evidently had some lover whose existence he had never suspected; and then he sent for St. Georges, who was brought into his presence by De Mortemart himself.

"So," he said, "you are an escaped *galérien*, monsieur. Well! You know what happens to them when retaken!"

"I know."

"What was your crime?"

"Nothing—except serving the king as a soldier."

"As a soldier!" he and De Mortemart exclaimed together, while the former continued, "In what capacity?"

"As lieutenant in the Chévaux-Légers of Nivernois."

"*Mon Dieu!*" exclaimed the commandant. "A picked regiment, and commanded by De Beauvilliers—*n'est-ce pas?*"

"He was my colonel."

"Come," said the other, relaxing his stern method of addressing St. Georges, and warming toward him, unknowingly to himself by the fact that this man in such dire distress was a comrade and had served in a *corps d'élite*—"come, tell us your history. We cannot help you—there is but one thing to do, namely, to send you to Paris for inquiry; but until you go we can at least make your existence here more endurable."

So St. Georges told them his story.

All through it both his listeners testified their sympathy—De Mortemart especially, by many exclamations against De Roquemaure and his sister, and also against la belle Louvigny—while the colonel spoke approvingly of the manner in which St. Georges had almost avenged himself on his foe in the inn. The description, too, of his existence in the galleys moved both young and old soldier alike; it was only when he arrived at the account of the destruction of Tourville's fleet that they ceased to make any remark and sat listening to him in silence.

It was finished, however, now, and when the colonel spoke his voice was more cold and unsympathetic.

"You have ruined yourself by the last month's work," he said. "I am afraid you can never recover from that. Did you not know that his Majesty has made it a rule that none who have served him shall ever take service under a foreign power and dare to venture into France again?"

"I know it," St. Georges said, "and I must abide by my fate. Yet, my child was here. I was forced to come, and there was no other way but this."

One thing only he had not told them, the story of what he believed to be his birth, the belief he held that he was the Duc de Vannes. Nor, he determined then—had, indeed, long since determined—would he ever publish that belief now. Had he kept his freedom until he had once more regained Dorine, it was his intention to have repassed to England and never again to have recalled that supposed birthright, or, as the child grew up, to have let her obtain any knowledge on the subject. He would work for her, slave for her, if necessary become tutor, or soldier, or sailor, as Fate might decree; but it must be as an Englishman, and with all connection with France broken forever.

And now, a prisoner, a man who would ere long be tried as an ex-*galérien*, as—if De Mortemart and the colonel did not hold their peace—a Frenchman who had joined England and helped her in administering the most crushing blow to France which she had suffered for centuries—he would never see his child again; what need, therefore, to publish his belief?

The hope that had sustained him for years was gone; the prayer he had uttered by night and day, that once more he might hold his little child in his arms and cherish and succour her, was gone, too; they would never meet again. Let him go, therefore, to his doom unknown, and, so going, pass away and be forgotten. And it might be that, with him removed, God would see fit to temper to his child the adversity that had fallen to his own lot.

CHAPTER XXXI.

ST. GEORGES'S DOOM.

THE *cours criminel* on the banks of the Seine had been crowded all day, and the judges seated on the bench began to exhibit signs of fatigue at their labours. They had sat from ten o'clock in the morning far into the afternoon, and, now that four o'clock was at hand, it appeared as if their sitting would be still further prolonged; and this in spite of the number of cases they had disposed of.

A variety of malefactors, or so-called malefactors, had on that day received their sentences : some for professing the "reformed religion," as they blasphemously —in the judges' eyes—termed it; some for being bullies and cutthroats; a student aged sixteen had been sentenced to imprisonment in the Bastille for writing on the walls a distich on Louis, stating that he had displaced God in the minds of the French ; * and a marchioness had been condemned to a fine of twenty pistoles and to remain out of Paris for a year for having poisoned her husband ; also a spy, a Dutchman, supposed to be in the service of the accursed Stadtholder and English king, had been condemned to death by burning, his entrails to be first cut out and flung in his face; and several petty malefactors—a drunken priest who had read a portion of Rabelais to his flock instead of a sermon ; a lampoonist who had written a joke on the De Maintenon ; an actor who had struck a gentleman in defence of his own daughter ; and a courtesan who had induced a young nobleman to spend too much money on her—were all sentenced to the Bastille, to Vincennes, and Bicêtre for various periods.

"Now," said Monsieur de Rennie, who presided today, when the last of these wretches had been finished off—"now, is the list cleared ? We have sat six hours." And the other judges, one on either side of him, repeated his words and murmured, "Six hours !"

---

* The distich ran :

"La croix fait place au lis, et Jésus Christ au Roi
Louis, oh ! race impie, est le seul Dieu chez toi."

For writing it the student remained in prison *thirty-one years.*

"Your lordships have still some other cases," the
procureur du roi said, addressing them, "which you
will probably be willing to dispose of to-day. There is
one of a man who is thought to have abandoned his ship
in the recent disaster at La Hogue, and to have escaped
to Paris, where he was captured in hiding; and another of three Jansenists who have blasphemed the
faith; also there is a man, an escaped *galérien*, brought
hither from Rambouillet by an officer of the Régiment
de Grancé for trial."

"Are the facts clear," asked the presiding judge,
"against this man? If so, the case will not occupy us
long, and we will take it to-night."

"Quite clear," the *procureur* replied, "so far as I
gather."

"Bring him in."

A moment later St. Georges stood in the dock set
apart for the criminals, his hands tied in front of him.
And in the court many eyes were cast toward him as he
took his stand. All knew that, for those who success-
fully escaped the galleys, there was but one ending if
ever caught again.

"Who gives evidence against this prisoner?" De
Rennie asked, looking at St. Georges under his bushy
white eyebrows. "And what is his name?—Prisoner, what is your name? Answer truly to the
court."

"I have no name," St. Georges replied; "I refuse to
answer to any."

The judge's eyebrows were lifted into his forehead
and down again; then he observed to his brother judge
on his right, with a shrug of his shoulders, "Contuma-
cious!" and then, because he was a man who disliked
to be thwarted, he exclaimed: "So much the worse for

you. Well, *M. le procureur*, who prosecutes—who is there as witness?"

"The officer who arrested him and afterward brought him to Paris. He can give your lordships the facts."

"Very well. Why does he not do so? Let him stand forward."

The officer stood forward, in so far that he stood up in the well of the crowd—his gold-laced, cockaded hat still upon his head, since as an officer of the king he was entitled to wear it in all other places but church— and briefly he answered the presiding judge's questions. Yes, he was a lieutenant of the Régiment de Grancé, quartered at Rambouillet—in his opinion, a miserable hole. His opinion on Rambouillet, the judge said, frowning, was not required; he would be good enough to give his name. His name was De Mortemart. De Mortemart! Perhaps, said the judge, he might be a relative of the Duc de Mortemart? Yes, the officer replied, he might be; in effect he was a son of that personage. The judge was pleased to hear it; the duke was universally known and respected, and—the acoustic qualities of the court were bad—would M. de Mortemart take a seat on the bench, where he and his brother judges could better hear him? The officer did not mind, though he was not inconvenienced where he was, but, of course, if their lordships desired. And so forth.

"Now," the judge said with great sweetness, when he had reached the exalted elevation, "would M. de Mortemart give himself the trouble to state how the fellow before them had fallen into his hands?" M. de Mortemart did give himself the trouble—telling, however, exactly what he thought fit, and also omitting many facts which he did not feel disposed to mention —to wit, he contented himself by saying that the "gen-

tleman " in the dock had been betrayed by a woman into
their hands—a " treacherous reptile " he termed her—
but he said nothing about St. Georges having acknowl-
edged that he had been a soldier of France once, and
had afterward fought on the English side against
France. To his young and chivalrous mind it was, indeed, a terrible thing that any Frenchman should join
with England against his own country, but—he did not
say so to the judge trying that man. The case was bad
enough against him without that.

In answer to further questions put with great politeness and an evident desire on the judge's part not to
bore the son of the Duc de Mortemart too much, he
stated that according to orders, he had escorted the
gentleman in trouble to Paris, and that he had ridden
by that gentleman's side all the way, treating him as
well as possible. Yes, he was bound to say he sympathized with the prisoner (he did not say that he
wished to Heaven the prisoner had availed himself of
many opportunities he had given him of escaping); he
thought he had been hardly treated—especially by the
woman who was, in truth, a viper. Did he mean to
say, the judge asked almost apologetically, that he had
allowed the prisoner to ride unbound by his side? Yes,
he did mean to say so; the prisoner had made no attempt, either, to take advantage of the license. Did
Monsieur de Mortemart think that was wise on his part
as an officer? Yes, on his part as an officer he did
think so. He *was* an officer; not "—and here he cast
his eye on the turnkeys and jailers in the court "—" the
canaille." And, in effect, the prisoner was before the
court; that justified him.

After this the judges ceased to ask the Duc de
Mortemart's son any further questions, but went on

with other matters. One of the *canaille*, a jailer, was put on the witness stand and questioned briefly. "Speak, fellow," said the president in a totally different tone from that which he had hitherto used to the duke's son, "have you examined the prisoner—is he branded?"

"He is, my lord, on his shoulder; an undoubted *galérien*."

"Enough! Stand down."

"Prisoner," addressing St. Georges, "what have you to say?"

"Nothing. Do your worst."

"No justification of your quitting the galleys?"

"Nothing that you would accept as such. Yet this I will say: I did not escape of my own attempt; the galley I was in was sunk by an English admiral off their coast; almost all were lost. I was saved and taken back to England."

"So! That may make a difference. What was the galley's name?"

"L'Idole."

Here the judge on the president's right hand leaned over to him and said : "This may be the truth. I had a nephew, an officer, on board L'Idole—she was sunk."

"Allowing such to be the case, prisoner, how comes it you are back in France?"

"I desired to return, and took the first opportunity."

"Ay, he did," suddenly roared out a voice in the court. "And ask him how he returned, my lord; ask him that!"

In an instant all eyes were turned to the place whence the sound came, and the presiding judge became scarlet in the face at any one having the presumption to so bawl at him in the court. "Exempts," he cried, "find out the ruffian who dares to outrage the king's justice by bellowing before us thus. Find him out, I say, and bring him before us!"

It required, however, very little "finding out," since he who had so cried was the man whom the *procureur du Roi* had spoken of as having abandoned his ship at La Hogue and fled to Paris, and was now present as a prisoner in the court to be tried for his offence. Nor was there much need to hustle and drag him forward, since he came willingly enough—he thought he saw here an immunity from punishment—if punishment be deserved—a chance of escape by the evidence he could give.

"Who is the fellow?" asked De Rennie, when, partly by the man's own willing efforts and partly by pushings and jostlings, he had been got on to the witness stand with two jailers on either side of him. "Who is he?"

"He is, my lord," the *procureur du roi* said, "the man who is charged with deserting his ship at La Hogue and fleeing to Paris. He says, however, he can give evidence against the *galérien* here which will also go far to absolve him of his desertion—if your lordships will hear him."

"Ay," said De Rennie, "we will hear him very willingly. But," he said, addressing the sailor, "tell no lies, fellow, in hope of escaping your own punishment. Understand that! And understand, also, that you must justify your own desertion."

"I need tell no lies," the man replied, a rough, bull faced and throated man, with every mark of a seaman about him, "to justify myself. And there was no desertion. *Mon Dieu!* was Tourville a deserter when he went ashore from L'Ambitieux? If so, then I am one, for I went with him."

"Tell your tale," De Rennie exclaimed angrily, the

man's utter want of respect irritating him, "and speak no slander against the king's officers."

"Slander!" the sailor repeated—"slander! How slander? I am Tourville's own coxswain; acted under his orders——"

"Go on!" roared the judge. "Your evidence against the prisoner. Your evidence!"

Briefly the man's evidence was this—and as he told it all in the court knew that the fate of the prisoner was sealed. After that nothing could save him.

The man *was* Tourville's coxswain—he produced a filthy, water-soaked paper from his breast to prove it— had been with him in Le Soleil Royal, had gone with the admiral when he transferred his flag to L'Ambitieux, had taken that flag from the lieutenant's hands and, with his own, hauled it up on the latter vessel.

"But," continued the man, "it was not for long. The English had got us in shoal water, their fireships and attenders came at us and burned us; their boarding parties came in two hundred boats—we could do nothing after the first resistance! And among those boarding parties"—and he lifted his finger and pointed at the prisoner in the dock—"was one in command of that man—that, standing there in the dock."

"Fellow!" exclaimed the judge, "this is a Frenchman. Beware!—no lies."

"I tell no lies. It is the truth. Ask him. He was on the deck of L'Ambitieux with a dozen other boat crews; we could not resist; their whole fleet came over our sides; the admiral and I left in the same boat, he bade us all save ourselves, gave us our freedom, disbanded us. Send for him, ask him if I am a deserter. Ask, too, that man, if he fought not against us on the English side."

"You hear," De Rennie said, looking toward St. Georges, "the charge against you—that you, a Frenchman, fought on the English side against your country. Answer the court, is it true?"

With all eyes turned on him—the pitying eyes of De Mortemart, the scowling eyes of the judges, and the vindictive eyes of most people in the court, who, having been hitherto inclined to sympathize with the prisoner, now only thirsted for his death—St. Georges drew himself up and faced his inquirer. Then, a moment later, he said: "It is true."

Those words were the signal for an indescribable hubbub in the court. Men muttered fiercely, "Burn him, burn him!" women shrieked to one another that no wonder the English devils had beaten France when Frenchmen fought on their side, forgetting the mothers that bore them; and De Mortemart, muttering between white lips: "My God! nothing can save him," left the court. The coxswain, too, who but a quarter of an hour before had heard hissed in his ears the words "lâche," "déserteur," "misérable," and other epithets, was now the centre of a group of turnkeys and exempts, all asking him why he had not told them before that he was a hero?

Meanwhile the *procureur du roi*, arrayed in his scarlet gown, sat at his table arranging his papers—there would be no further trials that day, he knew, the Jansenists and others would have to wait—and glancing up now and again at the other three scarlet-robed figures on the bench, conferring with their heads close together. Presently, however, a nod from De Rennie to the *greffier* caused that official to bawl out orders for silence in the court, and forced the muttering men and shrieking women to hold their tongues. They did so, willingly enough, too; they knew what was coming.

"Are your lordships prepared to deliver judgment?" asked the *procureur du roi*, carrying out the usual formula and pushing his papers away and rising as he addressed them.

"We are prepared," the president replied.

"I pray your lordships do so."

"The sentence of the court is that the prisoner be taken to the Hôtel de Ville, and from there to the Place de Grève, and there broken on the wheel till he is dead."

More murmurings, more exclamations from the nervous, excited crowd, and then a hush, while again the *procureur's* voice was heard:

"I pray your lordships to appoint a day and hour on which your righteous sentence shall be carried out."

"The decree of the court is that the sentence be carried out at the daybreak following the time when forty-eight hours shall have elapsed from now."

"In the name of justice I thank your lordships.— Prisoner," and the *procureur* turned to him, "you hear and understand your sentence?"

"Yes, I hear and understand it."

CHAPTER XXXII.

THE LAST CHANCE.

OUTSIDE the court all was sunshine and brightness on that June evening, and all the people streaming out in the warm air—that yet seemed fresh and cool after

18

the stuffiness within—chattered and laughed and chuckled at the exciting day they had had.

"For, *figurez vous*," said one, a hideous creature, "when we went to see the marchioness tried we could only hope she would be condemned, though all the while we know well that for the *noblesse* there is no serious punishment. *Ma foi!* what a punishment! Twenty pistoles—a sum she pays weekly, I'll be sworn, for absolution—and a *retraite* from Paris for a year. *Tiens!* she was not ill favoured, that marchioness; she will doubtless have a score of lovers follow her into the country. Say, Babette," and she turned to a pale-faced girl by her side, "shall we go to the Place de Grève to see that villain broken? Daybreak, after forty-eight hours; that will be daybreak on Monday. To-day is Friday!"

"Not I," the pale-faced girl replied. "For my part I could pity him—only that he fought against France. *It etait beau, cet homme la bas.* His mustache was enough to set a girl dreaming. And his eyes! *Ciel!* what eyes, when he faced the old *hérisson*, De Rennie!"

"Ah, bah! His eyes! Curse them, and him, too! He is a traitor."

"All the same, he is handsome. I wonder how many women love him?"

But now they stood apart from the courtyard to look at a troop of the Mousquetaires Noirs riding away from the precincts of the court itself—where they had been on guard all day—and to admire their trappings and bravery. And the pale-faced girl, who seemed—like many other pale-faced, cadaverous girls!—to have a great appreciation of manly beauty, tugged at her companion's arm, and bade' her observe the two handsome officers in conversation under the gateway.

"See, Manon, see!" she exclaimed. "There is the one who said he was son to the Duc de——"

"I hate all dukes," interrupted the other, "and all the *noblesse*. They grind the poor."

"Yet he seemed kind. He would have saved that one, I do believe, if he could. And how he spoke to the judge—as he himself speaks to others—like to a dog! And his companion, the officer of Mousquetaires who does not follow the troop. *Mon Dieu! il est beau aussi.* How many handsome men we see to-day!"

"*Ah! voyons*," exclaimed the other, grimacing irritably, "*les beaux! les beaux!* Nothing but *les beaux!* Some day, Babette, you will regret your admiration of the men."

"He looks pale and troubled, does that mousquetaire," the girl replied, taking no heed of the elder woman's reproofs; and then they passed on to the foul quarter of Paris where they dwelt, and where dukes' sons and handsome mousquetaires did not often obtrude themselves.

Had she been able to overhear the commencement of the conversation between De Mortemart and that officer of Mousquetaires she would probably not have wondered at the pallor which overspread the latter's face, nor at his look of trouble.

When the young fellow had fled out of the court, unable to remain and hear that doom pronounced on St. Georges, which he knew must come, he had gone straight to the guardroom with the intention of removing the three men of his troop whom he had brought with him to Paris in charge of their prisoner. Their work was done in Paris, he knew; it was best they should take the road back to Rambouillet at once. It was but eight leagues, and the summer nights were long; they could ride that easily and regain their quarters almost without halting.

But as he entered the room set apart for officers preparatory to summoning his men, he saw that which prevented him from doing so for some little time longer. He saw, seated in a deep wooden chair, his wig off, and fast asleep in that chair—with a flask of wine by his side—an officer of the guard for the day, whose face he knew very well indeed. The Régiment de Grancé was not always quartered at such dead-and-alive places as Rambouillet; it was sometimes accorded the privilege of being in attendance on the court itself—since it was officered from the aristocrats as a rule, the colonel generally being an exception, and selected because of his services—and at Versailles it had, not long ago, been thrown in with the Mousquetaires Noirs.

" *Tiens*, Boussac!" the young fellow cried, slapping the sleeping officer on the shoulder, and disturbing his slumbers; " rouse yourself, man; the court will be up directly—already your brother officer is chuckling that his guard hour will not last half a one."

" De Mortemart!" cried Boussac, springing from his seat and grasping the newcomer's hand with his own, while with the other he clapped his wig on. " De Mortemart—what brings you here? Have you got the route, is the regiment returned to Paris?"

" No such chance, *mon ami*, our luck is out. Neither Paris, nor, *ma foi!* a campaign for us—we are stewed up in Rambouillet for another year. And, *peste!* the only woman there worth a pistole has turned out the vilest of creatures. We cannot even sup with her now, or take a glass of ratafia or a cup of chocolate from her hands."

" That is not well. But what—what—brings you

here? Come, tell me," and drawing the wine flask toward him he poured out a drink for his comrade. "And you look sad, De Mortemart; is it because of the ' vilest of creatures '?"

Then, without more ado, his friend told what had brought him to Paris and in the vicinity of the *cours criminel.*

As he proceeded with his story—telling it all from the beginning, when la belle Louvigny had sent to the commandant, apprising him of an escaped *galérien* in her house—he marvelled at the excitement which took possession of his auditor. At the statement that the betrayed man was branded, was in truth an escaped galley slave, Boussac had sprung to his feet and commenced to pace the guardroom; when he described the scene he had witnessed between him and Madame de Louvigny, he could contain himself no longer.

" The man, De Mortemart, the man!" he broke out, " describe him to me." And without giving his friend time to do so, he went on :

" Tall, slight, long brown hair, curling at the ends, gray eyes—deep and clear. Gentleman to the tips of his fingers; a soldier above all."

" Ay, he has been a soldier."

" And his name—his name, my friend. It must be St. Georges. Come from England, you say, with the English fleet. It *is* St. Georges!"

" Nay, his name he will not tell. But this I know: he was once of the Chevaux-Légers of Nivernois."

" My God! it is he!" and overcome with excitement Boussac sank back into his seat again.

Rapidly De Mortemart told the rest—the coxswain's evidence; the certain doom that must be St. Georges's must be pronounced by now, since, outside, the clatter of the Mousquetaires could be heard, proclaiming already clearly enough that the court was up, the sentence awarded.

"I must know all!" Boussac cried, and followed by the other he rushed out. And then he learned the *galérien's* doom—wheel on the third morning from now.

No wonder the pale-faced girl thought he looked sad as he stood in the gateway bidding De Mortemart a hasty farewell.

"If I can," he said, "I must save him; must if necessary see the king. I am mousquetaire—I have the right of audience."

"Nothing can save him," the other replied. "He has served Louis, and he has fought against him—on the conquering side. That is enough!"

"Yet," said Boussac, "I will try. I can tell Louis something of his history that may—though the chance is poor, God knows!—induce him to hold his hand. Or, at least, to let the doom be something less awful than the wheel."

So they parted, the one to take his men back to Rambouillet, the other to try and save St. Georges, vain as he feared the attempt would be.

First, he sought a messenger, a trusty honest man he knew of, himself an old disbanded soldier, and told him he must ride that night on a message of life and death. Would he promise to let nothing stand in his way?—he should be well rewarded.

"Never fear, monsieur. To where must I ride?"

"To Troyes. You can obtain a good horse?"

"Ay! or get a *renfort* on the road. 'Tis thirty leagues, but I will manage it. What have I to do when there?"

"This. Make for the Manoir de Roquemaure, then

see at once *la châtelaine*, Mademoiselle de Roquemaure—
she rules it since her mother's death. Next, give her
this. Put it into her own hand and no other. In
the name of God fail not! Again I say, it is life or
death!"

"Fear not. I will not fail. In half an hour I am
on the road. Hark! the clock strikes from the Tour St.
Jacques; 'tis seven o'clock—ere it strikes the same hour
in the morning I shall be there and to spare—or dead.'"

"Brave man! Good soldier! I believe you. Go."

What the old soldier was to give into the hand of
Aurélie de Roquemaure was a letter containing the following hastily scribbled words:

"MADEMOISELLE: You spoke to me once of an unhappy gentleman, a *chevau-léger ;* asked me if he was
dead, and said you had some news would make him
happy if he knew it. Mademoiselle, he is not dead, but
dies on Monday, on the wheel—Monday morning next
at dawn! He has returned to France, fought against
Tourville on the high seas, is taken, and, as I say, condemned. If you have any power with the king, if you
know aught that may weigh with him, I beseech you
lose no effort. It is Monday morning, I repeat, at
dawn that he dies. Your respectful servitor,

"BOUSSAC."

The messenger departed—and about his fidelity he
had no doubt, so well did he know him—Boussac
mounted his horse and rode to where the three troops
of the Mousquetaires now in Paris on guard duty were
quartered. Then he made his way to the senior officer
in command, begged leave of him on urgent matters of
the last importance—so urgent, indeed, did he represent

them to be that he stated he was about to seek an after-supper audience of the king—obtained the leave, and, procuring a fresh horse, set out for Versailles.

"I will tell him," he said, "who St. Georges is, whom he believes himself to be. The late duke was Louis's friend in the days when the king's heart was young and fresh—surely he will, at least, grant a reprieve. More especially if I tell him all of De Roquemaure's villainy. As for the sister—if she is what St. Georges told me in his last letter he felt convinced she was—she will do nothing. Yet, *mon Dieu! mon Dieu!* who can look in those eyes as I have done and deem her so vile? Surely, surely, though he stands in her way so much, she will not let him go to his doom. Even though she knows for certain he is De Vannes, she will strive to save him. She must!"

It was no easy thing to approach Louis at the after-supper audience, free as the monarch generally made himself for an hour at that period, and in spite of an officer of the Mousquetaires being a more or less favoured person. For there were many who had greater claims than a mousquetaire to the royal ear, the royal salutation—a finger to the hat for a man, the hat lowered to the right ear for a lady—to the royal smile.

There were, to wit, the bishops, the ladies of the court, the marshals and the bastards, the ministers and many others. And to-night the king was, and had been for some days, so depressed, so for him almost angry, that few took this period for presenting petitions or requests. His great fleet was shattered by the hereditary enemies of France—since the Spanish Armada no fleet had ever been so shattered!—his power and might were broken, even if for a time only; and though he had told Tourville—with that royal graciousness which scarcely ever deserted him—that he was satisfied "he had done his best," he was in no humour for granting boons.

What hope was there that a mousquetaire should obtain aught from him that night; should even be able to approach him? Above all, what hope that such a request as Boussac's—that one of his own subjects who had helped in the shattering of his great fleet should be pardoned—was likely to be granted?

Yet, at last, the soldier who had waited so patiently for hours drew nearer and nearer to the circle in which the arbiter of the destiny of all in France sat, a crowd of courtiers and nervous petitioners behind and round him; at last, after having seen countless others bowed and smiled to, he was face to face with Louis, stammering and scarce knowing how to begin his request.

But the finger went to the hat, the king's smile—perhaps a little artificial now—shone on him, the king's soft, courtly voice said:

"Monsieur le lieutenant, have you a petition to make also? I am afraid it cannot be granted. Is it for promotion?"

"No, sire. It is for a man's life," and before he thoroughly understood, himself, what he was saying, he poured out his story before the king and the astonished listeners. And, at last, in a halting, laboured way it was told. Then the king spoke, while the shoulder-shrugging, grinning courtiers held their breath to hear his reply.

"Mon brave mousquetaire," he said, "you have been imposed on. De Vannes never married. I know it well—know, too, the woman whom he loved, who married De Roquemaure. And even if he had married and had this son, do you think I would pardon him for doing that for which he lies under sentence of death? Nay,

were he my own I would not do so. Ah!"—turning to
a beautiful blue-eyed woman who stood by the side of
Boussac, " Madame de Verneuil "—and the hand went up
to the hat and lowered it till the fringe touched his right
ear—" I rejoice to see you here to-night."

Boussac's audience was over.

CHAPTER XXXIII.

THE DAY OF EXECUTION.

THE night of Sunday had passed; already the holiday-makers were seeking their beds after a day spent in
the country—by some in the woods of Fontainebleau
and St. Germains; by others in the gardens of Versailles, where they had waited all day to see the king
come out upon the great balcony and salute his people;
by others, again, who had been to Marly to gaze in
amazement on distorted Nature; to gaze on the trees
stuck in the ground which would not grow here though
they had flourished for a century elsewhere, before being
uprooted to gratify a king's caprice; on artificial lakes
now gay with *caïques* and gondolas where but a few
years ago the frogs and eels had held undisputed possession; on a palace which reared its new walls where
starving peasants' hovels had been not long since.

The holiday-makers were going home to their beds
as all the clocks of the city clanged out the hour of
midnight; all were about to seek their homes ere they
commenced the new week—a week that to most of
them brought nothing but hard, griping toil, starvation,
and a heavy load of taxation imposed upon them by

THE DAY OF EXECUTION.

that king whom they stared at and reverenced, and by his nobility.

Yet not quite all, either! For some there were who, as they streamed across the Pont Neuf, or came in from the Charenton gate, or arrived back from Versailles or Marly, broke off in solitary twos and threes from the others and directed their footsteps toward the great *place* in front of the Hôtel de Ville—toward the *Place de Grève!* They, these solitary ones, had no intention of seeking their homes and beds that night—they could sleep long and well to-morrow night—instead they meant to enjoy themselves in the *place* until day broke, with the anticipation of what the daybreak would bring. For at that hour they knew they would see a man done to death upon the wheel; see limb after limb broken until life was extinguished by the final *côup de grâce.*

As they neared the great open space some cast their eyes up at the lights burning in the Hôtel de Ville and muttered to each other, wondering which room the man was in who would be led forth three hours hence; what he was thinking of; if he was counting each quarter as it sounded from tower and steeple; if—these speculations generally by women in the fast-gathering crowd —there were any who loved him? If he had a wife—a mother—a child? Any to mourn his loss?

"A traitor, they say," some whispered; "one who joined England against France." "A spy," others murmured, "who betrayed Tourville to the brutal islanders. Well, he deserves the dog's death! Let him endure it."

The quarters boomed forth again; at half past twelve the executioner and his assistants arrived in a cart. Ordinarily they came earlier when they had a scaffold to erect and a block to place upon it. Now, however, there was no block on which the man's head would need to be laid to receive the headsman's stroke. Instead, a great cannon wheel was lifted from out the cart, then next a wooden platform was constructed, having in it a socket of raised wood into which the wheel was dropped and firmly fixed by cords, three parts of it towering above that socket. Then a heap of ropes brought forth and flung down beside the wheel—they would secure the body tightly enough—following the heap two huge iron bars and a heavy iron-bound club. That was all, yet enough to do justice on the traitor.

"*La toilette de la Roue est faite,*" said one man, a joker; "soon his will be made also. 'Tis well the early mornings are warm now. He will not miss his clothes so much when they strip him to his singlet," and he laughed and grinned like a wolf and turned his eyes on the Hôtel de Ville. And still, as the moments and the quarters crept by, they chattered and talked about the coming *spectacle*, and wondered how the man felt in there who was now so shortly to furnish it. If they could have seen him, have been able to read his thoughts, they would have been little gratified—perhaps, indeed, a little dissatisfied—for he knew as well as they that his doom was fast approaching, that the clocks were telling of his fast-ebbing hours on earth; knew, too, that down below the wheel was being prepared, and bore the knowledge calmly and with resignation.

As they discussed down in the *place* what he might be doing and speculated on what his feelings were in those last hours, he above, at the iron-barred window of a room to which they had brought him after his sentence was pronounced, was gazing down at the crowd gathering to see him die. The feelings on which they speculated so much were scarcely such as would have satisfied them.

"The dawn breaks," he murmured to himself, as, although heavily chained both at the feet and hands, he leaned against the window and gazed far away over the roofs of the houses to, across the Seine, where the mists rose in the fields—"is near at hand. Another hour and daylight will have come—and then it is ended! So best!—so best!"

He shifted his position a little, still gazing out, however; then continued his meditations:

"Yes, so best. My last chance, last hope of life was gone when M. de Mortemart trusted me—let me ride by his side a free man instead of bound. Then I knew I must go on—come on—to this. I could have stabbed him to the heart more than once—have perhaps evaded even his three men—have escaped—been free—but how! By treachery unparalleled, by murder and deceit! And, afterward, a life of reproach and self-contempt. No! better this—better that wheel below than such a freedom!"

Looking down now at the crowd, his attention was called to it by a slight stir in its midst; he saw a troop of dragoons ride in to the *place* and observed them distributing themselves all round it at equal distance under the orders of an officer. Also he saw that a lane was made to the platform where the wheel stood—a lane among the people that ended at the platform and began he knew at the door of the Hôtel de Ville beneath him, from which he would be led forth.

"Courage," he whispered to himself, "courage. It will not be long; they say the first blow sometimes brings insensibility, and after that there is no more. Only death—death! Death with my little child's name upon my lips—that name the last word I shall ever speak; my last thoughts a prayer for her."

Gradually now he let himself sink to the floor, his manacles almost preventing him from doing so, and when in a kneeling position he buried his head in his ironbound hands and prayed long and fervently.

"O God," he murmured, "thou who hast in thy wisdom torn her from me, keep and guard her ever, I beseech thee, in this my darkest hour; let her never know her father's sorrow, nor share the adversity thou hast thought fit to visit upon him. And, since I may never gaze on her face again, see her whom I have so dearly loved, so mourned for, never hear the tones of her voice, be thou her earthly as her heavenly Father; sleeping and waking, oh, watch over her still!"

Then, because the thoughts of her were more than he could bear, and because he knew that the child whom he had loved so dearly—the child whose future life he had once sworn solemnly to her dying mother should be dearer to him than his own—would never know his fate nor his regrets, he buried his head once more in those manacled hands and wailed: "My child! my child! My little lost child! Oh, my child! my child!

"If I could only know," he murmured, later, "that you were well, happy—feel sure, as that woman told me once herself, and Boussac thought—that whoever has you in his keeping was not cruel to you, my little, helpless child, the end might be easier. If I could only know! O Dorine! Dorine!"

Looking up, as he strove with his two hands, so tightly chained together, to wipe the tears from his eyes, he noticed that the room was lighter now; the sky was a clear daffodil. Daybreak was coming; the day was at hand—his last on earth!

And again he whispered: "It is better so. But for her there is naught to hold me to life. Better so.

Now"—and as he spoke to himself, across the roofs of the houses the first rays of the summer sun shot up—" now be brave. The end is near; meet it like a man. And remember, her name the last word on your lips—the last ere your soul goes to meet its God!"

A murmur, a noise from the crowd below waiting for its victim, caused him to look forth again from the window, and to observe that some new officials had arrived. A horseman in a rich scarlet coat, over which, however, he wore a riding cloak—for the morning was still chilly—followed by two others in sober blue coats trimmed with silver lace, was making his way down the lane of people and was being greeted by the crowd.

Yet, to the doomed man standing by the window, he did not seem to be altogether popular with them, especially when he suddenly halted his horse, and turning round on the vast concourse behind him, said something to them, accompanied with a comprehensive wave of his disengaged hand—something that vexed and annoyed that concourse terribly, he could see, and hear, too—a vexation increased when, after the other had spoken a further word to the officer in command of the dragoons, they began to close in from the outside of the *place* round the assembled mob.

Then the horseman disappeared from St. Georges's view, evidently having entered the door beneath his window, and again the people murmured and shrieked.

" Has he given orders to clear them away," he began to speculate, " so that they may not witness my end?——" but his speculation was not concluded.

On the stone steps outside he could hear the tread of many feet, the clang of spurs and of swords as those who wore them mounted the stairs.

" They are coming for me," he thought, and again

he whispered: "The time is at hand. Courage! Be
brave!"

The keys turned grating in the locks, a great trans-
verse bar outside was moved with a clash, and the door
opened, the first person to enter being the newly arrived
horseman, followed by the principal official of the Hôtel
de Ville, and next by some of his subordinate officers,
as well as the jailers, one of whom carried in his
hands a large iron hammer and the other a great bunch
of keys.

And St. Georges, standing there facing them, looked
as brave a gentleman as any who had ever been led to
his fate.

"This is the condemned man?" the horseman asked
of the chief official; "the man who was sentenced at
the *cours criminel* on Friday last to die this morning?"

"It is the man, Monsieur l'Hérault," the official replied, his questioner being none other than L'Hérault,
the head of the police system.

"Remove his irons."

At this order the two jailers stepped forward, the
one unlocking the fetters that bound St. Georges's
hands, the other knocking away with the hammer the
iron pegs that ran through the steel ring which held the
chains round his ankles. And in less than three moments chains and fetters lay at his feet.

"Here is the warrant," L'Hérault said, handing it
to the governor of the Hôtel de Ville—for such the
principal official by his side was—"read it aloud to the
prisoner," and it was read accordingly. It ran:

"To M. l'Hérault, superintendent of our police, and
to the governor of our Hôtel de Ville at Paris:

"It is our royal will that the prisoner tried at our

cours criminel by M. Barthe de la Rennie, one of our judges, and sentenced to die on the morning of Monday, the 26th June of this year 1692, be released and set free unconditionally. And may——"

" What!" exclaimed St. Georges, reeling backward, and speaking in a hoarse whisper—"what! what does this mean? Who has written that?"

"The king," L'Hérault answered. Then he said briefly, " You are free."

" Free! Not to go to—to that?" and he pointed below.

" Not to go to that—though 'tis where escaped *galériens* usually go sooner or later. Your time is not yet come, it seems. I know no more, except that at midnight I was roused from my bed to ride here with this," pointing to the paper in the governor's hand, "and with this," putting another in St. Georges's. " It will," he continued, " bear you harmless in France so long as you offend no more."

" Sir," St. Georges said, and as he spoke L'Hérault looked at him, wondering if in truth this was an innocent man before him, " for your errand of mercy I thank you. Yet, believe me or not as you will, I had committed no sin when I went to the galleys."

Then he read the paper handed to him. It also was brief :

" The man bearing this is to be held free of arrest on any charge and to be allowed to pass in freedom through all and any of our dominions. His name is Georges St. Georges, and he is branded with the *fleur-de-lis* and the letter G. *Signé*, LOUIS R."

19

"What does it mean?" reiterated St. Georges. "Who can have done this?"

"It means," said L'Hérault, "that you have some powerful interest with his Majesty. Whomsoever you may be, even though you were one of the king's own sons, you must be deemed fortunate. However great your friends may be, your escape is remarkable."

"Friends! I have none. I——" but the sentence was never finished. The excitement of the last hour had overmastered him at last and he sank in a swoon before them.

When he came to himself the others were gone with the exception of one turnkey, who was kneeling by his side, supporting his head and moistening his lips with brandy. But in the place of those who had departed there was another now, a man at whom St. Georges stared with uncertain eyes as though doubting whether his senses were not still playing him false; a man also on one knee by his side, clad in the handsome uniform of the Mousquetaires Noirs.

"Boussac!" he exclaimed. "Boussac! Is it in truth you?"

"It is I, my friend."

Then, as St. Georges's senses came fully back to him, he seized the other's hand and murmured: "You! It is you have done this! Through you that I am saved."

"You are saved, my friend. That is enough. What matter by whom?"

CHAPTER XXXIV.

"I WILL NEVER FORGIVE HER."

ONCE more St. Georges was on the road, heading straight for Troyes, and by-his side once more rode a friend, as he had ridden over four years ago—Boussac!

When he had thoroughly recovered from the swoon into which he had fallen on hearing that he was free, he had again and again overwhelmed the mousquetaire with his gratitude—all of which the latter had refused to accept, and had, indeed, gently repudiated. Also it seemed to St. Georges that he avoided the subject, or at least said as little as possible.

"If," he said, when at last they were seated in an inn off the new Rue Richelieu to which he had led St. Georges, "there is anything to which you owe your freedom more than another, it is to the fact that the king must recognise that you are in truth le Duc de Vannes, the son of his earliest friend. Yet—yet"—he continued in an embarrassed manner—"he would not even allow that that should influence him—when—I pleaded for you.

"But it did—it did, Boussac, it did. He must have pondered on it afterward—perhaps reflected on how unjustly I had been treated by his vile minister, Louvois—you say he died in disgrace?—and that may have—nay, must have, turned his heart. O Boussac! how am I ever to repay you? Without your thought and exertions what should I have been now?" and he shuddered as he spoke.

"Oh! la! la!" said Boussac, "never mind about

me. The question is now what do you intend to do in the future?"

"Do!" exclaimed St. Georges. "Do! Why, that which I returned to France to do, fought against France for—obtain my child. Boussac, where is that woman now?"

"Woman!—what woman?"

"Ah! Boussac, do not joke. You know very well to what woman I refer. That young tigress—in her way almost as vile as the woman Louvigny!—the woman who stole my child."

"Mademoiselle de Roquemaure?"

"Ay, Mademoiselle de Roquemaure! That is the name. Oh Boussac! you have given me more than my life, far more. The power to wrench my child away from her keeping, to stand before her a freed man, the king's pardon in my hand, and tax her with her treachery."

"You will do that?"

"Do it! What am I going to Troyes for—to-night?"

"Ay, true! True! What are you going to Troyes for? Yet I should have thought, if you recover the child, it is enough. Why—say—bitter words?"

"Boussac, you—but, there, you are not a father; you cannot understand all I have suffered in these four years past. Why! man, the galleys, my exile, the death that yawned for me this morning, were easier than the loss of my little one. And, with her dying brother's own confession ringing in my ears still, as it will ring when I stand before her to-morrow, as I hope, you ask me what need I have to reproach her—to utter bitter words?"

The mousquetaire shrugged his shoulders; then

he muttered something about the recovery of the child being everything, and that reproaches brought little satisfaction with them; and after that he again asked St. Georges when he meant to set out for Troyes?

" To-night, I tell you—to-night. Yet "—and he paused bewildered—" I—I have no money. Not enough to get me a horse, at least. They have given me back all they took from me after my condemnation, but there were only a few guineas left."

" Where is the horse you rode to Paris on when De Mortemart brought you? "

" Ah! " exclaimed St. Georges, " a good horse— though, alas! at a moment when my life was in danger and a horse alone could save me, I—I stole it. Oh, if I can but get that again! "

" Why not? It is doubtless in the stables behind the *cours criminel,* where the guard stable theirs."

It was there; so that difficulty was soon solved, no objection being offered by the authorities to giving up the property of a prisoner who was so distinguished as to be acquitted by the king's order an hour before his execution; and then, when St. Georges had recovered it, he announced his intention of at once setting forth. He was impatient to be gone now he was so near; he calculated that by midday on the morrow he would have forced from Aurélie de Rouquemaure a confession of what she had done with Dorine. She was at Troyes he knew; Boussac, who professed himself well acquainted with her movements, having told him that such was the ' case.

" She is much at court now," he said; " I often see her. And she must be back at Troyes by now—I mean —that—she has been absent from there of late. But—

but she would be back by now—she—told me—she was——"

"What?" asked St. Georges, looking at him and wondering why he seemed so incoherent about the woman's movements; wondering also how he came to know so much about them, especially her recent ones—"what did she tell you when last you saw her?"

"That—she has been paying a visit—to—to—assist a friend—but——"

"Her friendship seems as strong as her hate—and greed," muttered St. Georges.

"But that," Boussac continued, still floundering a good deal in his speech, "she would be at the manoir last night—yes, last night."

"So. Then she will doubtless be there to-morrow also; she will require rest after rendering her friend so much assistance. I shall find her there."

"*We* shall find her there," Boussac answered. "I am going with you."

"You! Why?" Then he laughed—for the first time for many a day. "Do you think I am in danger now, with Louis's protection in my pocket, or," and his brow darkened a little, "do you fear that she is in danger from me?"

"*Mon ami*," Boussac replied, "I think neither of those things. The king's permission has made you safe —your manhood makes her so. Yet, let me ride with you. Remember"—and again he halted in his speech, as though seeking for a suitable reason for accompanying him—"we rode together when *la petite* was about to be lost to you; let us do so now when, I hope most fervently, she is about to be restored to you. And, my friend, I have obtained leave—we Mousquetaires are always fortunate in getting that. Do not deny me!"

"Deny you!—you! The man who saved me! I am an ingrate even to question you," and he seized the black gantleted hand of the other and wrung it hard.

After that there was no more to be said or done ere they set out—or only one thing. Boussac had mentioned that he had a friend, a dragoon officer, who was proceeding to La Hogue to join his regiment which was still there under Bellefond's command, and by him St. Georges sent twenty pistoles to be given to Dubois, the man who owned the horse which saved his life. He borrowed the money of Boussac, described the inn where he had seized the animal, and then mounted it for the first time with a feeling of satisfaction. "'Tis a good beast," he said, "and has done me loyal service; also it has well replaced another good one—that on which I rode from Pontarlier to Paris and never saw again. How long ago that seems, Boussac!"

"Ay," replied the other, "but it was winter then and the clouds were lowering over your life and her you loved—now 'tis summer, and all is well with you."

"I pray God! I have suffered my share."

All through that summer night they rode—resting their horses occasionally at country inns, then going on again, though slowly, and at dawn changing them for others and leaving them to rest until they should return that way. And so at last they neared Troyes, passing through the little town of Nogent, and seeing, ten miles off, the spire of the cathedral glistening in the rays of the bright sun.

"She will not know me," St. Georges had said more than once, as he thought of Dorine. "She was a babe when I lost her, now she is a child possessing speech and intelligence. May God grant it is not too late; that she is not too old yet to learn to love me!"

"Courage! *mon ami*, courage!" exclaimed Boussac, repeating a formula he had adopted from the first; "all must be well."

But—it was natural—as they approached their destination, the goal from which St. Georges hoped so much, his nervousness increased terribly and he began to speculate as to whether the child might not after all be dead; if, perhaps, she might not have lain in her little grave for long. "And then how will it be with me, Boussac? Oh! if she is dead how shall I reckon with the woman who possessed herself of her?"

"Courage!" again repeated the mousquetaire, "I do not believe she is dead. And if mademoiselle did seize upon her—well, she is a woman! a better nurse than the bishop's servant."

"Ah! the bishop's servant! That too has to be explained. What was he doing with her? I have wondered all these years—De Roquemaure's dying words told nothing. 'He had got her safe,' he gasped at the last. But why he? Why he! Oh! shall I ever know all?"

"Ere long, I hope, my friend," said Boussac, "ere long now."

As he spoke, they mounted the last hill that guarded the capital of Champagne and approached the summit. When there, they would be able to look down upon the old city—nay, more, from there they would scarce be a musket shot from the manoir, surrounded now by its ripening vineyards and its woods. She, the kidnapper of his child, would be in his grasp, must answer his demand!

Upon the summit of that hill still stood the gibbet

on which the peasant woman's husband had swung, but the body was gone—long since, doubtless—and the gallows tree was bare. "Perhaps," said St. Georges, "the poor thing obtained him decent burial at last. I hope so." Then, seeing a peasant coming along the road, he spoke to him, and asked him what had become of the corpse that hung there four years ago? The fellow looked up at him sullenly enough and stared hard for some moments; then he said:

"You are not De Roquemaure?"

"Nay."

"What affair is it then of yours?"

St. Georges explained briefly to him how he had met the dead man's wife and pitied her, and asked where she was.

"Mad," the man said. "Quite mad. Her brother keeps her." Then he muttered: "A curse on the De Roquemaures, and on him above all! His father was bad; he is worse."

"You need curse him no more," St. Georges answered; "he is dead!"

"Dead is he? Then he was the last; the woman counts not. Dead! Oh, that she whom he injured so could understand it! Dead, thank God! I would it were so with all aristocrats! France has suffered long."

A hundred years almost were to elapse ere the peasant's hopes were to be partly realized, and others like the De Roquemaures to meet their reward; but none foresaw it in those days. Later the clouds gathered, but even then the fury of the coming storm was not perceived.

"Give her this," said St. Georges, putting some of his few remaining pieces in his hand, he having provided himself with French gold for his English guineas.

"Or give it to the brother who has charge of her. I, too, have suffered at the hands of the De Roquemaures."

"And you forgive?" glancing up from the pistoles in his hand to the dark, stern face above him. "You forgive?"

"Not yet!"

Then he urged on his horse again, Boussac following him.

"But you will, my friend, you will," he said, as they rode down the slope. "In the name of the good God who forgives all, forgive her, I implore you!"

"Forgive her? I will never forgive her! I have forgiven that other who lies in a thousand pieces at the bottom of the sea, but her reckoning is yet to come. She stole my child from me, she lied to me in Paris, sympathized with me on my loss when, at the time, she knew where that child was; drove me to draw on Louvois, and thereby to my ruin. I will never forgive her! And if she now refuses to restore the child, then— But enough! Come," and shaking his horse's reins he rode down the vine-clad roads to the front of the manoir.

It frowned as before on the slope below it, presented on this bright summer morning as grim, impassable a front as on that winter night when first he drew rein outside it; beyond the huge hatchment now nailed on its front in memory of the late marquise nothing was changed. It looked to St. Georges's eyes a fitting place to enshroud the evil doings of the family he had hated so bitterly, and of the one representative now left whom he hated too.

Seizing the horn as he had seized it long ago in the murkiness of that winter night, he blew upon it and then waited to be answered. He had not long to do so;

a moment later the old warder who had once before opened the small door under the *tourelle* stood before him.

"Is Mademoiselle de Roquemaure in her house?" he asked sternly, while Boussac, sitting his horse behind him, uttered no word.

"She is in her house, monsieur."

"You know me. I have been here before. Say I have ridden express from Paris to see her and must do so at once."

"I will say so, monsieur. Be pleased to enter."

CHAPTER XXXV.

AT LAST.

It seemed almost as if he had been expected from his appearance being received in so matter-of-fact a way. Yet, he reflected, why should it be otherwise? Aurélie de Roquemaure could scarce know of all that had happened to him of late—above all could not be aware that he had become possessed of the information that she was the kidnapper of Dorine.

He had, however, but little time for reflection since Boussac was by his side, and, when they dismounted from their horses, had followed him into the large sombre hall to which the old servant had led the way. Yet, when the man had gone to seek his mistress, the latter took one more opportunity to plead that he should be gentle with her.

"Remember," he said, "remember, I beseech you, that you have but her brother's word for what you sus-

pect her of; he was a villain, ho might have lied in his
last moments for some reason—perhaps did not even
think those last moments were in truth at hand; might
have hoped to escape after all and profit by the lie.
Remember! Oh, remember!"

"I will remember," St. Georges said. Then, with
one glance at Boussac, he added, "But the villain did
not lie *then!*"

The domestic came back, and St. Georges learned
that the hour for his explanation, long sought and meditated upon, was at hand. "His mistress would see
monsieur," he said. He would conduct him to her.

In the same room where he had first set eyes on
Aurélie de Roquemaure he saw her again—the old man
ushering him in and then swiftly leaving the room.
They were face to face at last! As it had been before,
so it was now—her beauty as she rose on his entrance
was strikingly apparent, compelled regard. And the
four years that had passed since that first meeting had
done much to increase, to ripen that beauty; instead of
the budding girl it was a stately woman who now met
his eyes. And the contrast between them was great,
was all to her advantage so far as exterior matters were
concerned: he travel-stained, worn, and with now in his
long hair some streaks of gray; she fresh and beautiful
in the long black lace dress she wore, a rose in her
bosom, her hair undisguised by any wig and swept back
into a huge knot behind. "How beautiful she is!" he
thought, as he gave her one glance, "yet how base and
contemptible!"

With a swift movement she came toward him from
the further end of the room, her hands extended and
her eyes sparkling, exclaiming as she advanced: "You
are free! you are free!" But her greeting met with no

response from him. Could she have expected it, he wondered? Then he stepped back and coldly said:

"Yes, Mademoiselle de Roquemaure, I am free," while to himself he said: "So she knew that too. That I was trapped! God! That womankind can be so base!"

Staggered at the coldness of his first words, affronted at his refusal to take her outstretched hands, she drew back and looked at him calmly. Then she said, quietly, "I rejoice to know it," and, pausing, looked at him again.

"Mademoiselle de Roquemaure," he said, "I have not ridden here from Paris, from a prison which at one time I scarce thought to leave except for the wheel, to interchange idle compliments. I have come here with one set purpose, to learn what you have done with my child—the child you stole from the Bishop of Lodève's servant on the morning that your servant gave that man his death wound."

His eyes were intent upon her as he spoke, watching her eagerly. Yet, to his surprise, she neither started nor paled at his accusation. Instead, she said quietly:

"You know that?"

"Yes," he replied; "I know it."

"And your informant was——?"

"Your brother, or half-brother. With his dying words."

· "He was slain at La Hogue; ah, yes! you were there! I remember. Was it you who slew him?"

"No; but, pardon me, it is not about Monsieur de Roquemaure that I have come here. The De Roquemaures and I have had enough intercourse." And now he saw that he had touched her, since she grew pale as death. "There will be no need of any further when

once my child is restored to me.   Mademoiselle, I have
come to demand that child of you.   Where is she—what
have you done with her?"

For answer she advanced to a bell rope, and, pulling
it, said to the servant when he appeared, "Send Mademoiselle de Vannes to me."

"Mademoiselle de Vannes!" he exclaimed, "Mademoiselle de Vannes!   You call her that—you know——"

"I know."

He raised his hand to his forehead with a gesture of
bewilderment, then said, "And you keep her here?"

"She is here, monseigneur," as the door opened once
more; "here is your child."

Even as she spoke a bright-haired child ran into the
room and, rushing toward Mademoiselle de Roquemaure,
caught her by the hands and buried her face in her
dress, while she whispered :

"Aurélie, dear sister Aurélie, why do you send for
me now when I am so hard at work with Père Antoine?
And who is this stranger?   What does he want?"

"Who is this stranger?"   At those words St.
Georges's heart gave a throb—he said afterward that he
thought it would cease to beat—and the room swam
round with him.   He had found the child of many long-
ings—and he was a stranger!   A moment later he heard
Aurélie speaking.

"Dorine, this is no stranger.   Give him your hand;
kiss him."

Reluctantly the child advanced to where he stood,
and obeyed her in so far that she held out her hand;
but, either from coyness or some other cause, she did
not offer to lift up her face for him to kiss.   And he,
standing there, looking down on her, felt as if his heart
would break.   Then, overcome by all that was struggling

within his bosom, he dropped upon one knee beside the child and drew her toward him, she seeming terrified at his embrace.

"Ah, little one!" he said, "if I tell you how I have longed for this hour, prayed for it to come, surely you will say some word of greeting to me. Dorine, do you not know me? Dorine, Dorine!"

For answer, the child, still seeming frightened, drew further away from him and whispered that she did not know him, that she desired to go to Aurélie.

"You love her?" he whispered, too, for now his voice seemed to be failing him—"you love her? You are happy with her? I hoped you would have come with me——"

"With you!"—and now the tears stood in the child's eyes as she shrank still further from him—"and leave Aurélie?"

"Why not?" he asked almost fiercely, his despair driving him nearly to distraction. "Why not? Who is she? What share has she in you? You are mine, mine, mine! O child, I am your father!" And suddenly overwrought by his emotions, by the broken hopes he had cherished, the vanishing of the future to which he had looked forward, he sprang to his feet and turned to Mademoiselle de Roquemaure. "I see it all," he said; "understand all. Your brother uttered the truth at last. You stole my child because she stood in your way; you won her love afterward because——"

"Stop!" exclaimed Aurélie de Roquemaure, and as she spoke she drew herself to her full height and confronted him, while the child, trembling by her side, could not understand why her sister had changed so. "Stop and hear the truth since you force me to tell it. I stole your child because in that way alone could her life be saved, her safety at least be assured. My brother would—God forgive him!—have hidden her away forever; even then, as I learned afterward, the bishop's servant had stolen her from the inn in the city and was hastening to meet him. There was no time to lose; it was that man's life or hers, and—and—I acted by my mother's orders. Now, Monseigneur le Duc——"

But he whom she addressed thus had fallen on his knees before her, had endeavoured to seize her hand, and, failing that, was kissing the hem of her dress.

"Forgive, forgive, forgive!" he moaned; "I have been blind—blind! Let me go in peace and offend no more. She is yours, not mine; yours by your womanly grace and mercy—the love she has to give belongs to you by right of your womanly mercy. Better that I had died in Paris yesterday than live to repay you as I have!"

But now to the child's mind there seemed to come some gleam of light as to what was passing between the stranger and her mother; the words, "Better I had died in Paris," awakened her intelligence.

"Aurélie," she cried, "was this the gentleman whom you hurried to Paris to save?"

"To save!" St. Georges exclaimed, "to save! My God! do I owe my life to you as well?"

And Aurélie—her eyes cast down, her frame trembling from head to foot—murmured: "I could not let you die, knowing what I did, knowing the evil the De Roquemaures had wrought you. When Monsieur Boussac sent me word you were doomed, I determined to tell the king all."

.   .   .   .

So she had saved him! She, whom for four years he had regarded as a treacherous enemy, had saved not

only his child but him. And ere the day was over he
had learned all that she had done besides.

She told her tale to St. Georges and to Boussac as
they sat in the grounds of the old manoir, and made at
last all clear to the former that for so long had been
dark and impenetrable.

"The man who was your worst enemy," she said,
"was that vile Bishop of Lodève ; the next was Louvois
—for without them my unhappy brother would have
known nothing and could have attempted no harm
against you. He regarded himself as the heir of the
Duc de Vannes, and did not know of your existence
until Phélypeaux told him of it. And at the same time
the bishop said that he had another formidable rival in
the Romish Church——"

"The Romish Church ! "

" Yes, your father had become converted to it and was
received into it by Phélypeaux himself, the example of
Turenne having much influenced him. At first, on being received, he had, with the fervour of many converts,
bequeathed half of his great fortune to that Church,
the other half remaining a bequest to his heir—my
father, and after him my unhappy half-brother. But,
ere he set out on the campaign in which both he and
Turenne were to lose their lives, he wrote to the bishop
and told him that he had a son by an unacknowledged
marriage ; that he could not deem it right that he should
be deprived of what was properly his, and that he had
made a will leaving all his property to him. Then the
search for you began, though my brother was not concerned in it, being still a child. But the bishop sought
high and low, first for proofs of the marriage and next
to discover where the duke's son was. And Louvois
helped him because he had hated your father, who

20

298 IN THE DAY OF ADVERSITY.

despised him, as Turenne and many of the other marshals did."

"But you, mademoiselle," exclaimed St. Georges,
"how do you know all this? And did you know it
when we first met?"

"No," she replied, "but my mother suspected. By
this time my brother had heard something from Louvois,
who had found out all when the effects of the Duc de
Vannes, which he had taken with him on his last
campaign—his private papers and other things—were
brought back to Paris by the Comte de Lorge, Turenne's
nephew; had discovered that the son was named St.
Georges, his English mother's name having been St.
George, but could not discover where the duke had
bestowed him. Nor did he discover it until long afterward, when, happening to once more refer to the papers
brought by the comte, he discovered one he had over-
looked addressed to my mother; and he read it and
discovered thereby that the officer, who was serving in
the Regiment of the Nivernois, under the name of St.
Georges, was, in truth, the lawful Duc de Vannes.
Then in his cold, brutal manner he informed the bishop
where the man was who stood in the light of the
Church's gains, and alas! he told that other who expected so much, my unhappy half-brother. Also he
told them both that this man was to be transferred to
another regiment, and that he would set out from Pontarlier on a certain night. They might care to see him,
he continued; therefore he should receive orders to call
on the bishop at his family residence in Dijon, where he
happened to be then, and on my brother in this house
—though, not to arouse any suspicions, he was to present himself as a visitor to my mother. Also he told
them that which neither dreamed of until then—namely,

that Monsieur St. Georges was a widower, but had a child whom he would doubtless endeavour to bring with him. You must be able," she concluded, "to 'understand the rest."

"Ay!" said the Duc de Vannes, "I can understand. Only still, mademoiselle, I cannot conceive how you know all this."

"Yet the answer is simple. By one of those marvellous coincidences which happen as often in our everyday life as in the romances of Mademoiselle de Scudery, or the fables of Monsieur de La Fontaine, my brother had once asked my mother if she had ever heard of you, if your assumed name was known to her; the bishop supposing that she was greedy as he himself, had sent to warn her that you were on your way to Paris, and that it would be well if she could recognise in you any traces of your father and would send a word to Louvois saying whether she thought you were the man. But he overreached himself," Mademoiselle de Roquemaure added; "my mother's sympathies were with the son of him she had once loved so dearly, not with him who was the son of the man she had married. And as for Phélypeaux—she despised him!"

"Heaven bless her!" exclaimed the duke. "Yet still I know not how she unravelled all—how found out my birthright—my mother's name."

"That, too, is simple. Louvois died suddenly, as you know, in disgrace with the king. Some said by poison administered by himself, some from fear of the king's displeasure. Be that, however, as it may, his son, Barbézieux, was not allowed to touch any of his papers and all were handed to Louis intact. He confided them to De Chamlay, who refused Louvois's vacant post as minister of war but consented to go over his state affairs, and in those papers he found all; a copy of your father's letter to the bishop, the letter to my mother which had never been delivered—telling her everything and begging her to see you righted—his will and his marriage certificate, as well as that of your birth. Monseigneur, I have them upstairs—I showed them to the king the night before last—they are now at your disposal."

Boussac had strolled away ere the narrative was done —his delicacy prompting him to leave them alone— and as she concluded the Duke de Vannes dropped on his knee by her side, and, taking her hand, murmured:

"Forgive, pardon me! Bring yourself to say you forgive the evil I have thought, and let me go. Unworthy as I am to ask it, yet, if you can, forgive me and never more in this world will I offend your sight. And, for expiation, I give my child to you—you who have been so much more to her than I."

But Aurélie de Roquemaure, bending toward the kneeling man, said: "Nay. Why say that I forgive—I, who have naught to pardon? Only—do not go! Stay, rather, and win the love of the child whom you have loved so much through all your grief, through your long separation."

CONCLUSION.

THE Peace of Ryswick brought about many changes in both France and England. It opened each country to the other—for a time, though but a short one!—it enabled the refugees of each to return to their own lands, and for a few years England and her neighbours were not at open enmity.

Yet one refugee there was who never returned to France, but who, in the country of his adoption, and with his beautiful wife by his side and at his knee his children, took no part in the strife between the two lands or in their politics. Instead, he dwelt upon the estate he had bought in the heart of Surrey—with the money he had realized by the sale of his property in France—and there, a prosperous gentleman, passed life easily and well.

But there was no longer any Duc de Vannes in France—that old title was never revived after the death of the late owner of it on the plains of Salzbach—and in Surrey the handsome grave gentleman, who was known to be a wealthy *emigré* from across the Channel, was invariably spoken of and addressed as Mr. St. George.

And he was very happy thus!—happy when he thought of all the dangers he had passed through safely —though sometimes in the night his wife would hear him mutter in his sleep, " At dawn, at dawn !" and know that in his dreams his mind had gone back to that summer morning on the *Place de Grève*, when, putting out her hand, she would softly wake him; happy, too, in his children—in the one whose love had come back to him as he had prayed so long it might; happy in those others whom God had sent him: in the bright, handsome boy who bore his own name; and in the delicate, beautiful girl who bore her mother's— Aurélie.

And happy beyond all thought and early expectation when she, that mother, was by his side, or when, rising from her place near him, and stroking back the long hair from his forehead—now streaked with silver—and kissing him, would murmur:

"'If thou faint in the day of adversity, thy strength is small,'" and then falling on her knees beside him would whisper, "But your strength was great, my love, and in that strength you were able to endure."

THE END.

www.ingramcontent.com/pod-product-compliance
Lightning Source LLC
Chambersburg PA
CBHW031402270326
41929CB00010BA/1291